MARRIAGE AND DIVORCE IN THE JEWISH STATE

HBI SERIES ON JEWISH WOMEN

Shulamit Reinharz, General Editor | *Sylvia Barack Fishman, Associate Editor*

The HBI Series on Jewish Women, created by the Hadassah-Brandeis
Institute, publishes a wide range of books by and about Jewish women
in diverse contexts and time periods. Of interest to scholars and the
educated public, the HBI Series on Jewish Women fills major gaps in
Jewish Studies and in Women and Gender Studies as well as their
intersection.

For the complete list of books that are available in this series, please see www.upne.com

SUSAN M. WEISS AND

NETTY C. GROSS-HOROWITZ

Marriage and Divorce in the Jewish State

ISRAEL'S CIVIL WAR

Brandeis University Press   Waltham, Massachusetts

6/11/13
Lan
#40—

Brandeis University Press
An imprint of University Press of New England
www.upne.com
© 2013 Brandeis University
All rights reserved
Manufactured in the United States of America
Designed by Mindy Basinger Hill
Typeset in 10.35/14 Parkinson Electra Pro

University Press of New England is a member of the Green Press Initiative. The paper used in this book meets their minimum requirement for recycled paper.

For permission to reproduce any of the material in this book, contact Permissions, University Press of New England, One Court Street, Suite 250, Lebanon NH 03766; or visit www.upne.com

The publication of this book was generously supported by the Lucius N. Littauer Foundation.

Library of Congress Cataloging-in-Publication Data

Weiss, Susan M.
Marriage and divorce in the Jewish state: Israel's civil war /
Susan M. Weiss and Netty C. Gross-Horowitz.
    p.   cm.—Brandeis series on gender, culture, religion, and law)
(HBI series on Jewish women)
Includes bibliographical references and index.
ISBN 978-1-61168-363-9 (cloth: alk. paper)—
ISBN 978-1-61168-364-6 (pbk.: alk. paper)—ISBN 978-1-61168-365-3 (ebook)
1. Divorce—Law and legislation—Israel—Popular works.
2. Jewish women—Legal status, laws, etc.—Israel—Popular works.
3. Agunahs—Israel—Popular works. 4. Divorce (Jewish law)—Popular works. I. Gross-Horowitz, Netty C. II. Title.

KMK577.W45 2013
346.569401'66—dc23   2012027144
5   4   3 2 1

Dedicated to the women

whose stories we have told and

those whose stories we

were not able to tell.

CONTENTS

FOREWORD

Everyone interested in Israel's legal system knows that when the state was founded in May 1948, the religious establishment received the right to govern matters of personal status. That right was further embedded in the Rabbinic Courts Jurisdiction Law of 1953. The upshot of this political arrangement is that all Jewish Israeli citizens have to turn to Orthodox rabbis when they wish to marry, and to rabbinic courts when they wish to divorce, regardless of whether the couple is religious. From this division of authority between religious and civil components of society stemmed problems concerning who has the right to marry and how to end marriages in ways that do not coincide with Talmudic precepts. As a matter for Israeli society, discussions of marriage and divorce are particularly significant, since nearly everyone marries (97.7 percent of men and 96.8 percent of women) and approximately 15 percent of new marriages end in divorce. This book of seven chapters and a lengthy introduction explains concisely how the modern problem of *agunot* and *mesurevet get* (women whose husbands cannot or will not give them a divorce) has evolved.

Many people have written about the *agunah* problem. Two features distinguish this book. One thing that sets it apart from many other discussions is Susan Weiss and Netty Gross-Horowitz's attractive approach. First they explain all the inconsistencies and confusions in the religious laws that apply to divorce. Sadly, regardless of these legal problems, the rabbis approach "divorce with more reverence for the [laws] than concern for the plight of women denied a divorce." The Supreme Court of the State of Israel has not been of much help to women who feel trapped by the rabbinic courts. As the authors write, the Supreme Court "has to a large extent stood idle in the face of infringements on women's equality, dignity, and liberty of person inflicted by rabbinic courts in the name of religious laws." Exploring the tension between religious and civil courts internationally is the key concern of the HBI Project on Gender, Culture, Religion and the Law, which is the sponsor of this superb study.

A second distinguishing feature of the book is the unique perspective of its authors. Netty Gross-Horowitz is a journalist who has covered women's issues in Israel for several decades. Susan Weiss has practiced family law in Israel for over twenty years and was the founder of Yad L'Isha legal clinic, which acts on behalf of *agunot* in rabbinic courts. Weiss brought feminist legal methods to bear on the practices she saw in these courts. Following the model of Catherine MacKinnon, whose groundbreaking work transformed the unnamed discrimination against women in the workplace into the tort of sexual harassment, Weiss sought to name and remedy the inchoate anguish of women subjected to delay and extortion in the Jewish divorce process. The Center for Women's Justice, which she founded in 2004, has brought a series of influential cases that have resulted in the recognition of the tort of get refusal. This has raised the profile of the *agunah* issue, altered the notion of the harm it causes, and resulted in substantial damage awards to its victims. Weiss has become an internationally recognized expert on legal strategies for dealing with get refusal and brings her unparalleled experience and insight to bear in this accessibly written book.

Instead of lumping all *agunot* into one category, Weiss and Gross-Horowitz create a typology grounded in the stories of six different Israeli women. They rightly believe that first order of the day is to disentangle the conflicting laws and arrangements. To do this, they identified six Israeli women, whom they call Clueless, Scarlet, Ping-Pong, Accidental, Pawn, and Reluctant. They then take us into these women's homes and hearts to hear what they have to say, honoring the women's voices. Finally, Weiss and Gross-Horowitz reflect on the ultimate significance of their study. It shows, they argue, that Israel is at a crossroads in the choice of being a democracy or theocracy.

The mission of the HBI, of which the Project on Gender, Culture, Religion and the Law is a component, is to develop fresh ideas about Jews and gender worldwide. The project seeks to highlight innovative legal and scholarly work that reconciles women's rights and practices justified in terms of cultural or religious norms. This extraordinary overview of one of the pivotal problems in Israel today — the fraught relationship between religious and civil law at both the doctrinal and institutional levels — fulfills the promise of the HBI's efforts.

Shulamit Reinharz, Ph.D. DIRECTOR, HBI

Lisa Fishbayn Joffe S.J.D. DIRECTOR, HBI PROJECT ON GENDER, CULTURE, RELIGION AND THE LAW

ACKNOWLEDGMENTS

Without the women who agreed to tell their stories in print, these stories would have remained each one's own albatross, instead of contributing in some way to what we hope will be the women's eventual liberation, and the salvation of us all. Without the foundations and organizations that have supported the work of the Center for Women's Justice, which has represented these women and women like them, their stories would have been interred forever within the belly of the rabbinic courts. We are indebted to all these groups, though the ideas expressed in this book are not necessarily consistent with CWJ's mission or that of the foundations that support its work. Without our husbands to help us focus, we would probably have done something else. Without our editor, Ronnie Hope, to spot and suggest corrections for lacunae, inaccuracies, and clumsiness, the manuscript would have been full of them; any that remain are our fault alone. Without our copyeditor, Susan Silver, to polish the edges and synchronize the details, the project would have lacked the professional accuracy we hope it has achieved. And without the support of the Hadassah-Brandeis Institute and Phyllis Deutsch, our editor there and an indefatigable supporter of this project, nothing at all would have happened. Special thanks also to the Van Leer Institute library and its marvelous staff, who provided a quiet place to work. Netty thanks her family for their steadfast support. One's birth family plays an important supportive role after a marriage disintegrates. Susan thanks Tel Aviv University for providing much of the academic grist for the mill of this book.

Who Are We?

We both grew up in Orthodox Jewish families in New York City in the second half of the past century and attended the Yeshiva High School of Queens. Housed in a dull building in a decaying neighborhood, the school had an unspoken but foremost goal to teach us to be good Jewish girls and good Jewish mothers and to identify with the State of Israel as the homeland of the Jewish people. Obedient, attentive, and true to our calling, we got married in accordance "with the laws of Moses and Israel" — as the marriage liturgy goes — to good Jewish boys, bred nine children between us, and moved with our families to Israel in the 1980s, more or less for Zionist reasons.

In Israel life went awry for both of us, in different but converging ways.

I, Netty, became a reporter for the *Jerusalem Report*, a move that heightened my sense of feminism and community. The *Report*, an English-language Israeli magazine, did not relegate me to the woman's desk but gave me free rein to follow whatever muse beckoned. Subjects I covered were as diverse as the Dead Sea Scrolls and the Holocaust Restitution cover-up. In 1998 I interviewed President Bill Clinton in the White House about his ties to the Jewish community. His deputy chief of staff, Maria Escheveste, a Latina convert to Judaism who had just filed for divorce, had a question for me: could her husband, a Jew, withhold a *get* (a Jewish bill of divorce) from her? When I said that it was theoretically possible, she said rather plaintively, "But he wouldn't do that, would he?" The reaction of this powerful woman, sitting in her office in the West Wing, a headset perched on her head freeing her to do several things at once, underscored just how helpless a Jewish woman feels at the mere thought that her life may be put on hold and she may become an *agunah* — an "anchored" woman — because of a withheld get.

When I started out at the *Jerusalem Report*, I would not have labeled myself a feminist, even after I found myself one day at the Jerusalem Rabbinic Court, accompanying a friend struggling to get a divorce, because her husband had, for all intents and purposes, dumped her and the kids in Israel and returned to his shady commercial activities back in the United States. Located then in a dilapidated old Arab building on Jaffa Road, the court seemed to me to be an alien, outdated relic that was happily far from me and my everyday world. Later, however, I found myself, to my surprise and chagrin, in a similar struggle and back in the rabbinic court, now housed on King George Street in what had been, fittingly, the first home of the Knesset, where the laws conceding sovereignty over personal status to the rabbis had been passed. I slowly began to understand that what had at first seemed to me to be a quaint and harmless nod to tradition had in fact turned into a real system of law with real legal consequences.

Because I was the child of Holocaust survivors from Orthodox Jewish homes, my reluctant move to feminism was understandable. The trauma of the Second World War and its horrors were only a decade old when I was born. The huge price my parents paid for their beliefs was the biggest influence in my early life. Right or wrong, my parents, and like-minded survivors who were their friends, committed themselves to resurrect the world from which they had been sundered. Rather than discuss what might be awry in Orthodox Judaism, my parents celebrated its continuity. The State of Israel's embrace of tradition was taken for granted. Words like "pluralism" or "equality" were disparaged as naive, "American" ideas. Instead, everything was seen through the prism of survival: the war in Vietnam ("The Vietnamese are suffering"); the landing on the moon ("Why couldn't they spend all that money bombing Auschwitz?"); civil rights ("Too bad no one marched for us").

I knew certain gender-insensitive teachings existed in Judaism and clashed with the goals of the nascent women's rights movement of the sixties and seventies. Each wedding, when the bride donned a veil; each brit or bar mitzvah, when the value of manhood was consecrated; each morning, when boys and men in our school said a blessing thanking God for not making them female, told me that something was wrong with the interpretation of my faith embraced so wholeheartedly in the name of following tradition. But it was not until I got to the *Jerusalem Report* and met Jews from every walk of life that my mind began to open to different ideas about what being Jewish and Israeli meant.

My personal struggle to be inclusive of the past, but still modern, mirrors the Kulturkampf in Israel. My slow move to feminism reflects the reluctance of many of us Jewish women to confront their tradition until their tradition confronts them on a personal level.

I, Susan, an attorney, began my legal career in the United States with the Federal Trade Commission. Upon arriving in Israel with my husband, a couple of children in tow, less than perfect skills in Hebrew, and an American accent, I passed the Bar Association tests, but my legal career stalled until I began volunteering with Wizo and Naamat, two of Israel's oldest women's associations. Before I knew it, my volunteering had segued into a successful private practice with a specialty in divorce. One of my first clients was a woman who lost custody of her son because a rabbinic court was worried that she, a convert, might take the boy to visit with her father, a goy — a non-Jew. My client, acting against my advice, shockingly felt compelled to waive her right to appeal in exchange for a get. I had stepped into the rabbinic courts, and my life, my religious sensibilities, and my thoughts about the place of law in society all changed, immediately and forever.

I started exploring ways to respond to what I saw. I volunteered for the Israel Women's Network, the first Israeli feminist organization, set up by the legendary Professor Alice Shalvi in 1984, and sat on its committee on matters of halakha — the rules, traditions, and customs that have historically regulated the lives of religiously observant Jews — and rabbinic courts for a number of years. As a member of the committee, I was part of the initiative that established ICAR, the International Committee for Agunah Rights, a coalition of women's groups advocating for change within halakha to improve the status of women seeking divorce. I also took part in the ad hoc advisory committee that initiated and lobbied for the legislation that expanded the authority of rabbinic courts to penalize men who refused to give their wives bills of divorce, known as the Rabbinic Courts (Execution of Judgments) Law of 1995.

In the midnineties, while still volunteering at the Women's Network and working in my private practice, I was asked by Nurit Freid, the founder and director of what became known as the Monica Deniss Goldberg Program for Rabbinic Advocates, to teach a class to women who wanted to become rabbinic court pleaders. Professionals with an expertise in halakha, pleaders are allowed to argue divorce cases in rabbinic courts. Until Fried filed a petition with the

Supreme Court, the Israeli rabbinate had barred women from being becoming pleaders, and the profession was reserved for men who studied at yeshivot, institutions of higher Torah learning. (Attorneys, whether male or female, have always been permitted to appear in both rabbinic courts, irrespective of their halakhic acumen or religious affiliations; see Shamir, 1996.) I taught the female pleaders about the interplay between rabbinic and civil courts in Israel.

Inspired by the pleaders, who had been newly empowered within a rigidly gendered Orthodoxy, and hoping to use them to challenge the rabbinic courts' methods, I founded Yad L'Isha in 1997, a program that runs to this day under the auspices of Ohr Torah Stone, the umbrella organization for a number of educational institutions of higher Jewish learning. (The pleaders that it sponsors navigate the murky waters of the rabbinic courts, seeking bills of divorce for their clients. Under my auspices, we helped more than 250 women receive their gets. The work of Yad L'Isha was featured in the film *Mekudeshet*, or *Sentenced to Marry*, directed by Anat Zuria and produced by Amit Brauer.) As the director of Yad L'Isha, I also helped to rekindle the work of ICAR. And it was while at Yad L'Isha that I began studying sociology and anthropology at Tel Aviv University, another step in my quest to get a handle on and change what was happening in rabbinic courts.

I worked as the director of Yad L'Isha until 2004. But by then I realized that for things to change, I had to look outside the rabbinic courts. I understood, in the words of Caribbean American writer, poet, and activist Audre Lorde, that "the master's tools will never dismantle the master's house" (1984, p. 110). With this insight, I established the Center for Women's Justice (CWJ) in 2004. CWJ is a nonprofit organization whose mission is to find systemic solutions to the problems that confront Jewish women in Israel because of the interlocking of religion and state, including, most important, the problem of the agunah. One of our key strategies has been to demand that Israeli civil courts — labor courts, family courts, and the Supreme Court — respond to the infringements on the rights of women being perpetrated by Israeli rabbinic courts and the rabbinate in the name of God. As part of our overall activities, we sometimes accompany our clients in the rabbinic courts and often advise them on how to maneuver there. CWJ's work in, and relating to, the rabbinic courts has been most often undertaken by Rivkah Lubitch, a pleader who joined CWJ from Yad L'Isha. It is Rivkah's work that is featured in this book.

In response to my lifelong work in, and with, the rabbinic courts, I have become an unabashed feminist activist. But I had always considered myself a feminist. At age five, I wondered why Jewish tradition celebrated the births of boys and not of girls. I read *Ms.* magazine when I was seventeen. I thought women could be doctors, lawyers, and investment bankers and that men could do dishes. Yet no feminist leanings, no legal education, nothing, prepared me for work as a divorce attorney in the courtrooms of the State of Israel.

At different times and for different reasons, we both started asking the same questions: How did Israel get into the absurd situation where matters of personal status are decided by rabbis on the basis of archaic texts, most of which were written hundreds and thousands of years ago? What is at the root of this problem? What is going on?

Introduction

———

A woman in Israel can become a fighter pilot but can't get divorced.

Neta Ziv, director of the Cegla Clinical Law Programs at Tel Aviv University

(exaggerating to make her point)

———

In the mid-sixteenth century a young Jewish woman in Salonika named Reina, married to a man named Avraham, became entangled in a family drama. The background to the feud was that her widowed mother wanted to remarry, and Avraham's father opposed the match. From the writings of the brilliant scholar Rabbi Samuel ben Moses de Medina (Maharashdam in a Hebrew acronym), born in 1505 and died in Salonika in 1589, we learn that Reina, either in solidarity with her mother or because she had her own issues with her husband, involved herself in the argument and went so far as to request a divorce from Avraham, asking that he grant her a religious bill of divorcement, a *get*.

Reina claimed that her husband was impotent, that he did not ejaculate "like an arrow," and that she had deflowered herself on their wedding night using her own finger, wrote the Maharashdam, in his published questions and answers, known as responsa. Reina wanted a chance to remarry and have a son who would say kaddish for her, the prayer for the dead, after she passed away. Avraham, however, did not want to give Reina a get. Should he be compelled? This question was posed to de Medina, a revered authority who established an important yeshiva in Salonika. He acknowledged that earlier scholars were flexible about compelling the granting of a get when there was just cause. He noted that the earlier rabbis even held that a wife's mere assertion that her husband was "disgusting" to her was sufficient grounds. Still, the Maharashdam declared that a man may not be compelled to give a get in every instance.

Neta Ziv is one of the attorneys who represented Alice Miller in her successful petition to the Supreme Court to allow her to be admitted to the Israel Air Force's flying school.

He was skeptical of Reina's charges and wrote that the young woman may have been influenced by a circle of "bad women" (Shut Maharashdam, Even Haezer, no. 145).

Reina's saga, even though more than half a millennium old, is still relevant to Israeli women today. This book tells the stories of six different Israeli women who asked their husbands for Jewish bills of divorce and found themselves, like Reina, bound to their husbands' wills and to the same rules and regulations that guided the Maharashdam. Trapped in incomprehensible proceedings, subjected to humiliation and mental anguish, and faced with patently callous and unjust outcomes, these six women's tales are difficult ones. Some have happier endings than others. Some don't end at all. But they all paint a picture of a partial, but very real, theocracy gone awry.

It is the Rabbinic Courts Jurisdiction (Marriage and Divorce) Law of 1953 that introduces theocratic parameters into Israel's otherwise civil, and secularly inspired, compendium of laws. That statute requires all Israeli Jews to marry and divorce in accordance with halakha (or, literally *din torah*, or Torah law) — whether they be atheist, agnostic, Conservative, Reform, ultra-Orthodox, or postdenominational. Only Orthodox rabbis can marry them and only rabbinic courts run by Orthodox, male rabbis can decide when they are divorced. Those rabbis apply halakha. According to halakha, if a husband does not willingly agree to deliver a Jewish bill of divorce to his wife, or if he is missing, incapacitated, or physically unable to do so, she remains bound to him forever, an *agunah*. Women in the Diaspora affiliated with the Orthodox and Conservative movements will often insist on a get even if they are divorced in accordance with the civil laws of the state. In Israel, however, there are no secular, civil marriage and divorce laws. As far as marriage and divorce in Israel among Jews is concerned, halakha is the law of the land.

In this introduction we first briefly examine Israel's attitude to women in a broad perspective. Next, we offer a short history of Israeli divorce laws, including the biblical and rabbinic laws that underpin them, and provide some relevant statistics. We then explain why the writing of this book is pertinent today. And, finally, we will outline the structure of this book, clarifying why we have chosen these particular women and their particular stories. The introduction will enable the reader to enter, together with us, into the confusing world of the rabbinic courts as we begin to try to unravel what exactly is happening there and what needs to be done.

Women in Israel Today

Women pioneers made substantial contributions to the Zionist enterprise in the prestate and early-state days (although not properly acknowledged until the mid-1980s) (Herzog, 1992, 2004), and accordingly the right of women to equality was enshrined in the second article of Israel's Declaration of the Establishment of the State of Israel in 1948. It stated that the State of Israel would "foster the development of the country for the benefit of all its inhabitants . . . and will be based on freedom, justice and peace as envisaged by the prophets of Israel; it will ensure complete equality of social and political rights to all its inhabitants irrespective of religion, race or sex" (Provisional Government of Israel, 1948). On the website of Israel's Ministry of Foreign Affairs, law professor Frances Raday (2005) writes, "Israel's Declaration of Independence was one of the earliest state constitutive documents to guarantee social and political equality without discrimination based on sex. In 1951, the Knesset passed the Women's Equal Rights Law, which, although not bestowing constitutional authority on the courts to annul discriminatory legislation, was used as an interpretative tool by the Supreme Court in its role as the High Court of Justice to introduce an impressive range of equality rights for women."

Indeed, relations between men and women in Israel are generally very egalitarian, and over the years women have filled key roles. Golda Meir was prime minister in the early 1970s; Dorit Beinisch, former state prosecutor, is the retired president of the Supreme Court; Dalia Itzik served as speaker of the Knesset; Miriam Ben Porat, the first woman appointed to the Supreme Court, later served as state comptroller; and Tzippi Livni, former leader of the Knesset opposition, previously was foreign minister. One of the country's few Nobel Prize laureates is biochemist Ada Yonath. Israeli women can say and do exactly what they please. They dress as they want. They run supermarkets, law practices, medical clinics, and banks. Along with Israeli men, they enjoy universal health care, a relatively high standard of living, and a long life expectancy. A strong streak of tolerance and openness permeates Israeli society. Since 1970 women's studies programs have been offered at major universities. Rows of books on Israeli feminism fill shelves in libraries. Minority women have also slowly inched ahead, battling the conservatism of male-dominated Arab society, and in the last decade several Muslim women have been elected to the Knesset.

The downside is that a certain degree of machismo still thrives, and reports on violence against women still fill the media. But such behavior is now judged more severely than it was in the past, and criminal cases, to which a blind eye may have been turned decades ago, are now prosecuted. In recent years, high-profile politicians such as general-turned-politician Yitzhak Mordecai, cabinet minister Haim Ramon, and president Moshe Katzav have paid with their careers and reputations for carnal behavior that fell within the widespread reach of Israel's sexual harassment and criminal laws. Law makers sensitive to the demands of women have written progressive legislation that has limited pornography, such as the Communications (Telecommunications and Broadcasting) Law of 1982 (amended 2002), and expanded the definition of sexual harassment, such as the Prevention of Sexual Harassment Law of 1998.

But with respect to marriage and divorce, Israel is still ruled by laws that we can only describe as antediluvian. Long after most other countries have adopted civil laws that formalize the dissolution of marriages without reference to religious laws and customs, it is only in the overwhelmingly Catholic Philippines, in hard-line Islamic states like Iran and Saudi Arabia, and in what is otherwise the super modern and progressive State of Israel, that civil marriage and divorce remains elusive.

Jewish Divorce Laws

DIVORCE IN THE BIBLE

In the Bible there is a paucity of precepts dealing with divorce, mostly doing so only indirectly — laying down rules of conduct toward a woman whom a man has decided to "banish" or "send away." Leviticus 21:7 and 21:14 prohibit a priest from marrying such a woman; Leviticus 22:13 allows the banished, childless daughter of a priest to eat from the priestly tithes; Numbers 30:10 states that the vows of a banished woman must be honored. As for the conditions for banishment, Deuteronomy prohibits a man from "sending away" a woman whom he has taken as his wife if he wrongfully accused her of not being a virgin (22:19) or if he has raped her and thus was obligated to take her as his wife in the first instance (22:29). Deuteronomy 24:1–4 states that a man is not allowed to take back a woman he sent away if she has been, in the interim, with another man.

Most biblical scholars have assumed that in biblical times a man could "send his wife away" at will and that such sending away must be formalized with a bill of divorcement (referred to in Deut. 24:1 as *sefer kritut*) to make it clear that his banished wife was no longer his and could be "taken" by another man (Falk, 1964, p. 154). No provisions in the Bible were made for women to "banish" their husbands or to "send them away."

DIVORCE IN RABBINIC LITERATURE

The assumption that men could send their wives away at will continued through the Talmudic period. The Babylonian Talmud makes it clear: "A women is sent away [by her husband] whether she wants to be sent away or even if she doesn't want to be sent away, a man sends away his wife only if he wants to" (Yev. 14:1).

Nonetheless, already in the Talmud we see the sages becoming more attentive to the needs of women, attempting both to inhibit a man from sending his wife away for no reason, as well as to interfere under certain circumstances in which a wife may want to leave her husband (Hauptman, 1998). And while the Talmud still assumes that the key to releasing a wife from an undesirable cohabitation arrangement remains in the hands of her husband, who must send her away of his own free will (Yev. 112b), it also declares that there are cases in which rabbis can nonetheless "compel" (*kofin*) a husband to let his wife go — for example, when he suffers from afflictions that the Talmud assumes would makes it impossible for a woman to live with him, such as boils, leprosy, or bad breath; if he is a tanner (Ket. 77a); or if it he is infertile (Yev. 65b). And there are also circumstances in which the Talmud states that a man "should" let his wife go (*yotzee*) — for example, if he cannot support her (Ket. 47b, 48a) or withholds intimate relations from her (Mishna Ket. 5:7). And although the Talmud is silent, or vague, with respect to husbands who are violent, unfaithful, impotent, stricken with major defects, or just revolting, later authorities suggested that in limited and circumscribed circumstances — if husbands are, for example, *consistently* violent, *unrepentantly* unfaithful, *unquestionably* impotent, stricken with major defects *that the wife has not been told about before* marriage, or *sexually* revolting — some might argue that such husbands "should" release their wives.

The scope and application of the Talmudic grounds for interfering with a failed marriage on behalf of women were debated by the rabbis in the Talmud itself, as well as later. The issues they argued over included whether the inventory of grounds set forth in the Talmud for "compelling" a husband to release his wife was fixed, as contended by the Rosh (Rabbi Asher ben Jehiel, 1250–1327) (Shut Rosh 43, no. 3) or modifiable, as Rabbi Moses Alshikar (1466–1522) asserted (Shut Alshikar, no. 73); whether it can be claimed, a fortiori, that if a man can be compelled to give a get because he has bad breath, he can be compelled to do so if he puts his wife's life in danger (T. Yerushalmi, Git. 9:10); whether a woman who is revolted by her husband is entitled to a divorce at all if she has her eye on another man (Shut Rosh 43, nos. 6, 8); whether "should" means "compelled to" (Ket. 70a, *tosafot* at *yotzee veyitain ketubah*); and, in general, how much persuasion of recalcitrant husbands is permissible in light of the rule that prohibits forcing a man to grant divorce (*get meuseh*) (Git. 88b).

By the Middle Ages, and later on with the codification of halakha by Rabbi Joseph Caro (1488–1575) in the authoritative Shulhan Arukh, some of the most important rabbinic authorities began to take positions on these debates that greatly limited the circumstances in which rabbis were willing to intervene to convince husbands to release their wives. The greatly revered Rabbeinu Tam (Rabbi Jacob Ben Meir, 1100–1170), for instance, stated that persuasion of husbands should be limited to public ostracism, cited in Rema (Rabbi Moses Isserles, 1520–1572) (Even HaEzer 154:21, gloss to Shulhan Arukh) and that a man should not have to divorce his wife merely on the basis of her self-serving statement that she was repulsed by him (Ket. 63a, *tosafot*); this latter position was also supported by the Rosh (Teshuvot Rosh 43:8).

The Rambam, Rabbi Moses ben Maimon (1135–1204) proclaimed that the rule prohibiting the use of force against recalcitrant husbands was biblical in origin, and hence divine and immutable, citing, as proof text, Deuteronomy 24:1 (Mishna Torah, Laws of Divorce 1:2) although that verse does not deal with the issue of force but with the problem of taking back a woman who has been sent away. Rambam also claimed that the rule prohibiting a child born to a woman fathered by a man other than her husband (a *mamzer*) and his progeny from marrying fellow Jews was biblical in origin (Mishna Torah, Laws of Prohibited Unions 15:1) – something that, again, is not evident from the proof text. The Rambam also took the more woman-friendly positions that a husband could, under certain circumstance, be beaten until he agreed to divorce (Mishna Torah, Laws of Divorce 2:20) and that a woman repulsed by her husband was entitled to divorce (Mishna Torah, Laws of Marriage 14:8).

But Caro in the Shulhan Arukh, more often than not, took a conservative approach, holding that a court could *not* require a man to divorce his wife on the basis of his infertility until after she lived with him for ten years and was still barren (Even HaEzer, 154, no. 6); on the basis of his failure to support her if he could be compelled to do so (Even HaEzer, 154, no. 3); or if a woman claimed that she was repulsed by her husband, since although she could not be forced to sleep with him under those circumstances, it was his prerogative to decide if he wanted to divorce her or keep her as his maidservant (Even HaEzer, 77, no. 2).

In his contemporaneous commentary to the Shulhan Arukh, the Rema takes the strict position that a man is not required to divorce his wife on the basis of domestic violence, unless such violence was regular and persistent (Even HaEzer, 154, no. 3, gloss); on the basis of withholding conjugal affections, since this is hard to prove and the word of the woman should not be accepted in this matter (Even HaEzer, 154, no. 7, gloss) (Caro disagrees); or on the basis of infidelity, unless he admitted to it or there was proof of it, and even then, not everyone would agree (Even HaEzer, 154, no. 1, gloss). Like Caro, he maintains that if a woman claimed that she was repulsed by her husband, it was a husband's prerogative to decide if he wanted to divorce her or not (Even HaEzer, 77, no. 3, gloss).

With all the confusion, conflicting opinions, hesitation, conservatism, and dissonance with modern conceptions of marriage and divorce in these ancient, holy texts, the rabbis sitting on Israeli rabbinic court tribunals approach divorce claims with more reverence for them than concern for the plight of women denied a divorce. Rather than make decisions that may challenge what they see as immutable, divine rules or the opinions of revered rabbinic authorities, the rabbis cajole and delay, hesitant to issue decisions of any kind, particularly ones that may interfere with a husband's "free will." Even when decisions *are* made, confusion often reigns: grounds for supporting or denying a woman's request for a divorce are frequently vague and undeclared, different tribunals can take different positions as to what constitutes valid grounds, the same tribunal may take conflicting positions at different times, and a lower court tribunal may ignore the directives of the High Rabbinic Court (the equivalent of a rabbinic court of appeals) with impunity (see chapter 3). What's more, even when rabbis issue rulings against recalcitrant husbands, they often are unwilling to put any judicial weight behind them. Rulings that proclaim that a man "must" divorce his wife (*al ha-baal legaresh et ishto*) or that it would be a "good deed" (*mitzvah*) are not backed by judicial fiat (see chapters 4 and 5), even though the Rabbinic Courts Jurisdiction (Enforcement of Rabbinic Rulings) Law of 1995 allows for such coercive measures. And even orders "obliging" (*hiyuv*) a husband to give a get are not always enforced, with some tribunals insisting that only an order "compelling" (*kefiyah*) a get will warrant the application of significant pressure against a recalcitrant husband (Weiss, 2002).

To make matters more difficult still, if that's possible, many Israeli rabbinic courts will *not* compel a husband to divorce his wife — even if she has been able to establish grounds that they might accept for doing so — if he agrees in principle to divorce but insists, in exchange for the get, that his wife meet what the judges deem to be his "easily fulfilled" demands, citing the rulings of the same sixteenth-century rabbi consulted in the case of Reina (the Maharashdam) (Shut Maharashdam, Even Haezer, no. 41). The same applies to a husband's "reasonable" demands, citing the Maharik (Rabbi Yoseph Colon, 1620–1680) (Shut Maharik, Shoresh, no. 102). The Maharik-Maharashdam rules, together with the textual confusion and vagueness noted earlier, as well as the rule barring the "forced divorce," all foster a culture of extortion in Israeli rabbinic courts, where contested divorces are not solved by pressuring stubborn and recalcitrant husbands to give the get, but by pressuring women to give in to their husbands' terms (see chapters 3, 4, and 5).

DIVORCE IN ISRAEL

Rabbinic courts had been operating in the territorial area now under the sovereignty of the State of Israel long before its founding in 1948. For hundreds of years, the people living in the land were governed by the Ottoman Empire, which, ruling many different ethnic groups, specifically delegated the regulation of matters involving questions of personal status to religious communities, or *millets*, and allowed those millets to set up separate courts to determine how to formally enter into legal marriages and how to end them. In 1922, when the League of Nations gave the British the mandate to temporarily govern the land known as Palestine, they incorporated the millet system into the legal apparatus (Palestine Order in Council, 1922). The millet system remained in place for the entire British Mandate period, from 1922 to 1948, and in fact it still does. Kadis for Muslims, priests for Christians, or rabbis for Jews decide whether or not the rules and customs of their community allow for divorce in the particular circumstances of a case presented to them. No woman sat (or sits) on any bench of any court set up by any of these millets. The millet court system includes tribunals of first instance, as well as appeals courts set up at the insistence of the British to ensure a litigant's right of review, despite the objection of Jewish hard-liners that there was no reason to think that an appeals court can do a better job than a ruling court that had examined the facts and law carefully (T. Bavli Bava Batra 148b; Radzyner, 2004; see also chapter 3, where rabbinic courts clash).

As the possibility of the Jewish state became more real, the founding fathers had to decide whether or not to adopt the millet arrangement. In 1947, in anticipation of the declaration of the establishment of the state and the signing of the U.N. Charter (see chapter 7), David Ben-Gurion, then the head of the Jewish Agency (the representative body of the Jews in Palestine under the British Mandate), turned to religious leaders to work out the parameters of the place of religion in the state. In a letter dated June 19, 1947, and addressed to the World Agudath Israel Organization, the umbrella organization set up in 1912 to strengthen the worldwide Orthodox community, Ben-Gurion declared with unequivocal clarity, "The establishment of the state requires the approval of the United Nations, and this will not occur if the state does not guarantee freedom of conscience for all its citizens and if it does not make it perfectly clear that there is no intention to set up a theocratic government" (Rabinovich & Reinharz, 2008).

With this as the axiomatic precondition for what was to follow, Ben Gurion then addressed World Agudah's demands with regard to "personal status, the Sabbath, Kashrut, and education" and proposed guidelines that would frame Israel's Jewish character. He agreed, for example, that Saturday would be the state's official day of rest, that all public institutions would serve kosher food, and that religious educational institutions would be given autonomy and freedom, with the understanding that the new state could demand and supervise a core curriculum that included the study of the Hebrew language, history, and science. With regard to marital issues, Ben Gurion wrote, "All members of the committee appreciate the seriousness of the problem and the great difficulties involved. All bodies represented by the executive arm of the Jewish Agency will do all that can be done to satisfy the needs of those who are religiously observant in this matter and to prevent the division of the House of Israel into two" (58-59).

Suggesting that the new state would consider the implications of civil marriage and divorce when determining how to formulate its family laws, Ben Gurion seems to have been addressing the feeling of Agudath Israel then, and of the ultra-Orthodox to this day, that civil marriage would generate division among Israeli citizens, since it would legitimize marriages otherwise prohibited under halakha, allow for divorce without a get and thereby lead to the birth of *mamzerim*, and permit Jews to marry converts who were not converted under strict standards. Worst of all, it would facilitate assimilation by recognizing the marriages of Jews to non-Jews. Now often referred to as the origin of the "status quo" arrangement, the letter signed by Ben Gurion in June 1947 is often summoned to warn against any challenge to the delicate balance between the Jewishness of the state and other secular demands on it--though scholars have regularly pointed out the ephemerality of the status quo, which is actually changing all the time (Barak-Erez, 2009; Ripple, 1998).

Most interesting for our purposes, in 1947 the status quo with regard to the millet system may have been more liberal and afforded more freedom of conscience than it does today. Then, a person of the Jewish faith was not automatically subject to the jurisdiction of religious courts. Such jurisdiction was voluntary. Only if listed as a member of the organizational body known as "Knesset Israel" would a person be subject to such jurisdiction. Set up in the 1920s, Knesset Israel was established to represent the national and political interests of the "Hebrew People living in the land of Israel," and members were considered part of the Jewish millet. A Jew could opt out of the millet system simply by asking to erase his or her name from the membership list. This possibility of opting out was initiated, it appears, to accommodate both various demands of the ultra-Orthodox who did not want to be subject to the jurisdiction of what they viewed as the more modern, Zionist rabbinic courts and the liberal sentiments of the British who did not want to subject individuals to the rule of religious laws without their consent. The "Knesset Israel Regulation," adopted by the Mandate's High Commissioner in 1927 to make this absolutely clear, reads as follows, "Anyone who wants to erase his or her name from the books [of Knesset Israel] shall make a declaration to that end, either personally or by a power of attorney in writing to the National Board" (1927, p. 2221). But as it stands today in Israel, no person can opt out of his or her millet in favor of a secular, civil legal regime.

Different theories prevail about the history behind the signing of the status quo letter. Some claim it was signed under pressure of Agudath Israel, which, at the time, threatened to oppose the creation of the secular Jewish state, since it was not divinely ordained or religiously motivated. Other authorities, including sociologist Menachem Friedman, say that Agudath Israel was in a difficult spot, demographically, theologically, and economically after the Second World War and did not have the strength for such opposition to be effective and that its motives were more practical – to legitimize any future political involvement of the organization with the new state and to further its own interests (1990). In any case, the document was deliberately vague. The promises made were partial and subject to various interpretations. There was no assurance that halakha would govern personal status, and there was no undertaking to give jurisdiction to rabbinic courts (Harris, 2002).

And, in fact, Tel Aviv law professor Ron Harris points out that at the end of 1947 and beginning of 1948, unelected Jewish attorneys representing various Zionist organizational bodies put together a special committee to determine how best to set up a new, independent legal system. The committee was meant to decide whether or not to integrate *mishpat ivri* ("Hebrew Law," the term used by Harris to refer to the deliberate reconceptualization and moderniza- tion of the ancient halakha) with the laws of the new state in general and with regard to matters of personal status in particular, as well as to determine if, and how, to expand the jurisdiction of the rabbinic courts. It was not at all taken for granted that the millet system, which applied halakha, would continue as is, unmodified and unadapted (see also Shamir, 2000). But because of political and practical expediencies, a hasty, and to some extent offhanded, adoption of the millet system was made in May 1948 with the passage of the Law and Administration Ordinance. That law set forth the judicial and executive pow- ers of the new state. The norms and institutions implicit in this foundational law, claims Harris, took on a life of their own: "What the supporters of mishpat ivri and those who wanted to limit the jurisdiction of the rabbinic courts could have easily achieved before the implementation of the Law and Administration Ordinance of 1948 by relying on the support of many jurists and politicians and on the feeling that this was indeed the beginning of a new era, they were hard pressed to achieve in coming decades. They were hard pressed because legal structures, normative and institutional, even if set up without real thought, have an internal dynamic of their own. They do not only reflect reality but, at times, as in the case at hand, they create it" (2002, pp. 54-55).

Harris blames the failure to incorporate mishpat ivri at that crucial time in Israeli history as one of the reasons for the current polarization of Israeli courts, with civil courts defining what it means for Israel to be a "democratic" state and with rabbinic courts defining what it means to be a "Jewish" one. Whether Harris' vision of the bridging possibilities of mishpat ivri is accurate or not, and whether the continuation of the millet system is attributable to Ben-Gurion's express status quo agreement or to the not-very-well-thought-out consequences of a foundational law promulgated under the exigencies of time and war, the Knesset entrenched the millet system as the law of the land when it passed the Rabbinic Courts Jurisdiction (Marriage and Divorce) Law of 1953. That law states that matters of marriage and divorce of Jews in Israel shall be under the exclusive jurisdiction of rabbinic courts and that "marriages and divorces of Jews shall be performed in Israel in accordance with din torah [Torah law]" — referring to ancient, religious norms that are not imagined, as was mishpat ivri, to be necessarily in sync with or applicable to modern times. To this day, rabbinic judges draw on Torah law to support their positions, without any attempt to place those ancient texts in any type of context of time or place.

In addition to giving rabbinic courts exclusive jurisdiction in matters of marriage and divorce, section 3 of the 1953 law gave them parallel, but not exclusive, jurisdiction with civil courts to decide matters ancillary to divorce, such as child custody, alimony, and the division of marital assets. The court in which a suit was first filed would have jurisdiction. As a result, a "race to the courthouse" was set in motion, with divorcing husbands and wives literally racing to file papers in the court that they thought best served their interests. Women turn most often to civil courts and men to rabbinic courts, for reasons that will become abundantly clear in the course of this book. This race was further complicated by the fact that multiple civil courts were given jurisdictions over different ancillary issues. If a person wished to sue for divorce and to make sure that civil courts hear all ancillary matters, it was, and still is, a complicated, costly, and debilitating process.

In the 1950s and early 1960s a lot of the rabbinic courts' work involved figuring out how to free Holocaust-era women who were anchored because their husbands were absent and presumed murdered by the Third Reich (Krauss, 1962). Occasional tragedies, such as the dramatic disappearance in 1968 of the Israel navy's submarine *Ahi Dakar* with the presumed but unwitnessed death of all hands, many of whom were married, also called for rabbinic input to determine that the wives of the drowned seamen could indeed remarry, even though the bodies of their husbands could not be retrieved. In time, the focus of the courts' work changed from freeing widows to arranging divorces that were agreed on, as well as adjudicating those that were not.

By the 1970s more couples were getting divorced and more men were racing to rabbinic courts. According to halakha, women are not entitled to property accumulated by their husbands during marriage and, at best, can hope to leave with the property they came with and the predetermined, often symbolic, amount stated in the *ketubah*, or marriage contract. In 1973 the Knesset passed the Marital Property (Balancing of Resources) Law to protect the rights of women to marital property, specifically requiring rabbinic courts to apply the new law (para. 13b). But the law also proclaimed that marital assets would be divided "upon the dissolution of the marriage" (para. 5), thus binding the division of marital property to the giving of the get. This unfortunate and short-sighted language turned the well-intended law into a "dead letter," as Supreme Court chief justice Meir Shamgar would later refer to it in a well-publicized case (*Yaakobi v. Yaakobi*, 1995), since it effectively allowed men to deny their wives rights to marital property so long as they themselves were withholding the get. Women's advocates and rights groups began lobbying to change the law almost immediately after it passed.

In 1982 the minister of justice set up a committee, headed by former Supreme Court justice Elisha Scheinbaum, to make recommendations for improving the way family laws were being implemented. Made up of eight persons, only one of whom was a woman, the panel recommended that with respect to matters adjudicated in the civil courts, one judge be assigned to hear all aspects of a dispute (an arrangement often referred to as the "one family, one judge"). But Ariel Rosen-Zvi, a law professor, vocal advocate of women's rights, and a member of the committee, was not satisfied. Rosen-Zvi had an extensive background in Jewish law and would, a few years later, write two important treatises in the area of family law. He wanted the committee to stop "the race to the courthouse," which, he felt, caused litigants great pain. He also wanted to give exclusive jurisdiction to civil courts to deal with ancillary matters, in particular the division of marital property. In a separate letter attached to the recommendations, Rosen-Zvi suggested that the Knesset repeal section 3 of the Rabbinic Court Jurisdiction Law and thus confine rabbinic courts to the issue of the get alone: "The problem before us is not a political question, and not even a matter of religion. . . . It is a professional question whose solution requires, from a legal perspective, that order be made out of the chaos that reigns, and, from a moral perspective, that suffering be prevented" (Scheinbaum, 1986, p. 280).

Rosen-Zvi marshaled a series of arguments in favor of stopping the race to the courthouse, which he saw as a negative incentive to reconciliation that imposed a psychological burden on the parties. It also placed the sides into a whirlwind of litigation and deflected involvement with the real issues at hand, as well as dragging out the process and making it expensive. Moreover, Rosen-Zvi asserted that the "race" wasted court time, was duplicative, buttressed the power of the already powerful, allowed for the misuse of process on the part of duplicitous spouses willing to manipulate the law to their material favor, and harmed children. Rejecting the possibility of consolidating the ancillary matters within the rabbinic courts, he explained that they did not apply the same rules of evidence or procedure as those applied in civil courts, they ignored modern laws with respect to the division of marital property, and they felt compelled to rule in accordance with the ancient customs that the Supreme Court had rejected as inappropriate for a modern state. He added, "With respect to the interest of justice which is the goal of the judicial process, both civil and religious, the current situation is inadequate and defective" (quoted in Scheinbaum, 1986, p. 290).

It took twelve years after the publication of the committee's recommendations before the Ministry of Justice set up the family courts in 1998 in accordance with the Scheinbaum commission proposals. But this did not end the duality. Rabbinic courts still have parallel jurisdiction, along with the now-consolidated family courts, to deal with matters ancillary to divorce, such as child custody, support, and the division of marital property. Professor Rosen-Zvi's criticism is still relevant and the situation today is still "inadequate and defective." Recently, yet another Ministry of Justice committee recommended giving exclusive jurisdiction to family courts on all matters ancillary to the divorce, but no action has been taken. The rabbis predictably expressed their indignation with regard to the proposal.

In the 1990s new players in the legal arena applied further pressure against the hegemony of rabbinic courts and the rabbinate. In 1994 the Supreme Court forced the hand of the rabbinic establishment to allow women to become "rabbinic court pleaders," positions that until then had been held exclusively by Orthodox men who had studied in all-male yeshivot (*Training Institute v. Minister of Religious Affairs*, 1994). These women were well versed in halakha and dedicated to an Orthodox way of life, but they also had rich, secular academic backgrounds. According to Professor Ronen Shamir of Tel Aviv University, the female pleaders tended to treat halakha as a "dynamic body of knowledge which is susceptible to interpretation and reinterpretation" (1996, pp. 82–83). Also in the late 1990s and early years of the twenty-first century, various women's nonprofit organizations and legal aid clinics were established, which targeted the maltreatment of women in rabbinic courts for reform. These initiatives, together with existing women's organizations with broader agendas, banded together to resurrect ICAR, the International Coalition for Agunah Rights, which had been set up in 1989 by the Israel Women's Network to find "a solution to the problem of Jewish women and divorce within the framework of *halakha*" (n.d.). In 2008 ICAR — with the unswerving support and steadfastness of Professor Menachem Ben-Sasson, chair of the Knesset Law and Constitution Committee; the tenacious efforts of lobbyist Marc Luria; and some luck — managed to persuade the Knesset to amend the lamentable Marital Property Law to allow for the division of marital property without reference to the get, a move that, as mentioned, had been supported by women's organizations since the law was originally adopted in 1974 and which had been consistently and rigorously opposed by the religious parties.

The female pleaders, women's organizations, clinics, and ICAR, together and separately, all began to increase public awareness of the injustices being perpetrated in rabbinic courts, to apply pressure for change, and to appeal for help. At the same time, as Hebrew University law professor Pinhas Shifman explains, the Knesset, by way of legislation, and the family courts, by way of explication, had begun to extricate many matters from the framework of personal status law and establish in their place a secular, territorial regime, resulting in what he calls "legal schizophrenia," in which "two different juridical systems — that of religious law and that of secular law — are struggling and pulling in opposite directions" (1990, pp. 537–538). The mounting conflict of values between religious courts that have become more and more vigilant in applying ancient, patriarchal rules and modern family courts more and more keen to circumvent those rules and to protect the equal rights of women in marriage and divorce, has led to strained relations between the two court systems.

Since 2000 the tension between rabbinic courts and family courts has been exacerbated to the point of what the rabbis refer to as a "world war" by a newly conceived practice: women have started suing recalcitrant husbands for damages. Brought mostly by attorneys working at the Center for Women's Justice, these lawsuits claim that withholding a get is not a man's religious right but a civil wrong and that women are entitled to compensation for emotional distress and for the infringement of their basic right to dignity and liberty. The family courts have agreed, and about a dozen judgments have awarded significant damages, ranging from some thirty thousand to two hundred thousand dollars to the plaintiffs. (Similar, but much lower, awards have been made in favor of men against wives who refused to accept a get.) These suits have been greatly beneficial to women, who in almost all of these cases have either received their gets in exchange for a waiver of their material claims or been awarded damages. But rabbinic courts view these judgments as an invasion of their jurisdictional turf, a challenge to the rule against the "forced divorce," and an implicit criticism of the way rabbinic courts drag out contested divorces (see chapters 4 and 5).

Curiously, a heated debate about marriage and divorce laws in the Land of Israel took place as early as 1904, between two British Jewish writers, the anti-Zionist Lucien Wolf (1857–1930) and the Zionist supporter Israel Zangwill (1864–1926). In an article written in 1904 for the *Jewish Quarterly Review*, commenting on remarks by a certain Mr. Greenberg, Wolf mockingly asked whether biblical, rabbinic, or medieval marriage and divorce laws would be in place in a Zionist land: "Mr. Greenberg has given us another national custom for the observance of which we are said to require a political free-hand — the Jewish Law of Marriage and Divorce. May I ask him what law? Is it the Deuteronomic or the Rabbinic law of Divorce? Is it the ancient POLYGAMY which lingered among the Italian Jews as late as the seventeenth century or Rabbi Gershom's monogamous 'custom of the Gentile' of the tenth century, or Mr. Zangwill's recent repudiation of the marriage regulations of Ezra and Nehemia which even the Paris Sanhedrin upheld?" (1904, p. 22).

In an article responding to Wolf's, Zangwill wrote straightforwardly that Zionism was always a political movement and that the people who hoped to turn the state into a halakhic paradise were nothing but "religious dreamers" (1905, p. 414). But Zangwill did not foresee the historical events that were about to engulf European Jewry and how these events would impact Zionism. Nor could he imagine that "religious dreamers" would get an unexpected assist from successive Israeli coalition governments, which have had what were to them more burning issues on their agenda than personal status laws and have made numerous pacts with religious parties, not unlike the one Ben-Gurion may have entered into in 1947. Despite being a minority, the Orthodox and ultra-Orthodox parties hold the balance of power in the Knesset and have historically been willing to go either way on other issues, as long as they get the religious legislation and budgets they demand. The upshot is that Israel's marriage and divorce laws are far closer to the "halakhic paradise" of Zangwill's religious dreamers than Wolf imagined they might be over a century ago, as well as disturbingly closer to the theocracy Ben-Gurion had foresworn in his promise to the United Nations.

DIVORCE WITH REGARD TO HUMAN RIGHTS

At or about the same time Ben-Gurion promised the United Nations that Israel would not become a theocracy, he also asserted that Israel, once it became a state, would fulfill its obligations under the U.N. Charter, the foundational treaty binding all member states of the United Nations. On the day the British Mandate expired, May 14, 1948, the Jewish People's Council issued the "Declaration of the Establishment of the State of Israel" in Tel Aviv, proclaiming that the new state would "ensure complete equality of social and political rights to all its inhabitants irrespective of religion, race or sex; it will guarantee freedom of religion, conscience, language, education and culture; . . . and it will be faithful to the principles of the Charter of the United Nations" (Rabinovich & Reinharz, 2008, pp.72-73). In November 1949 the General Assembly accepted Israel's application for admission to the United Nations (resolution 273) and Israel signed the charter.

Israel is also a party to the Universal Declaration of Human Rights and subsequent treaties. Composed in response to the experience of the Second World War and adopted in Paris on December 10, 1948, by the U.N. General Assembly, the declaration's express purpose was to define the meaning of the words "fundamental freedoms" and "human rights" used in the U.N. Charter. The declaration consists of thirty articles, further elaborated on by the General Assembly when it adopted, in 1966, the International Covenant on Civil and Political Rights (ICCPR) and the International Covenant on Economic, Social and Cultural Rights (ICESCR). The declaration and the two covenants (together with two informal protocols) are referred to as the International Bill of Human Rights. In 1976, when the covenants were ratified by a sufficient number of individual states, the Bill of Human Rights took on the force of international law. Other treaties formulated and ratified by U.N. members further expand on the International Bill of Human Rights (*Fact Sheet No. 2*, rev. 1). These include the Elimination of All Forms of Racial Discrimination, the International Convention on the Elimination of All Forms of Discrimination against Women (CEDAW), the U.N. Convention on the Rights of the Child, the U.N. Convention against Torture, and others. In 1966 Israel signed the ICCPR, ICESCR, and CEDAW, all of which it ratified on October 3, 1991. In the official website of the Ministry of Foreign Affairs, Israel asserts that it "is a party to all six major international human-rights covenants."

Among the human rights delineated in the International Bill of Human Rights are the following: the right to freedom of thought, conscience, and religion (art. 18); the right to equality before the law (art. 7) and to participate in government (art. 22); the right for equality in marriage (CEDAW, art. 16); the right to privacy (Declaration, art. 12); the right to procedural fairness in law, due process, and fair and impartial trial (art. 10); the right to own property, and not to be deprived of it (art. 17); the right to liberty and security of the person (art. 7); the right to marry and found a family (art. 16.1).

Many states have constitutions that mirror, to some extent or another, the human rights set forth in international covenants and treaties and guarantee those rights to their citizens. Israel does not yet have such a constitution. Instead, it has a set of Basic Laws (currently eleven in number) intended to form the starting point of a future constitution and serve as the basis for defending human rights and civil liberties. The judiciary is supposed to secure the implementation of the Basic Laws, and the Ministry of Foreign Affairs is meant to monitor the extent to which Israel has implemented its various international commitments. Nevertheless, all of Israel's declarations, undertakings, and legislation in the sphere of human rights are qualified, making the true picture of Israel's commitment to those rights far less attractive than many Israelis would like to paint it.

As early as in 1948 the Supreme Court held that the Proclamation of Independence had no constitutional validity and cannot be used to invalidate laws and regulations that contradict it (*Ziv v. DeFacto Head*, 1948). Though the declaration has, at times, been cited in support of various progressive agendas (see, e.g., *Poraz v. Lahat*, 1988; and *Shakdiel v. Minister of Religious Afairs*, 1988), until the passing of the Basic Laws of Human Dignity and Liberty (1992) and of Freedom of Occupation (1994) the Knesset was free to pass laws that violated basic human rights and that could not be overturned by judicial review.

The Basic Laws of Human Dignity and Liberty and of Freedom of Occupation pledge to uphold "fundamental human rights in Israel . . . in the spirit of the principles set forth in the Declaration of the Establishment of the State of Israel." In theory, they enable the Supreme Court to invalidate (new) laws that infringe on those fundamental rights. Indeed, Supreme Court chief justice Aharon Barak declared that with the passage of those laws, Israel had "joined the community of democratic countries" and "become part of the human rights revolution that characterizes the second half of the twentieth century" (*United Mizrahi Bank v. Migdal Cooperative Village*, 1995, p. 379). But, in practice, the Basic Law: Human Dignity and Liberty does not refer specifically to the "right to equality" (Barak-Erez, 1995) and excludes from within its purview laws passed prior to its promulgation (para. 10), as well as laws and regulations "befitting the values of the State of Israel" (para. 8). To date, the Supreme Court has invalidated only a handful of laws on the basis of the 1992 and 1994 Basic Laws (*Office of Israeli Financial Planners v. Minister of Finance*, 1998; *Tzemach v. Minister of Defense*, 1999; *Oron v. Knesset Speaker*, 2002; *Gaza Coast Regional Council v. Knesset of Israel*, 2005; *Adalah Legal Centre v. Minister of Defense*, 2006; *Ploni v. State of Israel*, 2009; *Academic Institute v. Minister of Finance*, 2009), though the laws have been quoted to protect and expand the interests of women (to property, equal opportunity, and protection from rape, for example) (*State of Israel v. Ofir Beeri*, 1993; *Israel Women's Network v. Government of Israel*, 1994; *Miller v. Minister of Defense*, 1995; *Yaakobi v. Yaakobi*, 1995; *Plotkin v. Eisenberg Brothers*, 1997; *Center for Women's Justice v. Rabbinic Court Administrative Offices*, 2008).

With respect to the U.N. Bill of Rights and its "six major international human-rights covenants," Israel has consistently expressed its "reservations." A reservation is a unilateral statement purporting to exclude or modify the legal effect of certain obligations. Thus Israel has proclaimed its reservation with regard to article 7 of CEDAW, which protects the rights of women to hold political office, inasmuch as that article may relate to "the appointment of women to serve as judges of religious courts where this is prohibited by the laws of any of the religious communities in Israel" (res. 1); and with regard to article 16 of CEDAW, which protects the equal rights of women in marriage and divorce, "to the extent that the laws on personal status which are binding on the various religious communities in Israel do not conform with the provisions of that article" (res. 2).

The U.N. Committee on the Elimination of Discrimination against Women considers these reservations to be incompatible with the convention. It states that articles 2 and 16 of the convention are "core provisions" and claims that "neither traditional, religious or cultural practice nor incompatible domestic laws and policies can justify violations of the Convention. The Committee also remains convinced that reservations to article 16, whether lodged for national, traditional, religious or cultural reasons, are incompatible with the Convention and therefore impermissible and should be reviewed and modified or withdrawn" (*Reservations to CEDAW*, n.d.).

In sum, the Proclamation of Independence, the Basic Laws, and international treaties provide Israeli women with only attenuated protection against human rights violations, with Israeli courts deferring to religious laws, religious communities, the "values of the State of Israel," and sentiments referred to as "multicultural tolerance" (see, e.g., *Regan v. Transportation Ministry*, 2011). With historical errors compounding themselves on a daily basis, with room for judges to maneuver within the law, with express limitations in the Basic Laws with regard to prior laws and ones that protect the "values" of the state, with ideologically couched excuses, and with political pressure from religious parties, it should come as no surprise that the Supreme Court of the State of Israel has to a large extent stood idle in the face of infringements on women's equality, dignity, and liberty of person inflicted by rabbinic courts in the name of religious laws.

It is these infringements that we highlight in the chapters that follow.

DIVORCE IN BROADER CONTEXT, TERRITORIALLY AND CONCEPTUALLY

In her book *The Transformation of Family Law*, Harvard law professor (and former U.S. ambassador to the Holy See) Mary Ann Glendon describes how family law has changed in the United States and western Europe over centuries. Among other things, she shows how the regulation of marriage went from custom to law, from ecclesiastical control to secular regulation. She maintains that "from the sixteenth to the eighteenth centuries, in great parts of Western Europe, the Catholic Church lost its jurisdiction over marriage" (1989, pp. 30–31). A similar trend, as we have seen, has *not* occurred in Israel, where rabbinic control remains the law of the land. Thus it would seem, at first glance, that Israel lags far behind its Western neighbors and ideological allies.

However, closer scrutiny shows that the issues are much more complicated and fragmented. While Israeli law extends official recognition of "marriage" only to religious rituals performed inside Israel between persons of the same religious communities, in other ways, it gives somewhat lesser, but still official, recognition to different types of unions between consenting adults. The Ministry of the Interior registers couples married in ceremonies performed abroad as "married," including couples of different religions (*Punk Schlesinger v. Ministry of Interior*, 1962) and of the same-sex (*Ben Ari v. Director of Population Registrar*, 2005). Those couples enjoy much the same benefits that the state has to offer to couples married by Orthodox rabbis inside the state, including inheritance rights and the division of marital property (see Lifshitz, 2009). And more important, Israeli law, both statutory and judicial, recognizes "common law marriages" (the partners to which are referred to *as yeduim be-zibur,* literally, "those known to the public" as each other's husband and wife), extending benefits to women who live under such cohabitation arrangements that some authorities have claimed protect women better than if they were married (Shalev, 1995) and subject to the extortion of recalcitrant husbands, as described in this book. (But see Lifshitz, 2001, arguing that, while helpful, Israeli courts' recognition of cohabitation is at best a "patch" on an inadequate legal system.)

But just as in other countries studied by Glendon, it can be said that in Israel too there has been a historical shift in the relationship of the state to the family. To the extent that the Israeli state recognizes cohabitation arrangements as committed partnerships or unions, state involvement in the regulation of marriage and its dissolution has been progressively withdrawn, leaving the way people enter into such cohabitation partnerships and exit them primarily up to the individuals involved. Adults in Israel are free to enter and leave such partnership arrangements as they please, and the state interferes only to supervise the economic consequences of the dissolution of such arrangements.

But to the extent that the state mandates religious marriage and divorce as the "legitimate" and "legal" way to formalize the cohabitation of consenting adults, state involvement with the family has become an unbearable nightmare. The state, through the state-financed rabbinate and its rabbinic courts, gives people very little freedom indeed to decide how to construct a marriage, or who is authorized to consecrate it and legalize it. It gives them almost no freedom to divorce, leaving some women inside empty shells of "legal" marriages long after the partnerships have ended (chapter 4) and at the mercy of recalcitrant husbands; these men can disappear at will (chapter 1), make exorbitant demands (see chapters 1, 3, 4, and 5), or seek to control their anchored wives' sex lives (chapter 2). Whereas the Western world has moved from fault to no-fault for grounds for divorce, in Israel it is not at all clear what fault of a man, if any, is grounds for divorce. And even if fault grounds are established, rabbinic courts cannot declare the marriage over. Moreover, even if a couple marries in a civil ceremony abroad, the state mandates that the dissolution of such legal cohabitations will occur only in keeping with ancient religious rituals (chapter 6).

Hence, Israeli family law is a peculiar institution indeed, in which modern patterns of behavior, like cohabitation, both affect it and are ignored by it at the same time. On the one hand, Israeli civil laws dealing with cohabitation seem to be progressing in sync with changing social conditions that acknowledge that couples are constructing new families and unions held together by the emotional commitments of consenting adults and not by the law. On the other hand, the official marriage and divorce laws seem to be standing obdurately, and purposely, out of sync with modern behavior, harking back to a fundamental, patriarchal family order in which men take women and send them away according to their own terms, and women have very little, if anything, to say about it. This disarray, haphazardness, and conflicting set of values "owes something to the fact that the field of family law has become an arena for a variety of political, religious, and ethnic struggles," as Glendon put it with respect to the inconsistencies she detects in the family law regimes under her investigation (1989, p. 2).

In fact, the field of family law in Israel has become an arena for such a complicated political-religious-national-ethnic struggle, one that is being waged on the backs of women. In this struggle, civil courts, as Ron Harris has suggested, are distinguishing themselves from religious ones and in so doing are articulating what it means to be a democratic nation-state in a manner that is opposed to what it means to be a Jewish one. It also appears that different matters are at stake for the different courts and their constituents, with family courts interested in justice (among other things, the redistribution of family assets in a fair and equitable manner) and the religious courts interested in identity politics and the purity of the Jewish people (concerns of recognition and identity, of who is marriageable and who is not, and who is in and who is out of the Jewish people). Among the questions raised by this "world war" are the perennial ones: "Who is a Jew?" and "What is a Jewish nation?"

In 1958 Prime Minister Ben-Gurion asked Russian-born British Jewish philosopher Isaiah Berlin, along with fifty distinguished Jews from all over the world, to help answer these questions in reference to Ministry of the Interior deliberations on how to register the nationality and religion of children born to Jewish men married to non-Jewish women. Ben-Gurion asked his consultants to keep in mind four factors: that Israel is committed to ensuring the freedom of religion and conscience of its citizens; that Israel is the center of the in-gathering of exiles and therefore efforts must be made to "emphasize what is common and unites and to uproot that which is divisive and distancing"; that Israel does not have the same fears of assimilation that confront Diaspora Jewry; and that the Israeli people views itself as intimately connected with the Jews of the Diaspora. After all, he writes, "It is not happenstance that the state takes pains to deepen the Jewish consciousness of Israel youth, to root it in the past of the Jewish people and its customs and history, and to strengthen its connection to tradition and to world Jewry" (1958).

In his reply, Berlin said he did not want to add "his drop of fuel" to what he felt was destined to be, but had not yet become, a "major conflagration," a Kulturkampf. He also did not think it was a good idea to ask Jews in the Diaspora what they thought. "Israel is a sovereign State," he wrote, "founded to give full political and social expression to the Jewish nation," and it must act on behalf of that nation "without feeling obliged to seek advice of Jews beyond its borders. . . . [Unless], of course, the Jews are to be conceived as principally a religious establishment — a kind of church." Berlin expressed "his sympathy" with the view that the "civil status of the State of Israel must be sharply and definitively divided from Judaism as an established religion" and that "a modern liberal State is secular in character, and that the religion of its citizens is, in so far as it is a State and nothing else, indifferent to it." But, he emphasized, "It appears to me, and I am sure you will agree, that the status of the Jews is unique and anomalous, composed of national, cultural, religious strands, inextricably intertwined. To attempt either to affirm their indissolubility, or to attempt the separation of those strands, must inevitably lead to much deep and bitter disagreement. It seems to me that unless and until it becomes imperative, as it may one day, to face Jews with so crucial an issue, little advantage will be gained from doing so" (2009, p. 672).

In 1968 the issue raised by Ben-Gurion was presented to the Supreme Court by Benjamin Shalit, an army officer married to a non-Jewish woman, who petitioned the court to order the Haifa Population Registrar to register his children as "Jew" or "Hebrew" by nationality. The registrar had refused, stating that in accordance with internal directives, it could not register children as "Jew" by nationality if their mother was a non-Jew by religion. Like Berlin, the judges did not want to take on such an incendiary issue on such a small matter and urged the registrar to omit the problematic category of "nationality" from the registration form. When the parties disagreed, an expanded court held, by majority in January 1970, that parents had the right to register their children as they saw fit and that such registration had no bearing on whether, in fact, the children were Jewish or not (*Shalit v. Minister of Interior*, 1970). Six months later, in the aftermath of the ruckus the case caused, the Knesset changed the registration law to reflect the halakha. To date, by law, a child born of a non-Jewish mother cannot be registered as a Jew by nationality or religion.

In a similar vein, in May 2011 Israeli award-winning author and Palmah veteran Yoram Kaniuk, who is also married to a non-Jew, demanded that the Ministry of the Interior register his national status as "Israeli" and his religious status as "without religion," arguing that he, a secular Jew, is not "Jewish" as that term is now being defined by the state. This definition, he contended, stands in direct violation of the state's promise of religious freedom as set forth in the Proclamation of Independence and of the U.N. Charter and breaches the state's responsibilities and commitments to nonextremist Jewish denominations in the Diaspora (Mualem, 2011). When the ministry refused, he filed a petition with the Tel Aviv District Court asking that they order the ministry do as he requested. His petition was upheld, and the state is considering appealing it.

We agree with Kaniuk. "Judaism" is not the same as it was in 1958, or 1970. Things have changed. The strands of Jewish identity — nationhood, ethnicity, and religion — are unraveling willy-nilly. Each strand is distinguishing itself from the others, and in many respects this is happening at the expense of women and because of differences in attitudes toward women. In Israel and in the Diaspora, there are many Judaisms, many traditions, and many religious institutional expressions that reflect different identity politics and serve different needs, including those of individuals, different religious groups, and the state. The state can no longer ignore its commitment to the U.N. Charter and to its citizens to protect the freedom of conscience of individuals to believe in whatever permutation of Judaism, or construction of it, that speaks to them or serves their particular needs and to associate with whatever wider religious community, cult, or denomination they may choose. But the Jewish state cannot sacrifice its commitment to democracy and individual rights in favor of the identity needs of a particular individual, religious group, or, certainly not, fundamentalist movement. Moreover, it must find its own version of Judaism to reflect the values and moral commitments of its imagined national identity.

We believe that the day foreseen by Berlin has come and a culture war is upon us, ironically brought about by the state's attempt to avoid it. By giving a monopoly and coercive power to the rabbinic courts to decide issues of personal status, as well as allotting state funds to support them, the state has, inadvertently and with time, created a type of "church" in the sense described by Max Weber and intuited by Berlin — a formidable, religious institution that claims as its constituency, as a matter of right, all persons in the polity, as well as those beyond it (see Casanova, 1994). This new and unique church wants to use its territorially limited but vital state and political power to extend its control beyond state borders and to disseminate its religious beliefs, practices, laws, and truths over both its limited and loyal constituency of Orthodox Jews, as well as over a broader group that it refers to as the "Jewish People" (see declaration cited in *Sabag v. High Rabbinic Court*, 2004). The goals of this church and the interest of its transnational constituents are not congruent with the goals of the state and the interests of its territorially defined citizens, in particular its women, and the state can no longer afford to allow it to continue. The state must separate itself from the sociological church it itself has created, demoting it to a denomination within the public sphere of civil society but outside the realm of state-backed activities.

Most Jewish women in the Diaspora who want a Jewish divorce are not required by state law to undergo such a divorce, even if they married religiously (with the exception, interestingly, of Jewish women in Muslim countries who must divorce in accordance with religious rules). Mostly affiliated with the Orthodox and Conservative movements, such women desire a Jewish divorce because their group affiliations to particular religious communities bind them to customary laws — the halakha — and they do not recognize themselves as legitimately married or divorced except under those rules, the civil laws of their country of residence notwithstanding.

The Israeli rabbinate maintains that women in Israel who want a get are better off than their religious counterparts outside of Israel. In the Diaspora, courts cannot punish or incarcerate men who do not give their wives a religious divorce, whereas Israeli rabbinic courts can, they claim. Since 1995 the Knesset has delegated a vast array of powers to rabbinic courts to punish recalcitrant husbands, should they decide that the halakha so permits, by taking away their professional licenses, closing their bank accounts, restricting their ability to travel abroad, and even putting them in jail (Rabbinic Court [Execution of Judgment] Law of 1995). Therefore, argues the rabbinate, it should have jurisdiction over all Jews, wherever they may reside. When a citizen and resident of Monaco petitioned the Israeli Supreme Court in 2004, challenging the authority of rabbinic courts to prevent him from going home because he refused to give a Jewish divorce to his wife, also a citizen and resident of Monaco, the rabbinic court in its response defended its long, powerful state arm over men all over the world who refuse to give their wives a get. In a proclamation that resonated with Berlin's suggestion that there may be some who view Judaism as an established, transnational church, the rabbinic court declared,

> We reiterate our call to the Knesset not to stand idly by while cries of the agunot of Israel from around the Jewish world rise up to the heavens. Israel is the state of the Jews. Israel belongs to all Jews worldwide, even the Jews who are not yet citizens or residents of the state. So long as nations do not provide a legal solution for persons who are married in those lands under Jewish law and seek a Jewish divorce, the ear of the Israeli Knesset must be attuned to the cries of these miserable and unhappy women. The freedom of these women is in all

likelihood dependent on a decision that will be issued by a rabbinic court in Israel. Everyone who holds the principle of dignity dear to him – even those who are not observant of the Torah and its commandments – must garner all senses to help. Israeli Knesset must not seal its ears and shut its eyes to the troubles of these women (*Sabag v. High Rabbinic Court*, 2004, p. 826)

The Supreme Court, however, was not impressed. Justice Ayala Procaccia, writing for the majority, held that despite her sympathy for the plaintiff's situation, the jurisdiction of the rabbinic courts does not extend around the world, and they must, like all courts, limit themselves to their own territory. She vacated the rabbinic court orders that had restrained the man from Monaco, leaving him free to go. A few months after the decision, the Knesset amended the rabbinic court jurisdiction law to greatly expand the jurisdictional arm of the rabbinic courts to include, under certain limited circumstance, Israeli citizens who may not be residing in Israel or Jews residing in Israel who are not Israeli citizens (§4a). (But even in its current expanded configuration, the law would not allow for orders like the ones the rabbinic court issued in *Sabag v. High Rabbinic Court*, 2004.)

The rabbinic court's proclamation notwithstanding, civil courts worldwide have not stood idle while agunot suffer, and they have responded to their aid, mostly by refusing to provide legal remedies requested by a recalcitrant spouse, for example, in New York State (NY Dom. Rel., §253; McKinney, 1988); in Canada (Canadian Divorce Act, §21.1, and Ontario Family Law Act, §§2.4, 2.7; in South Africa (Divorce Amendment Act 95, 1996, §5a); in England and Wales (Family Law Act 1996, §9.3); and in Scotland (Family Law Act, 2006, §15). New York has even provided legislation that allows a court to penalize a spouse if he does not "remove barriers to remarriage" by taking such activity into account when dividing marital assets or determining spousal support (NY Dom. Rel., §236B, sec. 5h).

Foreign courts have also used tort law and contract law to help agunot. France was the first jurisdiction to allow women to sue recalcitrant husbands for damages (French Civil Code, §1382). A Canadian court awarded damages for breach of a husband's promise to give a get, separation of church and state notwithstanding (*Bruker v. Marcovitz*, 2007). A British court ordered a husband to pay increased alimony until he gave a get (*Brett v. Brett*, 1968), and a New York court declared "unconscionable" and void a unfair martial property arrangement that the wife entered into under pressure to receive a get (*Perl v. Perl*, 1987) (Weiss & Dainow, n.d.).

Most important, a formidable consensus of rabbinic authorities has held that women who have married in civil ceremonies, in particular those who could have married in religious ceremonies and chose not to, *do not* need a get to end their marriage. Their marriages are considered a "nullity." These include Rabbi Moses Feinstein (1895–1986), Rabbi Yitzhak HaLevi Herzog (1888–1959), Rabbi Ben Zion Meir Uziel (1880–1953), Rabbi Eliezer Waldenberg (1915–2006) (Breitowitz, 1993, pp. 74–75, nn. 212–216), as well as Rabbi Isaac HaCohen Kook (1860–1930) (Shut Ezrat Cohen, re: Even HaEzer, no. 38). A similar position was taken recently by former rabbinic judge Shlomo Dichovsky with regard to marriage of Israelis performed abroad (*Plonit v. Ploni [Benai Noah]*, 2003), although he claims that such marriages are not "nullities" but require a declaration of court to be dissolved (see, however, chapter 6). Similarly, rabbinic authorities have also held that parties who live together are not considered married, since it is their express intention not to marry and thus the halakhic proclamation that one does not cohabit licentiously but for purposes of marriage does not apply to them. These couples too do not need a get should they decide to part ways.

Thus, it is our opinion that Israeli women fare worse than their Diaspora sisters, since all of them, whether or not they are religious, must marry in accordance with ultra-Orthodox rules. And, as we see in these stories, these rules do not serve them well, despite the state-authorized long-arm of the rabbinic court — an arm that, it seems, the court more readily flexes with regard to tourists under pressure to return home than Israeli citizens.

Some Numbers

MARRIAGE

As of 2006 almost all Israeli men (97.7 percent) and women (96.8 percent) could be expected to marry at least once before the age of sixty-five. Of those couples who married between the years 2000 and 2006, about 88 percent did it in Israel and 12 percent abroad, most in Cyprus. Of those Israelis who married abroad about a third are couples in which both spouses are registered as Jews. In 2006, 3.8 percent of Jewish couples were living in a cohabitation arrangement (44,800 couples), the majority young and without children. A report published by Bar Ilan University states that cohabitation should be seen as a stage prior to marriage and not instead of it, despite a 33.3 percent increase from 2004 to 2006 of couples who cohabit and have children. Thus, although the state has given a nod of approval, albeit circumscribed and less than official, to cohabitation, and even though such cohabitation arrangements may be better for women than marriage, only a small number of Israeli couples choose to cohabit rather than get married (Halperin-Kaddari & Karo, 2009).

DIVORCE

An estimated 15 percent of new Israeli marriages end in divorce (*Americans for Divorce Reform*, 2002). More than 50 percent of divorces occur in the first nine years of marriage (Halperin-Kaddari & Karo, 2009, p. 44). Statistics collected by the rabbinic courts and collated by Halperin-Kaddari and Karo (pp. 73–80) show the following:

Between 2000 and 2007 Israelis filed an average of eight thousand contested divorce petitions a year in rabbinic courts and a similar number of uncontested divorce agreements.

In 2007 rabbinic courts issued 243 orders "obliging" divorce and 18 "compelling" divorce and imposed sanctions eighty-six times on recalcitrant spouses.

From 1995 until February 11, 2008, a total of 40,541 contested cases did *not* end in divorce. These included cases that the rabbinic courts referred to as both "active" and "inactive," with inactive cases being those the court closed administratively. (From our experience, women will sometimes allow their files to become "inactive" when tired of fighting or when their petitions are rejected; see chapter 5). Only 14.3 percent of these cases were considered "active."

Between 1998 and 2007 in 25 percent of active and inactive cases in which husbands were obliged to give a get, the husbands still had not agreed to divorce their wives. Since 1995, 5.9 percent of the contested cases that ended in divorce took three to four years; 12.5 percent took more than four years.

From these statistics one may conclude that rabbinic courts are ineffective in resolving contested divorce cases. Rabbinic courts issue few orders against recalcitrant husbands, and even when they do, such orders are not infrequently ignored. There are divorce suits that remain unresolved, and even when they are resolved, they take too long to complete. Many files are closed without explanation.

How many women are caught in the web of Jewish divorce laws? From these statistics, it is far from clear. One survey conducted by the Rackman Center in 2004 suggests that more than 40 percent of all Israeli women who had been involved in divorce proceedings claimed that they had been subject to pressures by their husbands who threatened to withhold the get and that nearly 7 percent of women who sought divorce have given up all hope of ending their failed marriages (Halperin-Kaddari & Adelstein-Zekback, 2012, p. 20; Halperin-Kaddari & Yadgar, 2010). Until rabbinic courts open their courtrooms and files to independent, professional researchers who will decide how to collect and collate data and how best to define who is an agunah, the numbers will remain incomprehensible and inexplicable, providing the courts with a veil of secrecy behind which to hide the true magnitude of the harm caused.

What is clear is that there are some women who stay in bad marriages rather than face the rabbinic courts and their daunting procedures and that there are those who walk out of bad marriages and don't bother ending them formally. And then, most important, all women who reach agreements with their husbands do so in the shadow of these rules and with the potential threat of the withheld get looming. Many will give up on their rights rather than face protracted divorce proceedings. Whatever the numbers, it is our contention that Israel's archaic and deleterious way of getting divorced must be changed.

CAVEAT, WITH RESPECT TO MEN

The focus of this book is the Jewish women who are separated from their husbands and cannot get the state to legalize the end of that relationship. The system discriminates against women in the name of religious law and facilitates the dominion of their husbands over them. It is this sad tale of discrimination and domination, buttressed by the "violent" power of the Israeli state, that we are telling, and not the story of Jewish men who are separated from their wives and cannot get an official divorce, although we are well aware that there are such men whose wives refuse to accept a get.

Since a decree attributed to Gershom ben Judah (ca. 960–1040), known as Me'Or Hagolah, "the light of the exile," Ashkenazi men cannot divorce their wives unilaterally and can also find themselves, like the women in this book, anchored to failed marriages. Nonetheless, we feel justified in writing from the perspective of harmed women and not, to paraphrase Martha Fineman, in the illusory light of equality (1991). Things are not equal. Jewish women who have relations with men other than their husbands, even if they are separated, and have children as a result are penalized. The children of those "illicit" unions, and their progeny forever, are considered to be mamzerim, who cannot marry other Jews. Unfaithful Jewish men are not so penalized. Extramarital relations of women are grounds for immediate divorce, whereas those of men are often forgiven and overlooked. Furthermore, Jewish law allows men whose wives are recalcitrant to take second wives, since bigamy is not prohibited in the Torah. Such dispensation is a specific exception under the Israeli criminal laws that prohibit bigamy (Penal Code of 1977, §179). Jewish women are not allowed to marry a second husband under any circumstances. Finally, and this applies to both Jews and non-Jews, men are generally more financially independent and secure and can more easily leave a failed marriage and pay the consequences than women, who are often dependent financially on their husbands.

Moreover, a woman's refusal to accept a get is not the same as a man's refusal to give one. One of the reasons for women refusing to accept a get is financial dependency on their husbands and the lack of a basis in Jewish law, and concomitantly Israeli law, for awarding alimony after the delivery of a get, which would protect and support a dependent, stay-at-home spouse in the event of divorce after a long-term marriage (halakha does not require a husband to pay alimony after a divorce). Once civil courts of law are empowered to declare a marriage over, and neither side can use the divorce as leverage, the legislature and courts will develop tools to grapple with the problems of economically dependent spouses in long-term relationships, including the issue of postget alimony, and how to divide up marital assets in a fair manner under those circumstances. Most important, even if the injustice suffered by "anchored" men and women were "equal" and even if the reasons for get refusal were the same, this would not, and could not, justify the continuation of a divorce regime that can leave both men and women legally anchored to failed marriages and open to extortion.

Why Now?

The question of the relationship between religion — and in particular strong religions or fundamentalisms — and the state is as relevant as ever. Though sociologists such as Peter Berger in the mid-twentieth century spoke of the "secularization of the world," today those same sociologists admit that they were in error and that religion has become a force increasingly to be reckoned with (Berger, 1997).

In the Fundamentalisms Project, a series of books based on a worldwide academic project sponsored by the American Academy of Arts and Sciences between 1987 and 1995 and published by the University of Chicago, Martin E. Marty and R. Scott Appleby define fundamentalisms as a set of strategies by which beleaguered believers attempt to preserve their distinct identity as a people or group, as well as their political power base, by selective and creative retrieval of the "fundamentals" of their distant past. Fundamentalists want to recreate the political and social order, often at the expense of women, in ways that promote the service and submission to their definition of the divine order and the preservation of their unique identity (1994). This definition, to a large extent, applies to the political leadership of the religious parties in the Knesset, in particular that of Shas and Agudath Israel, who, in turn, carry the swing vote in the committees that appoint Israeli rabbinic judges. And, as we see in the stories that follow, rabbinic judges, at the cost of justice and basic human decency, protect the "beleaguered" identity of their ultra-Orthodox group by defending what they believe to be the word of God inasmuch as it perpetuates the sacred helplessness of wives before their husbands' free will, terms for divorce, and the capacity and availability to deliver a get.

In none of the cases do the rabbis agree that the women should be allowed the right to divorce, independent of their husband's free will — even in the case of a civil marriage, where the consensus of rabbinic authorities would have allowed them to do so. All our agunot were dependent on their husbands for their freedom; they waited nineteen years (chapter 3), fourteen years (chapter 4), eleven (chapter 1), ten (chapter 5), five (chapter 2) and one (chapter 6) for a get after their marriages had to all intents and purposes ended. And, most interesting, we see how rabbis interpret texts and imagine halakhic categories that are completely new, or significantly distant from the consensus (see chapter 6), to protect their power base and political ends. The values of equality, dignity, and autonomy are far from their concerns.

In *Strong Religion*, one of the last books published as part of the Fundamentalisms Project, professors Gabriel Almond, R. Scott Appleby, and Emmanuel Sivan describe fundamentalist movements as one of the "significant political phenomena of our time." They describe how since 1979 these movements have risen to the highest level of state power in five countries: Iran (1979), Sudan (1993), Turkey (1996), Afghanistan (1996), and India (1996, 1998). They've infiltrated into parliaments, assemblies, and political parties in Morocco, Egypt, Pakistan, Jordan, the United States, and Israel and have formed powerful and deadly opposition groups such as Al Qaeda and Hamas. These movements challenge the centuries-long process that saw a retreat of religion from political power. The authors call for an end to Western myopia with respect to this potentially "dangerous phenomenon" (2003).

Giving religious courts power over the personal status of all citizens is, we believe, an expression of this dangerous phenomenon and is "Bad for Women," as liberal, feminist, political philosopher Susan Moller Okin argues with respect to multiculturalism in general (cf. Okin, 1999). It should not be supported in the spirit of multiculturalism, let alone be made the law of the land. Religion, especially in Israel, should have a respectable place in civil society, but it must defer to human rights and stand apart from state law (Casanova, 1994).

DISSONANCE

Another reason to raise this issue now: secular Israelis are doing what they want to do anyway as far as cohabitation and other issues are concerned, creating a rupture between government and "the people" that is likely to ultimately force a confrontation with the state. True, Tel Aviv's Rabin Square is not Cairo's Tahrir Square, but it doesn't have to be; there are free elections in Israel and many

Israelis voted in the past for the arch-secularist Shinnui party, which promised to combat religious coercion. It failed to produce change because of coalition politics, but nonetheless many Israelis simply ignore or find their way around religious legislation.

More and more shops (especially in the greater Tel Aviv area) are open on the Sabbath, in defiance of fines levied by government inspectors. Legislation such as the Law Prohibiting the Breeding of Pork (1963) and the Passover Law (1986), prohibiting the sale of unleavened bread or leavened bread products during Passover week, are essentially dead letters. And, as we have already mentioned, even personal status laws are slowly being eclipsed. Many Israelis don't marry at all and simply sign legal agreements in lawyer's offices or marry abroad.

And like secular Israelis, a growing number of liberal and open-minded Orthodox Israeli Jews are also distancing themselves from manifestations of state involvement with religion and halakha. They, as well as members of other religious communities including the country's small but growing Conservative and Reform synagogues, find themselves increasingly at loggerheads with the policy of state rabbinic judges over matters such as restrictions on the production of fruits and vegetables during a year designated for the land to lay fallow, conversion requirements, and personal status issues. They too call for the separation of rabbinate and state – attorney Dov Halbertal (2010), a former head of the chief rabbinate's office; Batya Kahana Dror, the executive director of Mavoi Satum, an organization that defends the rights of agunot and has spearheaded the attempt to set up alternative rabbinic courts; and Dr. Hannah Kahat, founder of Kolech, the first Israeli Orthodox feminist women's organization, being three prominent examples.

INADEQUATE RESPONSES

Today complaints about the plight of the agunot largely fall on deaf ears and certainly have no effect whatsoever on rabbinic judges. "I am empowered by the State of Israel and the Shulhan Arukh," thundered Dayan Haim Rosenthal once in a closed session of divorce proceedings. Indeed, the rabbinate proceeds serenely, as if there is no criticism whatsoever swirling about. The feeling is that everything is normal. If anything, the institution, they think, is greatly misunderstood, but it is here to stay.

Mainstream national women's organizations in Israel prefer to underscore their commitment to important, albeit traditional, women's issues, such as providing adequate day care centers, and only gingerly dip a toe into the murky waters of the get. The perceived evils of the occupation of the West Bank trump women's rights as far as some Israeli feminists are concerned. Inspired by American notions of equality between all people, these groups long ago assumed an agenda based on the logic that the conflict with the Palestinians has to be resolved before gender problems can be addressed.

Of course, there are women's rights groups and NGOs that are very engaged indeed and that try to pick up the slack on the get issue and champion the cause of the agunah (Center for Women's Justice, Kolech, Mavoi Satum, Rackman Center at Bar Ilan, and Yad L'Isha, to name a few, and more specifically, ICAR, the International Coalition for Agunah Rights, an umbrella organization). Many of these groups, but not all, are closely affiliated with Orthodox Judaism, and they stand behind several initiatives. Most represent individual women in their quest for a divorce. All have campaigned to educate Israeli couples to sign prenuptial agreements that are halakhically correct and would greatly limit the number of agunot by creating financial incentives for a man to deliver a Jewish bill of divorce to his wife in the event that their marriage has broken down. As outlined earlier, the Center for Women's Justice took a fresh approach by successfully convincing many Israeli (civil) family courts not to perceive get withholding "as a religious right, but rather a civil wrong," a move that warrants the award of compensatory damages, effectively changing the balance of power between religious and family courts. In 2008 ICAR did manage to convince the Knesset to amend the marital property laws to alleviate the double bind — no get and no property — that Israeli agunot had found themselves in when the law linked the division of marital property to the act of formal divorce. Recently, ICAR has also made strides to curtail the race to the courthouse.

We support all these efforts dedicated to liberating agunot, or at least ameliorating their predicament. But we want more. We feel that it is time to confront the difficult and inevitable challenge of disentanglement. Institutions are largely silent, politicians largely deaf, and no one listens to the agunot, but their plight throws Israel's problems with religious law into stark relief, with disentanglement looming ever larger and becoming more and more inevitable.

This Book

It is with the mission of disentanglement in our minds that we write this book. But first and foremost, our goal is to give a voice to Israeli women who have entered the Kafkaesque labyrinth of the state's rabbinic courts and have had a hard time getting out. It's about how these women are forced to navigate within a confusing and exasperating legal system and a daunting bureaucracy. The women we interviewed felt that they were trapped forever for reasons they do not understand, in a legal system where the rules are not clear and which seems to be run by divine fiat with which there is no negotiation. What are grounds for divorce if not the de facto end of a marriage? Who is making up the rules? What are those rules? What purpose are they serving? Who can the women go to for help? And when will it all end?

To write these stories we crisscrossed Israel to meet and interview six women of various ages and religious inclinations. Three are secular, two are religious Zionists, and one is ultra-Orthodox. Israeli religious divorce laws apply to all of them. The youngest one to sue for divorce was twenty-six when she filed her claim; the oldest was fifty-one. None wanted to be identified by their real names. The stories, told from the perspective of these women, are all authentic, though we have, both to make things clearer and to protect the anonymity of the women, taken liberty with details unrelated to the legal proceedings. All the attorneys and rabbinic pleaders we describe are composites of various professionals we have met over the years — with the exception of Rivkah Lubitch, who is, as we have already mentioned, a very real person. All the women were represented or advised at one stage or another by the Center for Women's Justice. Each agunah story is a narrative of pain and bureaucracy, chosen because it underscores a different aspect of the problem.

In "Clueless" (chapter 1) our agunah is Every Jewish Woman who marries like a member of the tribe and is ignorant of the legal consequences of that act. When her marriage breaks down, her husband refuses to give her a get and eventually disappears, leaving her in limbo for almost a full decade, because he cannot be found. Her story highlights the taken-for-granted circumstances under which Israeli Jewish women enter into Orthodox Jewish marriages — the only ones that can be performed in Israel and recognized by the state — without understanding the implications.

We purposely begin with Clueless's story because she represents the typical Israeli Jewish woman who marries within the borders of the state. The state takes away her freedom of choice, forces religious acts on her, and fails to explain the consequences of them to her. All Jewish women who marry in Israel, as well as all Jewish women who marry in Orthodox ceremonies anywhere, may become anchored to failed marriages if their husbands are missing, unable, or unwilling to deliver a bill of divorce to them. Many, if not most, are clueless regarding this possibility, and we want to raise their consciousness with this story.

In "Scarlet" (chapter 2) our agunah cannot obtain her get, even though her husband is the one who first filed for divorce. After she agrees, he does an about-face and his lawyer draws on key rabbinic authorities who lived from the thirteenth to nineteenth centuries to argue that a husband has the right to withhold a get as punishment for what he contends is his wife's wayward behavior. Scarlet's husband also insists on conducting a "sex-trial" to brand her and her alleged lover with what is tantamount to a modern-day Jewish version of Nathaniel Hawthorne's scarlet letter. Scarlet's story highlights the patriarchal underpinnings of halakha and how it maintains domination over the bodies of women, even after marriage is over.

We have chosen to tell Scarlet's tale after that of Clueless, because her story, like Clueless's, could happen to every Jewish woman. In addition to showing how the long patriarchal arm of halakha extends over Jewish women even after they are divorced, Scarlet demonstrates the veto power of the get in the hands of a spouse who does not want to give or accept one. It is a power often misused by attorneys as leverage, and it is a power greater in the hands of men than in those of women. When attempted to be used by women, it can easily boomerang against them. We wanted to feature the get as a tool of delay and dominance.

In "Ping-Pong" (chapter 3) our agunah spends nineteen years in the rabbinic courts being batted from one tribunal to another in the quest for a get. She goes from district rabbinic court to the High Rabbinic Court and back again, ping-ponging from one court to another. Confusion and disagreement reign regarding what grounds the courts will accept for her divorce. Even after she receives her get — more than twelve years after she started her long journey — the Ping-Pong agunah's nightmare is not over. Her husband asks the court to rescind the get when she tries to raise a challenge to her divorce settlement. The rabbinic court declares that she needs another get and that her status as a divorcee under halakha is held in abeyance. Her story is about the confusion, dissonance, and contradictions inherent in Jewish divorce laws; the power bestowed by rabbinic courts on husbands over their wives even after divorce; and the fact that none of the logic underlying those ancient rules in any way resonates with modern sensibilities.

Few divorce cases are tried and decided in rabbinic courts. Since the objective of most rabbinic courts is to convince the parties to end their marriage by agreement without the court's intervention, most hearings are more like extended negotiations — similar to those described in Clueless — than attempts to establish the facts or to argue what the law is, or should be, in a particular case. Ping-Pong's saga, though extreme, enables the reader to understand what happens when a woman insists that a rabbinic court render an opinion. Indeed it might be better for a wife to ask for a rabbinic court to mediate an agreement on her behalf than to decide a case on the basis of halakha, given the narrow and limited circumstances under which a court will compel a husband to give a get. Ping-Pong's story allows us to follow closely, as the halakha is deployed by a virtuoso pleader who knows how to manipulate the rules and the rabbis.

In "Accidental" (chapter 4) the agunah leaves her husband after living with him for only three short, very unhappy months. Fourteen years later, with her husband stonewalling in the rabbinic courts, the Accidental agunah is still legally married to him. The story brings to the forefront the public policy question that begs itself with regard to all the cases told in this book and with regard to Israeli divorce law in general: if a marriage is over in fact — irrespective of who may, or may not, have been responsible for the breakdown of that marriage — what purpose, if any, is being served the state, or the parties, or the Jewish people, by refusing to declare that marriage over by law?

To a large extent, Accidental is the exaggerated point at which we might have ended the story part of our book if all we had wanted to do was to focus on the error of applying ancient religious rules as the laws of divorce in a modern country. No modern divorce regime can justify the official continuation of a marriage fourteen years after a couple has separated, unless, of course, the purpose of that regime is to sustain the dominion of men over women and to allow vengeful husbands to capriciously curtail the liberty and autonomy of their wives.

As Ping-Pong in chapter 3, Pawn in chapter 5 stresses the vacuous nature of rabbinic court decisions. Though the court declares that the husband "must" divorce his wife, this decision, by the court's own definition, is essentially meaningless. It is a mere recommendation and if a husband ignores it, it does not mean that he is a "get refuser." But Pawn is more than the story of singular women caught in an ancient religious system that is no longer working in a relevant way. Pawn enables us to show that the issue at hand is greater than the sum of its individual parts. In chapter 5 the agunah is moved around helplessly in a power struggle between rabbinic and civil family courts over the question of what to do with a woman's claims that a husband's refusal to give a get is a "tort," a twisted, immoral act that entitles her to damages under civil law. When Pawn files for damages in family court, one rabbinic judge declares that a "world war" has erupted. What is at stake in this war is not only the continued domination of men over women (however denied) and not only the question of who should be given the job of deciding these cases; it is a war over what is valuable and meaningful and who has the authority to articulate what it is that has value and meaning. Pawn brings to the articulated fore the culture war that rumbles unspoken throughout all the cases. What should take priority — the autonomy of women to determine their lives or the "purity of the Jewish people" and its freedom from mamzerim? Are the needs and fundamental interests of a transnational "church" more important than the policy considerations of the Israeli Jewish nation-state with its limited borders and modern sensibilities?

In "Reluctant" (chapter 6), our final agunah is not clueless. She does not want to legalize her relationship with the man she lives with and adamantly refuses to get married through the rabbinate. Yielding to the pressure of her partner and her tradition-minded mother, she agrees reluctantly to formalize the relationship with her partner in a civil union in Cyprus, a move increasingly common among Israelis, even some Orthodox ones, unwilling to submit to the dictates of state religious courts and authorities. But when the two decide to break up, the rabbinic court refuses to issue a formal judgment dissolving the marriage and, instead, insists that the husband give his wife a get to legalize their separation. When he refuses, they put him in jail, despite the woman's protestations. This story depicts the concrete impact of religious institutional power on the very bodies of women and men when backed by the state.

We end with Reluctant's story because we want to emphasize the point that rabbinic courts should not operate alongside civil ones. Rabbinic courts will wield the authority given to them by the state in manners consonant with their interpretations of religious law, at that particular moment, and with their interests in the matter at hand, whatever they may be. They do so without regard to how the brandishing of that authority may infringe on the rights of others — to liberty or to freedom from religion. In chapter 6 the rabbinic court refused to end the couple's marriage in manners consistent with contemporary values and procedures, even though the High Rabbinic Court had, in a previous case that had "backed the rabbinic court to the wall," suggested that it would do so.

Finally, in "Israeli Divorce Laws and Human Rights" (chapter 7), we use the stories we have told to pinpoint the human rights violations perpetrated by Israel's rabbinic courts, infringement not only of the right to marry but also of the rights to property, equality, liberty, freedom of conscience, and due process. The chapter illustrates how these narratives of pain not only express the problems of individual women harmed by group customs but also implicate the state in violations of fundamental freedoms and compromise Israel's claim to be a democracy. We end with this chapter, which enables us to summarize the implications of the previous ones and to make our recommendation for tikkun olam — social change and a better world.

In the meantime the halls of the religious courts are full of powerless women. Nobody is listening to them. Resignation and apathy reign. Reflecting the cultural chaos in the country, many Israeli Jews are reluctant to condemn the system that can effectively ruin their lives or the lives of their loved ones. "The current situation is the only arrangement we have now," one of our interviewees mused, as if it were beyond our power to demand a distinction between the strictures of a state bureaucracy and one's private religious beliefs, between state and religion. The following narratives of pain clearly illustrate different aspects of the problem. Our topic speaks to the moment we are living in. Israel must decide: *is it a democracy or a theocracy?*

ONE

The Clueless Agunah

---

*Male domination is so rooted in our collective unconscious
that we no longer even see it.*

Pierre Bourdieu, *Masculine Domination*

Shackled hand and foot, Eitan was escorted into the Jerusalem Rabbinic Court
by two wiry police officers. "Our second today," one of the cops told Rivkah, the
reserved but resolute rabbinic pleader who had orchestrated this much longed-
for moment for her client, Shira, Eitan's wife. "This is my regular beat. Me and
my partner, we bring in about five of these sonofabitches every week, to the Beit
Din. Go figure them out. I prefer thieves. These husbands, they make me sick."

Eitan was an unkempt, middle-aged man with little hair. He weighed at least
150 kilo, about 330 pounds, in a not-very-tall frame, and the heavy chains on his
legs chafed against his swollen ankles, annoying him. He hadn't always been
so big. When he married Shira, he weighed barely 100 kilo. Pleasantly pudgy
at that time, one might have said, if one wanted to be kind. Like a teddy bear.
At least that's what Shira thought then.

Beginnings

In 1987 Shira Mazal Yosef, of medium height, with darkish skin tone, married Eitan Avimelch Azulai, her first and only boyfriend, when she was only
twenty. They had known each other since she was a freshman and he a senior
at their high school, located in the heart of Maoz Zion, a small locality on the
outskirts of Jerusalem, where they lived. After a mutual friend introduced them

at the water fountain, it took what seemed an eternity, says Shira, before Eitan finally stammered that he liked her sweater. A perky, pumped-up sort herself, she smiled bashfully and took his long silences for braininess. "He's too smart for small talk," she confidently told her mother when the latter commented on his awkward manner. Their first date was at a local movie theater. On a sticky summer night, he held her hand in the darkened theater. Shira liked the silent type, and Eitan's easy pace was fine with her. To be honest, she hadn't had much experience with boys herself. After the movie, he bought ice cream cones. As they licked their cones and spoke of the future — he said he wanted five kids — it all seemed so romantic and idyllic.

Though from a secular family, when she married Eitan, Shira was a virgin — *bitultilah*, as it is written in Aramaic in the ketubah. It was different then, in the eighties. Though virgin brides are a rare if not extinct phenomenon today, even among those who might claim to be Orthodox, back then brides whose families hailed from conservative Muslim countries were still *bitultalot*. Both Shira's and Eitan's family rode on the Sabbath and ate pretty much what they wanted outside their homes, but they prided themselves on their conservative ways and respect for traditional customs.

But an outsider would never have guessed that Shira was a traditional sort after a glimpse of her wedding gown. She and her mother loved the dress, sewn by a local seamstress, who copied it from a bridal magazine and added all imaginable embellishments. It was strapless and backless — not what they wore in Tripoli or Fez, where the groom's and bride's families came from. The only nod to the past was Shira's thick antique veil, which her maternal grandmother, Mazal-Tov, had worn on her wedding day.

A sensible girl with a brown ponytail who normally dressed in jeans and a sweatshirt, Shira had dreamed for years of renting a gauzy number straight from the ateliers of famous Israeli wedding-wear designers such as Galit Levi or Pnina Tornai in North Tel Aviv. But the dresses she sampled at those upscale establishments were too costly. Her father worked as a clerk for the city's collection department, running after people who didn't pay their parking tickets, and her mother was a secretary. Renting a fancy gown was beyond their means, costing the equivalent of a few thousand dollars, compared with the few hundred dollars that a local seamstress requested.

All of Shira's ideas for the wedding came from *Mitchatnim* (Marrying), a quarterly magazine published by the Israeli equivalent of the Yellow Pages. It advertises every conceivable item or service for that special day, from a choco-late waterfall for the dessert table to D.J.'s, lighting engineers, caterers, flower providers, dress designers, and rabbis. Israel is carefully portrayed as a paradise of Eros and love, where storybook weddings are the norm.

Mitchatnim has no editorial policy with regard to how one should marry, and the ceremony section is rich with possibilities. Recent copies, for example, include a practical guide on the technicalities of marriage in Israel provided by the Jewish Life Information Center (ITIM), an independent, nonprofit organization that helps couples navigate the religious bureaucracy. There are listings for Havaya, an organization that claims to provide a "meaningful" lib-eral Jewish wedding, and for Reform marriage, neither of which is formally rec-ognized in Israel as a valid, legal marriage, as well as for a group that arranges civil weddings in Prague (which are recognized); for Tzohar, an organization of Orthodox rabbis who conduct weddings with less stress on formal ritual for secular couples (recognized); and for a private Orthodox rabbi who promises to show up a half an hour early and tailor the ceremony to individual desires at no charge (recognized). What there is no mention of in *Mitchatnim* is divorce, or of the legal consequences of marrying in the Orthodox way — "in accordance with the laws of Moses and Israel," which is the only way possible to get mar-ried in Israel, officially, for Jews.

Shira had no idea that by marrying in accordance with the laws of Moses and Israel she was stepping into a medieval arrangement. Most secular Israeli Jews have a peculiar relationship with religion to begin with. More nostalgic, or perhaps superstitious, than pious, with a dollop of nationalism, they cir-cumcise their sons, have a Passover seder, and fast on Yom Kippur. By and large, they also gladly comply with the laws that require Orthodox rabbis to officiate at weddings, even if these rabbis insist that brides immerse in a *mikveh* (ritual bath) prior to the ceremony and cover their naked shoulders with a shawl under the *chuppah* (marriage canopy). Most secular Israelis have his-torically supported policies that enhance Israel's Jewish character, as long as those policies don't affect them on a daily basis, like interfering with driving and shopping on the Sabbath or eating a cheeseburger. They will fight reli-gious encroachment if they feel an overly Orthodox presence like a yeshiva in the neighborhood might ruin the value of their homes. But some of them are known to revere "holy" men. (A recent T.V. documentary showed well-known secular multimillionaires swearing allegiance to their guru — a faith healer-rabbi from the Negev known as the "X-Ray" for his purported ability to predict the future.)

Even if someone had bothered to suggest that Shira sign a prenuptial agreement, she probably would have declined immediately. It's bad luck to think about divorce when getting married. The couple had no money to worry about. Besides, in Shira's mind, Eitan was solid as a rock, and he loved her. True, there was some small tension at the beginning after her future mother-in-law made disparaging remarks about Shira's dark skin. But that was it, and the couple glossed over it.

They asked Rabbi Rafi Abitbul, a prominent Maoz Zion figure, to perform the wedding. A man with a large black hat, trimmed beard, and expressionless face, he was a vocal and respected member of Shas, the ultra-Orthodox Sephardi-Mizrahi political party founded in 1984. Like many other non-Orthodox Mizrahi Israelis, Shira's and Eitan's families supported Shas. They were thrilled and honored that Rabbi Abitbul had agreed to conduct the wedding service. The possibility of having a makeshift civil ceremony, or being married by anyone other than a strictly authentic and Orthodox Sephardic rabbi, never entered anyone's mind.

The night before the wedding, Shira's mother, who was almost as excited as Shira herself about the upcoming event, accompanied her to the mikveh. The attendants were very nice and showed them a special bridal room for undressing. The mikveh is a step pool in which Jewish men and women have, throughout the ages, immersed themselves for ritual purification purposes. It was mentioned in the Bible, with respect to the cleansing of a person who had come in contact with a corpse or another defiling object. Recently, some non-Orthodox women and men have rediscovered the mikveh as a place of spiritual renewal and have developed cleansing ceremonies that revolve around immersion after traumas or before life-cycle events. Today, ritual immersion is considered optional for men according to halakha, but obligatory for observant women, seven days after the completion of their menstrual cycle.

In Israel all Jewish brides, whether secular or religious, are told by the rabbinate when they register their impending marriages that they are required to immerse the night before they wed. Before performing the ceremony the officiating rabbi expects to see a note from the woman in charge of the mikveh, confirming that the bride has undergone the ritual, and the rabbinate in turn requests that the officiating rabbi send in the note along with a copy of the ketubah and authorization of the wedding ceremony to be attached to the file that documents the couple's wedding.

A dispassionate outsider might indeed argue that it is unconscionable for the state to require women to dip themselves in ritual pools before exercising such a basic right as the right to marry. Imagine governments of the United States or England or Finland asking its women citizens, before they get married, to strip naked, brush their teeth, remove all makeup and nail polish, clean their navels with a cotton swab, and step into a designated pool under the watchful eye of another woman. One can just hear feminists all over the world screaming of trampled civil rights and sexual harassment. But in Israel women abide by such rules mostly because they have become part of a series of marriage rituals that sweep women off their feet, carrying young brides with the momentum of preparations, any claims to the contrary occluded by the mysterious pull of ancient tradition.

Many Israeli women think a one-time premarital dip is not such an imposition and might even bring good luck for fertility. "*Lo nora*" they say in Hebrew, meaning "not so bad." Brides are often accompanied to the mikveh by an entourage of women friends and relatives bearing gifts and cakes. But there are some Israeli women who prefer to circumvent the procedure altogether and will do so by turning to lenient rabbis who do not ask to see proof of mikveh attendance, by asking other women to fictitiously undergo the ritual in their place, or even by offering bribes to rabbis to turn a blind eye to their evasion. But such circumvention is the exception and not the rule.

Shira initially thought she would be uncomfortable standing naked in front of the *balanit* (bath attendant — its root comes from the Talmudic word for bathing or anointing). The balanit is always a married woman. Her *sheitel* (as the wig worn by Orthodox women is called in Yiddish) askew, she studied Shira's body and plucked a few stray hairs from her naked back. Then she told Shira to do a better job removing her eye makeup with the baby oil and cotton balls that she handed to her. Her manner was friendly but firm. The attendant covered Shira with a white sheet, telling her to drop it at the last possible minute before entering the water. The water was warm. Shira noticed a solitary dark hair floating on the surface, as well as a dead fly. She faced the attendant and immersed three times, her head below water. Then she recited a blessing: *Barukh ata adonai eloheinu melekh ha-olam al ha-tvilah* (Blessed thou art God, King of the Universe, on the [sacrament of] Immersion). The balanit asked her to dunk in the water once more. Shira wondered if God was actually watching her. The voice of the balanit interrupted her thoughts.

"Kosher!" shouted the pious, matronly balanit heartily at the young, very naked Shira as she climbed up the stairs from the depths of the pool. The woman held out the white sheet to cover her again and gave her an extra towel. Shira went back to her room and dressed. "We wish you a happy life with your beloved," the balanit and other attendants shouted to Shira when she reappeared after drying her hair with a blow-dryer. Her mother had baked a special honey cake to share with all the women at the mikveh that evening. The attendants lit incense candles to celebrate the occasion and sang traditional wedding songs as they ate. Shira felt weird. She had just undressed and immersed herself before strange, bewigged women, and now she was eating cake with them. But she also felt a sense of mystical spirituality, her very clean body now sanctified to her husband, to the rabbinate, and, in an odd sort of way, to the State of Israel, which had obligated her to undergo the procedure.

At the wedding hall the next day, Shira had made sure that a chuppah bedecked with white flowers would be erected in the garden. It was still warm enough to sit outside and Shira had always wanted an outdoor wedding. Solemnly, she walked with her parents to the canopy. In keeping with Israeli mores, some guests continued chatting and eating hors d'oeuvres, but others were sitting around on folding chairs and clapping and ululating joyfully when Shira walked by, a large filmy wrap covering her sleeveless shoulders. Rabbi Abitbul was already standing beneath the chuppah, smiling and joking with Eitan, who had been escorted there by parents and friends, men who were holding the poles supporting the canopy. When Shira was at his side, Eitan squeezed her hand and beamed at her. In his nasal twang, the rabbi read aloud six of the seven special nuptial benedictions, as well as the ketubah, with one blessing reserved for Shira's uncle, a rabbi. Eitan then read out his line: "*Harei at mekudeshet li b'taba'at zo k''dat Moshe v'yisrael*" (You are hereby consecrated unto me with this ring in accordance to the laws of Moses and Israel.) Shira was silent, as she was expected to be throughout the service, without even the "I do" of other ceremonies. The audience, led by the rabbi, sang out, "*Mekudeshet, mekudeshet, mekudeshet*" (Consecrated, consecrated, consecrated). Who would ever have dreamed such a honeyed moment would end in catastrophe.

After the wedding party the couple drove in a rented car decorated with ribbons and balloons to a hotel. Eitan was sweet and gentle. Neither had experience as lovers, but everything went smoothly. But then Eitan called his parents, and someone else, and told them that he and Shira had just consummated their marriage. Shira was appalled but decided to be polite rather than express her acute discomfort. "Why are you so insecure?" she finally asked. Eitan shrugged and said he wasn't insecure; he just wanted them to know that he was "a man." Shira noted that Eitan was attracted to strong male figures. She attributed this to his own father's behavior, always putting his mother down, always demanding that she be accountable to him. It wasn't until Eitan's mother began to work independently as a home health-care aide that she was able to spend money freely without reporting to her husband. In fact, her first check was a gift to Shira and Eitan — a long weekend in a hotel in Eilat, Shira's dream.

Middle

Their first child was born two years after the wedding. Shira recalls that during this period she and Eitan got along, "sort of." She found Eitan to be alternately bellicose or broodingly withdrawn. Shira's mother advised her to be a loyal wife and to ignore his volatile mood swings. She recalls that one day she perked up when Eitan said something "normal," expressing happiness that she had become pregnant so quickly. It was a son, and Eitan seemed excited by the prospect of being a father.

Eitan started working as a refrigerator and washing machine repairman for a local service company. But he got little satisfaction from his work. Each day he would awake and listlessly call his boss for the roster of customers on his shift. Shira, on the other hand, had begun working as an assistant to a kindergarten teacher, and she loved it. She started to dream of opening her own kindergarten and decided to go back to school at night to study early childhood education. Her mother took care of the baby while she was studying.

But just about the time Shira went back to school, Eitan started vanishing for days at a time. He said he was off making money but would not elaborate. At first, Shira attributed this behavior to the jitters of new fatherhood. But soon she became alarmed. During the daytime, Eitan was often glassy-eyed and distant. Shira began to suspect that Eitan was having an affair. "Maybe he's gay?" she wondered, because of his attraction to strong men. "Don't let your imagination run away with you," advised friends to whom Shira tearfully confided. Trying to be optimistic, Shira hoped that the birth of another child would give Eitan stability. Four years later she gave birth to a baby girl, and two years after that, another son.

But the arrival of children put added strains on the couple's marriage. A few months after their third child came, Shira returned to her job at the kindergarten, cultivating a safe place for herself, where she felt empowered and in control. At about the same time, Eitan revealed that he had decided to give up refrigerators and washing machines for good and wanted to dedicate a good part of his time to the study of mysticism and forms of spirituality such as communication with the dead, meditation, and "exorcizing evil spirits." These studies, he claimed, gave him great intellectual and emotional satisfaction. Eventually, he said, he'd be able to teach. What's more, he had become very attached to Shalom, the man in charge of the program of study, and had started helping him recruit students and raise money. Eitan had become Shalom's right-hand man, and the work required his around-the-clock commitment.

Relieved that Eitan's absences were attributable to studies and not infidelity, Shira at first tried to indulge his new interests. But soon he became more and more engrossed in his new studies and was spending less and less time at home, neglecting almost all his domestic duties and having practically no contact with their children. It gradually became clear that Shalom, whom Eitan once described as his "rebbe," or rabbi, was more like a cult leader than a spiritual guidance counselor and that Eitan was more like a groupie than a yeshiva student, as he preferred to refer to himself. Eitan's new career path also meant that Shira would be the family's main breadwinner. Meanwhile, her dream of having her own kindergarten was slowly coming true. Though it lacked an outdoor area, the couple's small apartment was declared safe by local inspectors, and she received a license to operate a small preschool. In the back of her mind she worried that the children or their parents might be afraid of Eitan and dreaded the thought of them being in contact.

Shira became increasingly unhappy and distant, and so did Eitan. He began to mistreat Shira, hurling insults at her in front of their children and yelling at her for every minor perceived infraction, if he spoke to her at all. Shira tried to reason with him and pleaded, "Why are you doing this?" But very soon she realized that no degree of reasoning would help, and she began to contemplate her options.

In Court

In 1999 Eitan's temper took a turn for the worse, and one day he pushed Shira against the wall, bruising her badly. She filed a complaint with the police, who took out a court order barring him from approaching Shira or the family home for three days and charging him with battery. After the three days were up, a family court, granting Shira's request, extended the order for another month. Deeply insulted and denying that he had done anything wrong, Eitan moved in with Shalom, his ersatz rebbe and now business partner. After the month was over, he refused to move back home. Later, Shira would write in court papers that Eitan's disengagement from her and the children "caused them great grief."

With Eitan refusing to pay for child support or any household expenses, Shira had no choice but to sue him. A friend recommended a local attorney, a nice-enough and competent-enough young woman named Pazit, with a penchant for miniskirts, who had just graduated from a local legal college. In accordance with standard protocol, Pazit sent Shira rushing off to family court to petition it for permission to sell their small apartment and divide its assets, to order Eitan to pay child support, and to declare that Shira was the custodial parent of their three children. Shira was not entitled to alimony, Pazit explained, since she worked. Jewish law, which Israeli family courts must apply with respect to support determinations, states that a man is entitled to his wife's earnings unless she chooses to keep them, in which case she does so in lieu of his obligation to support her. Shira wanted to keep her salary. It was modest, but at least it was hers, and she had control over it. "Only after you're well entrenched, deep in the family court," Pazit continued, "will we sue in the rabbinic court for a get. I don't want any confusion about who is deciding what in this case."

"Why must I sue in two different courts?" Shira asked, concerned about the expense and time involved. "Because," answered Pazit firmly, "family courts have no jurisdiction to decide whether you are married or divorced. You need to go to a rabbinic court for a get. And even though a rabbinic court could by law also hear your claims regarding the family apartment, child support, and custody, trust me, you do not want to be there. In family court, cases end. In rabbinic courts, well, *elohim gadol* [God is great]. You never know how long it will take."

And in Shira and Eitan's case, God was very great indeed.

The family court case was not all smooth sailing, but it ended. Eitan put up a not-very-gentlemanly fight over the children, arguing that Shira was an unfit mother. He even appealed his custody case all the way up to the Supreme Court, enlisting a disreputable psychologist to that end. But Shira won custody, and the court ordered Eitan to pay 3,200 shekels a month in child support, plus 1,000 for housing costs (about $1,200 in total). The court also ordered the sale of the family apartment and division of the remaining equity between Shira and Eitan, leaving Shira with only a few shekels but happily disentangled from any monetary relationship with Eitan. Later she was able to rent back the apartment, with her beloved kindergarten, from the buyers. Litigation in the family court took about three years, including the appeal.

And, as Pazit had predicted, in the rabbinic courts the case did not end. In May 2000, shortly after the family court documents were in place and hearings set, Shira sued, as advised, for divorce in the Jerusalem Rabbinic Court. The court is housed, ironically, in the old Knesset building just off King George Street in the hub of commercial, downtown Jerusalem. Here, for almost eleven years and at immense cost to the Israeli taxpayer, the three rabbis who sat in this particular tribunal churned water — *tahnu mayim*, as the saying goes in Hebrew — while deliberating the divorce case of Shira Yosef-Azulai versus Eitan Azulai. (The state pays rabbinic judges the same salaries that it pays civil court judges. The difference is that three rabbinic judges sit on a single case, making the cost of a hearing of a divorce case three times the amount of its civil counterpart. In 2011 the state's total budget for the running of rabbinic courts staffed by one hundred judges was close to 140 million shekels, or about $40 million.)

The first hearing was set for August 8, 2000. When Eitan did not show up, the rabbis issued an arrest warrant for him and ordered him to post a 10,000-shekel (about $2,800) bond to ensure his appearance at future hearings. But neither Shira nor the police could locate him.

"We need to petition the court to appoint a private investigator to locate Eitan," Pazit suggested. "Without Eitan, there can be no get. And without a get, you will never be divorced."

"Can't a rabbinic court just declare my marriage over?" Shira wondered, thinking about some of the divorce trials she had seen staged on the imported soaps aired on Israeli T.V. As she recalled, a court simply stamps the papers "divorced" and that's it.

"No. It doesn't work that way in rabbinic courts. We need Eitan. The halakha is that a marriage is over only when a husband delivers a bill of divorce, physically, to his wife."

"Well I don't care about halakha. I am not religious. Let's just go to family court," Shira suggested. "That's a civil court, and they don't have to decide things according to halakha, no?"

"No," Pazit answered testily, always surprised that the answer was not obvious to her clients. "There is no civil divorce in Israel. You can get married and divorced only in accordance with halakha. It does not matter if you are the Baba Sali [a holy Moroccan rabbi] or Dana International [a famous Israeli transvestite pop singer]. The family courts have no say in the matter."

On October 16, 2001, more than a year after the first hearing, the rabbinic tribunal accepted Shira's motion and ordered the court's administrative office to hire a detective, at the expense of the state, to locate Eitan. Eight months after that, on June 18, 2002, the court issued an order to the cell phone company, at Pazit's request, to produce a list of calls that Eitan had made and received for the past six months; and on June 27, 2004, two long years later, the court extended the order to cover calls made by Shalom, Eitan's guru. Shira called the detective periodically for news, but there was none. Eitan, it seemed, had vanished, swallowed into the depths of the earth "like toxic waste," Shira liked to say.

Then, in September 2004, four long years after Shira had first filed for divorce, Shalom unknowingly called up Shira's cousin to solicit business for some new software that he was peddling. Her cousin, by pure luck, recognized his voice and invited him to his office for a meeting. The police were informed and followed Shalom home from the meeting to find Eitan watching T.V. in a house in a remote farming village. They arrested him and brought him to court the next day, shackled and escorted by two police officers.

At the hearing, Eitan, despite the restraints, acted as if he were still in a position of power. Fact is, he was. He complained that the cuffs on his legs were too tight, and the rabbis directed the police to loosen the chains. Eitan wasn't alone. His father came too, and so did Shalom and Wachtfogel, his attorney, a squat man with a mustache and slight limp. But it was Eitan who, as per Wachtfogel's suggestions and orchestration, dictated the pace and content of the proceedings. He had a long list of conditions for giving Shira the get, including demands that Shira agree to transferring jurisdiction in matters of custody and child support to the rabbinic court from the family court, lowering the amount of child support payments for the couple's three children to 1,900 shekels (about $550 — less than half the amount that had been awarded already by the family court), and waiving her rights to collect on the debt that he had incurred for nonpayment of child support for the past four years. Under pressure to get on with her life and to set herself free from the elusive Eitan, Shira agreed to everything.

"Might as well " Pazit advised her. "It's going to be hard to collect any money for child support from Eitan, under the best of circumstances."

But despite Shira's concessions, Eitan still refused to give a get on the spot. He needed more time to "think." And it was already three o'clock, way past the time the rabbis normally would have allotted for sitting in the courtroom. They wanted to move on to their other commitments, one as the head of a local yeshiva, one as the rabbi of a local community, and another to his wife for a late lunch. Incredibly, at the end of the very unsatisfactory hearing, the court simply ignored Shira's and Pazit's desperate pleas to keep Eitan under lock and key, and they freed him, without bail, after he gave his word that he would show up the next day.

"But why are you trusting his 'word'? He's not going to show up," Shira yelled, distraught because Eitan had not given her a get on the spot and at the thought that he might go underground again. The court brushed off her supplications, giving her the feeling that they thought she was being stubborn and hysterical and that they were not going to imprison a man who suffered from having such a difficult wife. Although Eitan had ignored previous court orders to appear, withheld the get, and remained hidden for almost four years, the judges' minds were made up. Shira imagined all the money that the state and she had spent on private investigators, lawyers, and the like, disappearing shekel by shekel. And as Shira anticipated, Eitan did not show up the next day. She was back to the beginning or, as she would soon learn, worse than that.

Perhaps feeling they had erred by letting Eitan go without bail, the rabbis set another hearing for November 30, 2004, just two months away. Eitan did not come, but he did send his lawyer, Wachtfogel. Instead of asking where his client was or why Eitan hadn't shown up, the rabbis astoundingly allowed Wachtfogel to continue to negotiate in his name. Wachtfogel now wanted Shira to agree to further lower child support payments by another 200 shekels, to a total of 1,700 (a little less than $500) for all three children, and to lower the sum by a third each time one of them turned eighteen. He also asked for cosigners to guarantee Shira's agreement not to sue for any increase in child support in the future. Again, Shira, under pressure, agreed, and Wachtfogel, again, cryptically promised a response from his client to the new agreement within ten days.

But ten days came and went and nothing happened. Wachtfogel did not inform the court whether Eitan agreed to the latest offer or not. Eitan, again at-large, was not available to give, or be compelled to give, Shira a get. At Pazit's request, the court set still another date for a hearing, March 3, 2005. Again Eitan did not show, but Wachtfogel did. This time he demanded that Shira commit to pay a fine of 50,000 shekels (about $14,000) should she breach the terms of the previously agreed-on contract. Wachtfogel also demanded that Shira provide various statements from her bank and from the National Insurance Institute that confirmed that Eitan had no outstanding debt to the bank or the institute, which had made child support payments in his stead for years. And he wanted Shira to promise to indemnify Eitan if the bank or institute sued him nonetheless.

Drained of financial means and figuring that nothing would come out of the proceedings anyway, Shira had arrived at the March 2005 hearing without legal representation. She decided to ignore Eitan's new demands and repeated her original request that the court compel him to give her a get. But the rabbinic judges angrily dismissed her and told her to obtain representation. They wanted her to respond through a lawyer to Eitan's latest offer.

Feeling dejected, Shira returned home empty-handed. She had a new boyfriend, and he wanted to get married. She had nothing new to tell him and no idea when, if ever, she would be divorced. She knew she was going to lose him. He wanted a kosher wedding and a kosher relationship. And this was not possible so long as she was still married to Eitan by law, if not in body or spirit. She could not marry under halakha, that was clear. She could not even marry civilly, say, if she flew to Cyprus. Pazit had explained to her that the religious marriage entered into in Israel was recognized internationally as a legal marriage. If she married abroad without a divorce, she could be prosecuted for bigamy.

More time went by, and her boyfriend had enough and took off. Shira was beginning to wonder whether she should just give up on ever receiving a get. Why waste money on attorney's fees that got her nothing? Anyway, she was getting too old to have another child, and she did not need to worry about having a mamzer. She could just find someone to live with who wouldn't care that she was still officially married. But Pazit suggested that they ask for another hearing; if not, she explained, the court would close Shira's file for lack of activity and forget about her completely. "You will not even be a sad statistic," Pazit informed her. "You need to show your face at least once a year in court. Even if you go without me." And besides, Shira needed closure and was sick of fending off Eitan's creditors who came looking for him at her apartment. She really did want this get. And so did the children.

On July 4, 2006 (another year had passed), a new hearing was set, at Shira's request. Again, Eitan did not come, sending Shalom in his stead this time. Unperturbed that Shalom had no legal standing, the rabbinic judges treated him with respect, as if he were a professional representing Eitan's legal interests. Not only did they ignore the fact that Eitan did not bother to show up, and refrain from issuing any judgment against him, but they also allowed Shalom to put forward new terms for the divorce. Shira, who had come without Pazit, was not interested in listening to, and did not want the court to hear, any more new terms or conditions for obtaining the get.

But the presiding judge insisted. He angrily warned her that she was the one responsible for what was happening. And he told Shira, in these words, "If Eitan agrees [to give the get] but just has certain conditions and you refuse, then you are 'chaining' yourself." This is a common admonishment made by rabbinic judges to pressure women into agreeing to their husband's terms for divorce. Pressuring men is against the halakha. Pressuring women is permitted, as per the Maharashdam-Maharik rule (see introduction). The idea behind this rule is that if a husband agrees, in principle, to give a get, the court cannot apply any pressure on him so long as the judges deem his terms reasonable or easy to comply with. If a woman rejects her husband's terms, she is accused of creating the impasse. Rarely, if ever, will rabbis decide that a husband's terms are unreasonable or not easy to comply with. Thus, for all intents and purposes, the Maharashdam-Maharik rule places full negotiating power in the hands of the husband and absolves the court of having to take any responsibility for determining the conditions for divorce, even in the most heinous of circumstances.

Husbands like Eitan can thus procrastinate and delay forever, making sure that the rabbis will issue no order against them so long as they are "negotiating" the terms for divorce (see similar strategies in chapters 3, 4, and 5). And thus, the rabbis transfer responsibility for the ongoing abuse onto the helpless victim. With a turn of phrase, the rabbis can turn reality upside down and declare the verdict without a trial: it is not men who are doing the anchoring, but women who anchor themselves with their stubbornness. Shira was responsible for what was happening, not Eitan nor the rabbis, who had refused to issue any decision and who had released a shackled Eitan without bail.

Despite it all, Shira didn't give up. She knew she could not really get on with her life emotionally, socially, or financially with Eitan weighing like an enormous albatross around her neck. She requested yet another hearing, and it was scheduled for February 2007. Neither Eitan nor Wachtfogel, nor even Shalom, showed up. The rabbis determined that the police should again be told to bring Eitan, but since there was no address, they referred the case a to the special internal unit of the court in charge of searching for missing husbands, telling it to appoint a private investigator to locate Eitan. Meanwhile, they scheduled still another hearing, with the summons to be delivered to Wachtfogel.

At the next hearing, a month later, Eitan failed to show up, apparently out of fear of being arrested, but his father, Shalom, and Wachtfogel did show. Once again Shira, now cowed and afraid to display any bravado or frustration lest the rabbis withdraw their latest order to appoint a detective to find Eitan, agreed to waive (again) all fees and fines associated with nonpayment of Eitan's debt to her and the children and to lower support payment because one child had already reached the age of eighteen. Shalom (again) told the court that "within a number of days" Eitan would respond, probably affirmatively, to this latest offer to end the stalemate and give Shira a get. But again there was no response. After almost another year had gone by, Shira asked for still another hearing, which was set for February 2008. Again Eitan sent Shalom and Wachtfogel to unveil his latest conditions.

Eight years after the proceedings in their court had started, the rabbis were more convinced than ever that Shira and Eitan had to divorce, and they set a date specifically for the delivery of a get for March 13, 2008, ten days hence, even though Eitan had agreed to nothing. "The financial dispute between the couple will be settled *after* the get procedure," the court ruled. Concerned that Shira might have Eitan arrested for nonpayment of child support, the court also issued an order barring her from doing so throughout that day. But Eitan still failed to show up. Wachtfogel explained that he was afraid the police might arrest him anyway. The now furious judges finally ordered Eitan forcibly brought to court and not released on bail until the case was heard. But the missing husbands unit failed to locate him.

By now, Shira had hooked up with the Center for Women's Justice, the Jerusalem-based women's advocacy group that represents women denied gets in high-profile cases (see prologue). It assigned Rivkah Lubitch, a rabbinic pleader, to her case. Appalled and astounded by the way the case had been handled by the rabbinic judges, Rivkah suggested that Shira file a complaint with the Ombudsman's Office of the Israeli Judiciary. Established in 2003, the Ombudsman's Office occasionally provides redress for persons who feel injured by judicial actions and investigates complaints against judges. Shira's complaint, filed on August 10, 2008, stated that, after eight years and nineteen hearings, the rabbinic court had not rendered even one decision in her case. Moreover, Shira told the ombudsman, she had been the object of degrading remarks by the judges and had been pressured to make sizable concessions to receive a get. She also said that the court had not taken decisive action to ensure Eitan's appearance in court.

Three months later, the ombudsman, former Supreme Court justice Eliezer Goldberg, found Shira's complaint to be correct, in part: the judges had egregiously allowed the case to go on for too long and eight years was "doubtlessly an unreasonable length of time" for a case to be heard yet left "undecided," he ruled. Shira had indeed been spoken to in a "degrading" fashion by at least one rabbinic judge. By allowing the case to linger, Goldberg argued, the appeals process had been thwarted. He chided the rabbinic judges for not producing a decision "after efforts to persuade the parties to reach an agreement had failed." Had the lower court reached a decision, that decision could have then been appealed, the ombudsman reasoned, and another court might have been more aggressive in scheduling hearings that could have ended the case earlier. He lamented that the rabbinic court "did not use the tools at its disposal in order to enforce the husband's appearance at an earlier stage . . . not eight years later," and, as a result, Shira was a "victim of the legal system."

The report vindicated Shira, which was in itself highly satisfying but had few practical consequences. What Rivkah had hoped was that it would put the rabbinic court on notice that they were being watched and, perhaps, prod it into issuing more substantive rulings against Eitan in the future. A few months after the report, in 2009, the rabbinic court held another hearing. Once more, Eitan did not show and the court issued no ruling.

The End

It was a quiet, gray day in autumn of 2010. Ten years had elapsed since Shira filed for divorce and nothing had happened, apart from the departure of her boyfriend. The court's arrest warrant against Eitan was still in force, but neither she nor the police had any idea where he was. Shira was doing the dishes when she got a call from Eitan's cousin, Tirza, a short-haired feminist who wore Birkenstock sandals and was always eager to know how Shira was faring. Tirza always said she was distressed "out of her mind" that everyone was helpless before what she described as a "well-oiled patriarchal bureaucracy fueled by religious fanaticism." Shira liked Tirza, though her feminist fervor had seemed exaggerated when they first met. Now, it made more and more sense to Shira, and she was very happy to hear from her, even happier when she heard why Tirza had called this time.

"I saw him," Tirza told Shira. She said she was shopping in a mall in Beer-sheba and had just spotted Eitan in a jewelry store with a woman. Shira jotted down the name of the store and immediately called the court-appointed private investigator, who used his connections to contact the mall's security officer, who in turn located Eitan and his companion on tape from the mall's closed circuit T.V. and approached the jewelry store for information about the two. That night, Eitan was arrested at the woman's apartment and taken to jail, in his pajamas.

The next day, Eitan appeared before the rabbinic court, once again in manacles, remarkably defiant. "You have no right to hold me in prison," he told the rabbis. "I am not a criminal. You have not ordered me to give a get. So I am not in contempt of court. If you do not release me, I will appeal. And by the way, I am not interested in giving the get." But he was no longer addressing the same three rabbinic judges who had heard his case for ten long years, but new, younger ones, who had read the ombudsman's report. "We are holding you under arrest to make sure you appear in court for all scheduled hearings," they responded. "Not because you are in contempt of court, but because of your attendance record. We intend to keep you in jail so long as we are conducting hearings in your case. And remember, if we do not make a decision, you cannot appeal."

"You are pressuring me to give a get," retorted Eitan, well aware that a *get meuseh* (a forced divorce) was invalid.

"We not forcing you to give a get," they answered. "Just to show up for hearings. This hearing has ended. We'll see you on Sunday." That was a Thursday, and Eitan would have to spend a long weekend in prison with, as Rivkah would later write, other criminals, cockroaches, and mice.

Sunday came and Eitan was brought back to court in chains. His father also came.

"Ok, I'll do it," he told the rabbis, with his father's encouragement. After a weekend in jail and ten years underground, Eitan came round to giving Shira a get, without any terms or conditions.

In Israel, the one-and-a-half-hour get procedure is a ceremony at which a woman can find herself alone, at what may very well be the most emotional moment of her life, with a room full of men — a tribunal of rabbis, her husband, the scribe who writes the get, and the two witnesses to the writing and delivery of the get, who must be men. Women are not barred from attending the ceremony, but, aside from the wife (and even she can be bypassed if she sends a male agent), no woman is necessary, or has any capacity, to act as the orchestrator, agent, or witness to a ritual of this importance. But first, before the divorce ceremony begins, the rabbis verify the couple's names and their father's names by an initial set of witnesses so that the parties to the get be properly identified in accordance with halakhic rules.

Shira had not brought any witnesses with her, since she had no idea that Eitan would relent that day. Unprepared, her brother was promptly called at work to provide elementary testimony over the phone regarding his sister's and father's names. (The willingness to take testimony over the phone underscores how malleable the judges can be when they want to. To paraphrase the Orthodox feminist Blu Greenberg, "Where there is a rabbinic will, there is a halakhic way.") Her brother identified her as Shira, the daughter of Beni, also known as Benjamin, Ben, and Bentzi. No mention was made of her mother's name. Eitan's father testified to his own name and to his son's names.

Next, the rabbis asked the husband to proclaim out loud that he was declaring null and void any and all "previous vows" he may have made to stay married, or not to stay married, to Shira. He was also asked, repeatedly, if he was giving the get of his own free will to make sure that he was not being coerced in any way (for example, by being put in jail) but was doing so of his own volition. Even if Eitan had been physically in jail when the get ceremony was being enacted, such legal language and formalisms are a prerequisite to giving a get. Rabbinically sanctioned force exercised in accordance with halakhic norms is not considered coercion and will not void a get, as it is presumed that at the precise moment the get is given, it is being given freely, as the husband states. Sometimes, but not always, the rabbis will also ask the wife if she consents to the divorce — an innovation of medieval times when it was determined that a man could not divorce his wife, as he could in biblical times, against her will (see introduction). The rabbis did not bother to ask Shira. The answer was obvious.

The get itself is written by a scribe in ink with a feather quill on parchment. Since, according to Jewish law, a man is supposed to write the get by himself, the husband must temporarily purchase the tools from the scribe and then lend them back and appoint him as his agent. The husband and scribe remain closeted together while the get is written. The wife stays in the corridor, waiting. The short document states that the divorced woman is "permitted and allowed" to marry any other man, except a *kohen*, a member of the priestly tribe considered to be at the top of the unspoken Jewish caste system. As part of the ceremony, the husband repeats part of what is written in the get. As in the wedding ceremony, the wife is silent. The get is then placed by the husband in the woman's cupped hands. She raises it in the air and walks several feet, signifying possession and acceptance of the document. After that, the rabbis tear the get, some say to suggest the finality of the proceedings; others say to deface the get so that its validity can never again be questioned. Its pieces are filed with the court. The rabbinic court informs the Ministry of the Interior of the divorce and arranges for the newly divorced each to receive a divorce certificate, which arrives by mail several days later. The get, a woman's writ of manumission, stays with the court.

When Shira took the get into her hands, she could not cry or laugh. She hurt so much, she was numb.

"All's well that ends well," one of the friendly clerks told Shira.

"It's a pity I can't agree with you," Rivkah snapped back. "All is not well. Shira endured much unnecessary suffering, wasted much energy and money, and missed out on innumerable relationships because of the unbearable ease with which this rabbinic court released Eitan from custody in 2004 and dragged her case out for ten long years."

TWO

The Scarlet Agunah

———

At some brighter period, when the world should have grown ripe for it,
in Heaven's own time, a new truth would be revealed, in order to
establish the whole relation between man and woman on a
surer ground of mutual happiness

Nathaniel Hawthorne, *The Scarlet Letter*

———

Jonathan Cowan met Allison Coopersmith while scuba diving in Eilat. Jonathan, a modern Orthodox British Jew, came to Israel in the 1980s while still a student. Allison Coopersmith, also British, was in Israel on holiday. Both are children of Holocaust survivors. Jonathan, who comes from a long line of illustrious Torah scholars and rabbis, is a taciturn man with muted emotional responses. He grew up in Golder's Green, the heavily Jewish suburb of London, and spent years studying Talmud at the illustrious yeshiva of Gateshead in northern England. Allison is a redhead with a then-nascent sense of humor that blossomed with age and tribulation. She grew up in Hendon, another Jewish London suburb, where she attended a government school in the mornings and a private, liberal Jewish seminary in the afternoons. Only in her early twenties when they first met, Allison was totally mesmerized by Jonathan, who seemed to be just the opposite of her beloved but ordinary father. Her father had only two interests in life — making money and watching the evening news from his adored lounge chair. Jonathan was a renaissance man who could talk about anything and had an opinion about everything, from British politics to jazz, the latest technology, Muslim fundamentalism, and so on.

For Allison, one sticky point with Jonathan, who was at the time a physics student at the Technion in Haifa, was his desire to live permanently in Israel, or make *aliyah* (Hebrew for "ascent"). She admired his romantic determination to live in the Holy Land and his individualistic spirit, but she wasn't sure at all about making the move herself. She preferred English manners and tea and crumpets to Israeli brashness and falafel. Moreover, she was not sure if she could live a religious lifestyle, Jonathan's condition for marriage. Shabbat was nice, in her mind, but strict kashrut and mikveh were questionable.

Still, Allison overcame her reservations and the wedding was held, at Jonathan's request, in an Orthodox synagogue in London. Days before the ceremony they went to a county clerk who, after verifying that neither was married, issued a state marriage license. The officiating rabbi mailed the endorsed license back to the clerk after the ceremony, and Jonathan and Allison received their British marriage certificate in the post, pronouncing them man and wife in the eyes of the state. The couple enjoyed all the trappings of a British wedding. Allison wore a streamlined Edwardian-style gown with covered buttons up the back. Jonathan sported tails. A chauffeured Rolls-Royce ferried them from synagogue to dinner hall, where a costumed master of ceremonies toasted the couple. But despite all the festivities, Allison's spirits fell irredeemably after Jonathan, saying he was too shy, refused to sit beside her on a bench fashioned as a sort of throne for the two of them.

The throne incident foreshadowed what was to come. Jonathan was rarely, if ever, by her side, preferring the company of his books or of mysterious business partners whom Allison never met. Allison's parents had been anxious about the union from the start, mostly because of Jonathan's nationalistic political and religious views. Their daughter, they fretted, had been raised in a Reform home where Zionism was hardly emphasized.

A divorced older cousin who had resisted pressure from her former spouse to move to Israel mentioned that she had avoided it, among other reasons, because "men have the upper hand in Israeli divorces." Allison did not realize that it was a veiled warning. Like many Reform Jewish brides she had never heard of a get and had no idea what it was, or of its ramifications, let alone that in Israel there was no civil divorce. The Israeli *aliyah* emissary in London said nothing about it. Allison ignored her father's warning that her fiancé's family was "very weird," and she attributed his dislike of the family and disapproval of Jonathan to parental skittishness.

Shortly after the wedding, Allison's parents were alarmed when they learned Jonathan had insisted that Allison sign over all her money to their joint account, only a few thousand dollars at the time, while he refused to do the same. Back from their honeymoon in Turkey, she bitterly complained to her mother that Jonathan had disappeared to go on private excursions, acted unlovingly, and once even pushed her down a flight of stairs. Her mother, a practical woman not given to sentimentality, suggested a divorce before "children come along and complicate matters." Allison did not reject the idea out of hand, and she pondered about the etiquette of returning wedding gifts. But what Allison's mother did not know was that Allison was secretly pregnant; despite her grumblings, she made up her mind to work things out. In the interest of domestic harmony, Allison agreed to do whatever it took to keep Jonathan happy: keep a kosher home, wear a head covering outside the marital abode (inside, she refused and Jonathan relented), and immerse monthly in a mikveh seven days after her menstruation had stopped.

These new habits frightened Allison's parents. Their daughter had turned Orthodox, and they found this alienating. But they were advised by their female Reform rabbi back in London to maintain a respectful silence. Whatever made Allison happy should make them happy, they rationalized. But Allison was actually very, very *un*happy, a fact she hid well. Jonathan could not find an academic position in one of the top Israeli universities and became a disgruntled teacher of statistics at one of the lesser community colleges. Though he could easily have found a job in industry, Jonathan refused to look for a position outside teaching. He liked the flexibility it afforded him.

After the wedding, with all its pomp and ceremony, the couple moved to an undeveloped, no-frills religious settlement in the occupied territories, close to the Tel Aviv suburb of Petah Tikvah, but Allison did not want to stay there. She worried that few of her friends and relatives would travel there to visit her. She also thought that the men in the community had a radicalizing influence over Jonathan. Eventually they left the settlement and moved to a small house in Netanya, which Jonathan purchased in his name alone, a small detail that he did not bother to tell Allison about.

Ten years came and went, and the couple, despite their differences, managed to have five children. Allison's parents loved the spirited kids but worried about their daughter's ability to cope with all their demands and Jonathan's at the same time. They tried to visit as often as they could, even though Jonathan made them uncomfortable. At the end of each visit, Allison's father would slip a few thousand pounds into her purse just before they left. She cried each time she saw the bills, knowing that her father understood that Jonathan wasn't taking care of her and probably never would.

Determined to gain independence from Jonathan and her parents' favors, Allison began to look after several apartments owned by wealthy British Jews for supplemental income. (Later on, Jonathan would falsely accuse Allison in rabbinic court of meeting lovers in these apartments.) As her business expanded, Jonathan's complaints became more frequent. She was out a lot with clients; dinner was never on time. He became increasingly jealous, increasingly angry, and increasingly unhappy with his marriage.

After twenty years of marriage, when their oldest child was in the army, Jonathan, graying, listless, and secretive, announced to Allison that he wanted a divorce. He told her that one day she would thank him for his role in actively dissolving the marriage. His aging parents were alarmed, because they did not want to see him middle-aged and alone, but they stood by him as they always had. They rather liked Allison, but their son's attitude ruled out any emotional attachment to their daughter-in-law. They were always a tad suspicious that she married Jonathan for his family wealth, which they had no intention of sharing with her.

Parrying

By the time Jonathan proclaimed to Allison that he wanted a divorce, he had already consulted with a number of attorneys, picked one, and filed all the paperwork in court, hoping that suing first would give him a tactical advantage over Allison. In the "race to the courthouse" (see introduction) most men run to the rabbinic court, where it is presumed that they will have the upper hand, while most women run to the family courts. These presumptions, while usually true, are also overstatements. Each case must be evaluated on its merits. Each case suggests numerous tactics and possibilities for creative (and expensive) divorce attorneys who exploit the complicated system to their clients' (and their own) advantage.

Israeli divorce attorneys are by and large a notoriously unattractive lot, although some are thoughtful officers of the court who try to balance the material and psychological interests of their clients with the professional goals of their case. Many others approach each case as a joust they must win or die. No collateral damage is too large a sacrifice in the zero-sum fight. Acting on the unrestrained directives of their clients, they can turn formerly beloved spouses and children into cannon fodder for bloated egos and targets of repressed feelings of vengeance. Jonathan chose the biggest, the best, and most expensive gladiator of them all, one whose pivots and parries dazzled even some of the most astute family court judges. And the judges, often bored by the monotony of their cases and frustrated by the inability of people who once loved each other to show compassion, can be blinded by the dust of the fray engendered by some of these litigious gladiators or else weighed down by the notion that the loser will appeal any decision the court eventually makes.

Jonathan picked Shimmy Padan, a short, charismatic man who liked seafood and car racing and was a favorite among the divorcing who's who of the Israeli entertainment industry. Padan advised Jonathan to split jurisdiction between the two court systems. First, they'd sue in family court, where Jonathan would ask the court to award him sole custody of the couple's three minor children (a move that would particularly infuriate Allison) and to divide the marital property, from which they excluded the Netanya house, an asset that, they correctly claimed, was purchased mostly with funds gifted by Jonathan's parents. And to top it all, they would demand that Allison vacate the marital home immediately or pay rent. Next, with the family court petition in place, they'd file for divorce in rabbinic court.

Jonathan was giddy at the thought of Allison receiving the writs. He had wanted to "put her in her place" for years. He hired a man to serve Allison with the family court papers. "These are divorce papers, and I don't think your husband likes you too much," the process server chuckled as he placed the documents in her hand. Religious court documents demanding her appearance in a divorce action arrived by regular mail a few days later.

First Allison called her parents, and then she hired an attorney, one she hoped was a match for Padan. She chose Benny Davidson, who was as tall as Padan was short and a fellow Brit, who she thought could talk to her parents and explain what was happening, since they were paying the bill. A religious man, who like Jonathan had studied at Gateshead, Davidson was a favored choice among new British immigrants and had a reputation of being as shrewd and as cutthroat as he looked boyish and innocent.

"Great," Davidson told her, scanning Padan's court papers quickly. "Shimmy Padan made a wrong move, suing for division of marital property in family court. I'm surprised. He should have just sued for everything in the rabbinic court so that it would take jurisdiction over the house. It's far more likely for a rabbinic court to deny a wife the rights to a house registered in her husband's name than it is for a family court to do so. I fully expect the family court to award you some percentage of the house, if not half, as well as to give you half of all the other assets, if we can find them. Until the family court rules, stay in the house and insist on your pristine dedication to Jonathan and your marriage. If you leave the house, we won't have any control over its disposition. Possession is nine-tenths of the law. Meanwhile, I'll prepare a motion for an accounting so we can start finding the other assets that Jonathan must have hidden under the *balatot* [floor tiles], God knows where."

"And with respect to the rabbinic courts," Davidson continued, "the main thing is that the rabbinic judges should 'fall asleep,' so to speak, and forget about this case. That's not hard for them because they never rule anyway. And whatever you do, don't agree to accept the get."

"But I want the get," Allison told him.

"If you are divorced from Jonathan, the halakha is that the two of you cannot stay in the house together. One of you will have to leave or else the get will not be valid. And why should Jonathan leave? He will never leave *his* house. Over his dead body. Also, if you accept the get, you are in the street, because he is arguing that the house is his, just his, and you may stay there only as his wife. Once you accept the get and are no longer his wife, his financial obligations to you ends. I need you to stay in the house and refuse a get so that we have control over what happens with the house and have leverage over Jonathan."

"But I want the get," Allison repeated.

"Not yet. Patience." Davidson told her. "Trust me."

All this did not sit right with Allison. But with the different courts involved and with all the different claims that can be made in one constellation or another, and with the get as leverage, the divorce contest in Israel is a complicated, cerebral enterprise. It is a game that Allison had no idea how to play. She relied on Davidson.

In the initial papers filed with the Netanya Rabbinic Court in 2004, Jonathan stated that he was entitled to divorce Allison because she had "violated the laws of Moses and Judah," as those rules and customs were set forth in the code of the Shulhan Arukh. According to the code, a man could divorce his wife if she caused him to violate the rules of the Torah (the laws of Moses) or if she were blasphemous and immodest (the customs of Judah). Padan and Jonathan came up with a long list of the ways that Allison had caused Jonathan to violate the laws of Moses. They said she had stopped immersing in the mikveh altogether, deliberately misled him about when she did or didn't have her period, no longer kept a kosher kitchen, and made only minimal preparations for Passover. All of this, they charged, she did maliciously and willfully to cause Jonathan to sin and transgress the commandments of the holy Torah. With respect to the customs of Judah, they claimed that Allison had immodestly and blasphemously cursed Jonathan; questioned the authenticity of certain biblical stories, such as the existence of Abraham, the sacrifice of Isaac, and the parting of the Red Sea in the Hebrew's flight from Egypt; mocked the intelligence of rabbinic judges; and dressed immodestly, for example, by having stopped covering her hair and by walking around in her underwear in the house.

Historically, such allegations not only entitled a man to divorce his wife — which, for a good part of Jewish history he could do without any reason at all (see introduction) — but also allowed him to do so without paying his commitments under the marital contract. They are grave allegations from a religious perspective, and though some rabbinic judges simply gloss over them, others take them seriously, especially when they are made by religious men.

Davidson denied all of the Moses and Judah allegations and, in line with his delaying tactics, asked the court to help the couple reconcile. The rabbinic tribunal assigned to Allison's case, notorious for not making any decision to end a marriage, happily ignored all of Jonathan and Padan's allegations of sinful behavior and accepted Davidson's denials at face value. They would not even let Jonathan try to prove his claims. "We suggest you try counseling," they wrote in their first decision. Davidson continued to deny and delay, happy that the rabbis were cooperating with his attempts to use Jonathan's desire for divorce as leverage to make sure that Allison would not forfeit any rights she might have to the marital home and the other assets accrued during the marriage.

But I want a get," Allison continued to say to Davidson. "Why don't I just agree that I am not an appropriate Jewish wife, accept the get, and get on with my life?"

"*Le'at, le'at.* Slowly, slowly," he replied. "My plan is working. If you agree to the get right now, Jonathan will never agree to give you any share of the apartment or anything. If he wants the get, he'll give you your part of the house and the marital property."

But it didn't seem to Allison that Davidson's plan was working quite as smoothly as he claimed. When Jonathan saw that he failed to make an impression on the rabbinic judges, he upped the ante and charged flat out that Allison had betrayed him with other men. This annoyed Allison, who had never been unfaithful, although with her marriage in total shambles, she certainly was considering it now. Not to mention that her non-Orthodox British parents were genteelly encouraging her to find a boyfriend. "You are still young and vital. You are not going to live your life like some pious, high-minded wallflower because of some silly paper," they urged, referring to the get. Davidson reassured Allison that so long as she denied all charges of infidelity and insisted that she wanted a reconciliation, the rabbis would not force her to agree to divorce (even though, theoretically, such baseless allegations by her husband were themselves grounds under halakha for her to sue for divorce, had she wanted it). The rabbis were not going to force a divorce on Allison, who had, with her subtle humor and good nature, managed to endear herself to the rabbis more than the stern Jonathan. Thus, the rabbinic judges assumed Allison was telling the truth when she said she did not want the divorce (although they implored her, repeatedly, not to "play games") and accepted her denials; they ignored Jonathan's ranting, thinking that he was lying to force a get on a faithful wife of long standing.

"This is good," Davidson explained. "Our delaying tactic is working. Eventually, Jonathan will want to marry someone else, and he will crack and give you a get and your share of the property."

But three years later, in 2007, nothing had moved, and the rabbinic tribunal had issued no real decision. Hearings continued in the rabbinic court, but they were hollow and empty. Allison would persistently deny Jonathan's baseless allegations, and the court would, unremittingly, do nothing, again and again. Allison had gotten nowhere, which is exactly what her attorney had wanted, but which she was beginning to think was, in fact, part of Jonathan and Padan's grand plan. *They* wanted to delay. And Jonathan did not really want to give her a get. He wanted only to do the very opposite of whatever it was he thought that Allison wanted, and thus he could rely on the rabbinic courts to do nothing whatsoever to resolve the impasse. Ironically, this had been exactly Davidson's strategy all along. But now Davidson's delaying tactics seemed counterproductive to her. They were having a boomerang effect. She was stuck in a marriage that she had long ago wanted to end.

Allison decided to confer with another source. Asking around for recommendations, she got to Center for Women's Justice pleader Rivkah Lubitch and schlepped to Haifa for a consultation. She wanted to know what Rivkah thought of Davidson's maneuvers. "Many attorneys operate in this manner," Rivkah told her. "But I, for one, never play around with the get." With Rivkah's words reverberating, Alison girded her strength for a confrontation with Davidson. She would tell him to agree to a get, even though she had not yet reached an agreement with Jonathan on their marital property and even though the family court had not yet issued any substantive ruling in the matter. The civil court had been hampered by a blizzard of delaying tactics employed by Padan and Jonathan, which included endless appeals and even requests to recuse the judge (they failed). The family court had long ago denied Jonathan's request for the custody of their minor children, but the property case, like the divorce proceedings, had become bogged down in the minutiae of procedure and law. Finally, Allison insisted.

"Tell them," she told Davidson, "that although I did not mix up my meat and milk dishes, never questioned the divine authorship of the Torah or the revered status of rabbinic authority, and did not sleep with another man other than Jonathan, *ever,* I agree to the get and want to be divorced from him. In any event, I am not managing to soften Jonathan's position regarding our property, including the house, with your recommendation to reject the get and delay. I might as well have my freedom." She would leave the house, knowing that it would be hard to get Jonathan out of there should the court award her any part of it. But she needed to get on with her life and did not want to spend the rest of it in court, paying Davidson for the privilege.

Davidson reluctantly agreed with her and changed tack. He began pressing for divorce. And, as was only to be expected, Jonathan now changed course and withdrew his offer of a get, taking a new position altogether. Allison now officially became an agunah, a status that she had unwittingly been in, and had even unknowingly contributed to, for the past three years. To justify withholding the get, Jonathan outrageously contended that according to halakha he needed to be married so that he could prove that Allison was unfaithful and convince the rabbinic court to issue a ruling preventing her from marrying a man whom he had identified as her lover, Tom. And what's more, he claimed, he was *not* obliged to divorce Allison if he thought she had slept with another man. Though he admitted that the halakha prevented him from having sex with Allison if had she been unfaithful, he insisted it was his right to choose whether to divorce her, or keep her in limbo, as his "maidservant," so to speak, if not as his lover.

Jonathan wanted the court to hold a trial on this issue and wanted an opportunity to cross-examine Allison about her sexual activity. After three years, exasperated and perhaps hoping to placate Jonathan so that he would now agree to divorce, the rabbis complied and, despite Davidson's objections, set a date for trial. Davidson argued that Jonathan had stated explicitly that the marriage had broken down, that he believed Allison was an adulteress, and that he wanted a divorce. Allison agreed to the get. Of what purpose was a trial, besides lasciviousness? But the rabbis grumpily rejected all Davidson's arguments. They agreed with Padan's logic that Jonathan had to be married to Allison to have standing to prove that she may not marry her alleged lover after divorce. They set down two days for trial, an unusual amount of time for trial in a rabbinic court.

The Sex Trial

Jonathan hired private investigators. "If she's having an affair, she is coming home late or sleeping over at Tom's, and we will submit logs," they assured him. Padan agreed zestfully. He liked ruses, and he had developed a personal dislike of Allison. Soon her comings and goings were being monitored by P.I.'s, and she was wondering why strange men with laptops, cell phones, and even pet dogs were seen outside her building and Tom's residence at all hours. The P.I.'s also installed what is referred to in P.I. parlance as "big ears," which would allow them to pick up sounds inside Tom's bedroom. The findings were inconclusive. But the investigators and Padan said that if Allison thought that they possessed some evidence and became convinced that they had "the goods," in their words, on her, she might crack and admit to greater offenses. It was therefore important to "psych her out," reasoned Padan, and he lugged into rabbinic court a large suitcase filled, he hinted, with incriminating photographs — an old shysters' trick.

Carrying a James Bond-type attaché case himself, Jonathan bragged in court that he had hefty proof of an affair between Allison and Tom, but as it was illegally obtained from Tom's apartment, he could not show it unless Allison agreed to waive her right to privacy — which she refused to do. Jonathan subsequently pressed Allison to take a lie detector test. She again refused, taking the position that the test results were inadmissible. One rabbinic judge was suspicious of Allison's self-righteous denials and reliance on legal loopholes and leaned sympathetically to Jonathan's side. "Why would you refuse to take a lie detector test or waive privacy rights if you were innocent?" he quizzed Allison curiously. "What are you afraid of? What are you hiding? Though we can't force you to undergo a polygraph or waive your rights to privacy, we can reach certain legal conclusions from your refusal to do so."

Short of Allison denying all allegations of infidelity, Davidson preferred to let Shimmy Padan try to prove Jonathan's case without any preliminary testimony from Allison. Rules of evidence and procedure are fluid in rabbinic courts, and rabbinic judges rarely hold formal trials, so testimony is taken in a haphazard, disorganized manner. Padan was out of his usual, rigidly controlled element of the predictable family courts. Thoroughly secular, Padan was far from being a rabbinic pleader versed in religious law, and he had never conducted a trial around such an esoteric, halakhic matter. But, he assured his client, such a trial was "a piece of cake."

"Are you sure?" asked Jonathan. "The rules are a bit different in rabbinic court."

The lawyer shot back a sarcastic look. "Didn't I promise you that the civil trial would take years and that I would bury the judge in paper? Didn't I? I know what I am doing," he bristled.

But Allison was a formidable opponent. She had been well coached by the seasoned Davidson in parrying cross-examination. Padan had to be careful with her. Allison might arouse a measure of sympathy if he pushed her too hard. Initially Padan's instinct was to have a bewigged Orthodox female lawyer associated with his firm do the questioning. But Jonathan dismissed the idea. "Your colleague's performance at the family court trial was a disaster. *You* do the questioning," he told Padan. Also, the associate had confided in Jonathan that she was not comfortable asking "immodest questions." But Padan's initial instincts proved correct. The sight of the formidable, pugnacious Padan bombarding little Allison, a slender woman, with questions and facing off in court bothered even the rabbinic judges.

One of the main issues at the trial was the question of whether or not Allison had ever performed oral sex on Tom. It seems that Padan was trying to establish that Allison was making what he thought was the irrelevant "Bill Clinton" distinction between intercourse (sex) and fellatio (not sex), when she claimed that she had not committed adultery. Perhaps Allison had not had sexual intercourse with Tom but, Jonathan and Padan assumed, surely she must have kissed Tom and even performed oral sex on him, acts the rabbis would condemn. Padan's questioning of Allison on these matters would last several hours.

The three elderly rabbis were seated behind Allison as she testified. They asked Padan to behave in a gentlemanly manner and to make his questions gentle, not crude. Allison was the only woman in the room among a sea of men — two male attorneys, three male rabbinic judges, a male stenographer, and Jonathan. Religious rules bar female judges altogether, and most jobs in the rabbinic court system (including clerical positions) are held by Orthodox men. Given the intimate setting and the testimony that was about to unfold, this all-male scene made Allison somewhat uncomfortable, and she wished that her own lawyer had been a woman. Backed by all these men and their laws, Jonathan felt confident that he would be calling the shots. He felt in control — of the marriage, of the divorce, and even of what would happen beyond all that. Under the cloak of state-backed halakha, he would dictate the terms of the divorce (if it were to occur at all) and thwart any intention Allison may have of marrying Tom.

Before the trial, one rabbi escorted the couple to his chambers and impassionedly warned them both — as if Allison had any say in the matter — that their dispute had "escalated beyond control." He said that, in a similar case a few years back, word got out that the couple had an adultery trial and nobody wanted to marry their children. (That the rabbis themselves could simply refuse to hear Jonathan's so-called evidence and compel him to give a get apparently never occurred to them.)

Padan rose from his seat to show Allison to the lectern. The skullcap he had perched on his head for the rabbis' sake looked like an inverted Chinese takeout food bowl, she thought. Thoughts raced through her mind of great women who underwent such trials. "I am like Anne Boleyn," she said to herself, referring to the second wife of Henry VIII of England who was convicted of trumped-up charges of adultery with several men, including her brother. Like Boleyn, whose husband ordered her executed along with her supposed lovers, Allison felt doomed and outmaneuvered. She knew she needed to gird herself for what was about to happen, and she mustered all her strength to appear confident, even flippant, in the courtroom. It was a good performance. Fact is, Allison was frightened of Padan and deeply unnerved by the trial and what ensued.

The venetian blinds at the rabbinic court were drawn but one or two bent slats afforded Allison a glimpse of the street below. She saw fellow Israelis walking, waiting for traffic lights to change, buying things in stores. People are doing normal things, she thought. If they only knew that a few feet away, I am in a rabbinic dungeon undergoing a medieval ordeal. She wanted to shout for help, but she composed herself. Padan made sure that his crisp white shirt was neatly tucked into his pants, suggesting that he was about to enter the limelight. Davidson sat holding his head in the palms of his hands and keeping his eyes clenched shut, as if he were in deep thought or perhaps making believe that it was all a bad dream.

The following description of a fragment of Allison's adultery trial is reconstructed from the court protocol and an interview with Allison, because the religious, male stenographer chose not to take down a verbatim account.

"Mrs. Cowan," Padan began, careful to use Jonathan's surname for Allison, thus underscoring her married status. "Tell me, how long have you known Tom?"

"A number of years," said Allison, trying to face the rabbis when she spoke, as Davidson had told her to do.

"Where did you meet?" he asked.

"In the neighborhood, school, just around. . . . Actually, Tom comes from London, like me. He is a divorced man. I knew him as well as his family, vaguely, before I came to Israel."

Jonathan had a yellow legal pad and showed Padan something.

"Get to the point," harrumphed one rabbi testily.

"Mrs. Cowan," Padan continued, "isn't it true that Tom accompanied you at night to parties [neshafim] or formal public celebrations to which you wore heavy eye makeup and evening clothes?"

"No," said Allison. "I have never been to a ball in my life [neshef can mean a formal ball as well as party], and I have no evening clothes to speak of. I have just a few dressy items, which I wear to weddings. They hang in the back of my closet. I wear moderate eye makeup. Mascara from Maybelline — that's an American firm."

Davidson jumped up and shouted, "This is a waste of time! Who cares what she has hanging in her closet and what kind of mascara she uses?"

Padan continued, "I want to establish that Tom and Mrs. Cowan went out in the evening together. Like a married couple. They went to parties, dinners, and his apartment. And believe me," he chuckled, pleased with himself, "they didn't spend their time alone reading poetry. Trust me."

"Is it true Mrs. Cowan that Tom took you out to dinner?"

"We didn't go out, as you put it," said Allison. "And there were no dinners. But I did make dinners for thirty years as Jonathan's wife and the mother of his children. He doesn't look thin or underfed, does he?"

"Okay," said Padan, who was, he thought, coming in for the kill. "Did you ever visit Tom's apartment?"

"He showed me his apartment. Sometimes I watched T.V. there because Jonathan canceled our cable subscription and then our T.V. stopped working. I like to know what's going on in the world, especially in foreign markets. This affects my work."

"Did you ever kiss him on the mouth?"

"I don't recall . . . but I did kiss him on both cheeks. This is customary way of extending a greeting in our circles. I might even give you such a kiss. Well maybe not you. . . . But everyone does it."

"Mrs. Cowan, did you touch or kiss his sex organ?" asked Shimmy forthrightly, as if the term "sex organ" were commonly spoken in a rabbinic court. One rabbi seemed upset.

"You promised your line of questioning would be gentle," the rabbi interrupted.

"No, I did not do that," responded Allison. "Are you crazy?"

"Sirs," said Padan to the rabbinic judges, repeating the request he made before the trial began, "I have photographs here and audio recordings that would indicate that this woman is lying through her teeth. I want to enter them as evidence. But I can do so only if she waives her right to privacy, otherwise she might press charges," declared Padan.

Allison answered quickly, "I do not waive any such rights, and I will press charges immediately with the police if anything illegal has been done. I will not condone a crime."

"Again, did you kiss him on the lips?" asked Padan.

"No," said Allison.

"Did you suck his sex organ?"

"No," she answered. "I don't do those things."

"Oh, don't play Little Miss Innocent with me. You know that you gave him a blow job."

"I don't know what you are talking about," said Allison. "I told you, and this court, I don't do those things."

"I think I've heard enough," said the presiding judge, and he ended the session.

After Allison's testimony, Jonathan managed to convince the court of his right to submit embarrassing videos of Allison walking around their house in her underwear. He insisted on showing them to prove Allison's loose and halakhically inappropriate behavior, in violation of the customs of Judah. He brought in a computer for that purpose, which he set up on the rabbis' podium. All attempts by Davidson to disallow the submission of the material as irrelevant fell on deaf ears. The rabbis viewed the fifteen-minute segment uninterrupted. Allison was mortified. But there was no reference or hint of Tom in the video.

The court also subpoenaed Tom as a witness, at Jonathan's request. But on the day scheduled for Tom's testimony, one judge failed to show up. Rescheduling Tom was feasible but would take months. Padan decided to waive his interrogation of Tom and asked the court to render a decision without it. He was confident that Jonathan's and Allison's testimony were determinative, and he asked to submit his summation of the proceedings in writing.

In his papers, Padan argued that he had proved that Allison slept with Tom — though she had admitted nothing, and Jonathan had submitted no incriminating evidence, such as pictures of Allison and Tom or even records of phone conversations between them. Padan argued that Jonathan's and Allison's own testimony were enough to prove the case. And he asked the court to issue a declaratory statement that Allison was forbidden to be with Jonathan, her husband, *ba'alah*, as well as with Tom, her illicit lover, *bo'alah*, in accordance with Talmudic law [T. Bavli, Sotah 27b]. These biblical Hebrew terms reflect crude, ancient gender identities and attitudes. *Ba'alah* is Hebrew for "her husband" and also means "her owner"; *bo'alah* means "the man who has penetrated her." The terms are still used today in rabbinic courts and, even more astonishingly, so are the halakhic principles set forth about 1,500 years ago. If adultery on the part of a wife is proved or admitted, a rabbinic court will issue a ruling proclaiming that a woman, once divorced, cannot remarry her husband or marry her lover. That decision becomes an official part of the wife's divorce file, and there have been circumstances in which there was notification of such a decision on her divorce certificate.

In Allison's case the judges were either persuaded that adultery had not taken place between Allison and Tom or felt that the evidence was inconclusive, or perhaps they were just wary of an appeal by Davidson or an outcry from women's organizations; they denied Padan's request to label Allison's divorce certificate with the equivalent of a Scarlet A. They were nevertheless unequivocally convinced that Jonathan *believed* that adultery had taken place. Therefore, finally, they suggested to Jonathan that he divorce Allison. When he refused, the court issued a ruling that he was obligated to do so — a *hiyuv get*.

But Jonathan had a surprise for the rabbis. In his mind, the lower court had no right to issue any order against him, let alone a hiyuv. He directed Padan to engage an expert in halakha, a rabbi with an advanced degree in law, to help him appeal to the High Rabbinic Court. Jonathan wanted to claim he had the right to punish Allison for her bad behavior by not divorcing her, ignoring the fact that it was he who originally asked for divorce. The Jewish law expert agreed that there is basis for this argument and helped write an appeal that was more than eighty pages long (including attachments) and had to be specially bound since it could not be stapled together. The most interesting parts of the appeal were labeled "C: Setting Her Eyes on Someone Else and Getting a 'Prize' from the Court" and "D: Abhorrent Behavior and Its Implications," which contained citations from revered halakhic authorities whose words are often quoted by the courts.

First, it cited the Rosh (Rabbi Asher ben Jehiel, 1250–1327), who wrote, regarding a woman who "had her eye" on someone else, "For what reason should we compel a husband to divorce such a wife and release her. She must not have relations with her husband and *she should be like a living widow*. After all, she has no obligation [according to halakha] to procreate! Why should we compel a man to divorce his wife because she goes after her heart, has her eye on someone else, and wants him more than the husband of her youth, and desires to fulfill her passions. Why should we compel a man to divorce her? *God Forbid, no rabbinic judge should rule in this manner!!!*" (Shut Rosh 43:8). Then the brief quoted the Rambam, who, they observe, thinks that a woman has the right to demand a get if she is "fed up" with her husband but would not compel a man to divorce his wife if she behaved improperly, for example, by teaching Torah to young children (Shut Ramabam, no. 45). So, a fortiori, he certainly would not compel a man to divorce his wife if she had dalliances with another man, as Allison allegedly did.

And, it added, the Noda BeYehudah (Rabbi Yechezkel ben Yehuda Landau, 1713–1793) makes it clear that a misbehaving wife should not be rewarded with her freedom: "If she was intentionally unfaithful, she cannot force him to divorce her, since she was the one who faltered and made herself prohibited to him. A person who sins cannot be rewarded, and she must forfeit her marriage contract and all its provisions. Nonetheless, the choice is in the hands of the husband to decide if he wants to [divorce her or to] leave her lonely for the rest of her life . . . forsaken forever" (Mahadura Tanina, Even HaEzer, no. 12).

And, finally, the brief cited the Maharik (Rabbi Joseph Colon ben Solomon Trabotto, 1420–1480) for the proposition that Allison should "rot till her hair turned white," which was that sage's recommendation in a much lesser case, in which he was asked whether it was proper to compel a man who had already married someone else to give a get to his betrothed fiancée who had wrongfully jilted him. (Today, Jewish engagement and marriage occur almost simultaneously to avoid this dilemma.)

But Jonathan had backed himself into a wall. First, he initiated the divorce proceedings, but now he was refusing to grant his wife a get. He had gone too far even for the rabbis. The High Rabbinic Court still treated him, and especially his attorney Shimmy Padan, whose social standing among the Israeli elite was common knowledge, with respect. They allowed them their day in court, but they were not about to interfere with the decision of the lower court.

The case had become unmanageable. Advised that he would probably lose the appeal and fearful that the lower court would support a travel restraint order against him, Jonathan, in a volte-face, agreed to give the get, on two conditions: one, Allison must move out of the marital domicile within two days; and, two, the couple's youngest child, by then aged seventeen, must not meet with any "romantic" male friend of Allison until the child reached the age of thirty. Told by the rabbis that this was not enforceable, Jonathan then tried to convince the court to apply the order until the child was twenty-one. When that still didn't convince the court, Jonathan agreed that the ban should last only until the child's eighteenth birthday, the legal majority age, just a few months away. Davidson recommended that Allison accede to these conditions and asked that the get ceremony be enacted that very day. In accordance with the first term of the agreement they subsequently reached, Allison could not return home without Jonathan's permission, and she had to make complicated arrangements to take her clothes from the house.

So it came to pass that in March 2009, five years from the date Jonathan first filed papers, the couple was hastily divorced. No mention of Allison's presumed lover, Tom, the bo'el, was made in Allison's official divorce judgment or on her divorce certificate, thus freeing her to marry Tom, if she so chose. But the trial, in all its prurient detail, is still part of the court record.

The divorce case has ended. Recently, the family court issued a ruling on the disposition of Jonathan and Allison's property — seven years since Jonathan first filed suit in 2004, and more than two years since the final hearing in the family court case. But Jonathan is appealing the judge's decision. Meanwhile Allison lives outside the marital home, and Jonathan has dominion over it and all its contents.

Although he had objected to the adultery trial as superfluous and irrelevant in Allison's specific case, at no time during the lengthy divorce proceedings did Davidson, or anyone else, question whether the court had the right, in principle, to hold a trial on Allison's sexual life, to show a video of Allison in her underwear, or to prevent Allison from marrying a third party as punishment for her alleged adultery. All involved acquiesced in the power of the state, deferring as it does to the rabbinic courts and the halakha, to discipline and punish the bodies of married women.

The grip of the Israeli state on Jewish women is not limited to its ability to punish them for adultery. As a precondition to their marriage, all Jewish women are required by the state — through its abdication to the rabbis — to immerse in a mikveh, to undergo a course on when and how to conduct their sexual lives with their husbands, and to set the date of their wedding in accordance with their menstrual cycle (see chapter 1) — although these rituals and precepts may be anathema to some of them and certainly are foreign to many of them. One rabbi recently refused to perform a wedding when the bride could not present a mikveh attendant's certification that she had undergone the required ritual immersion. The state pays for, and builds, ritual baths that service Jewish married women. In accordance with a recent directive of Chief Rabbi Yonah Metzger, it has refused access to women who are single or divorced who for all sorts of religious and spiritual reasons like to use the mikveh. And, as we have seen in Allison's case, the state authorizes the court to conduct "sex" trials to try to bar women from engaging in sexual relations after marriage with a man who may have been their lover. Should the trial prove the adultery allegations to be true, rabbinic courts note the fact on some of the woman's divorce papers, thus literally and figuratively branding a woman with the equivalent of a Scarlet Letter.

"If I'd claimed that Jonathan cheated on me, would that have been grounds for divorce?" Allison asked Davidson, curious.

"A man's infidelity is not necessarily grounds for divorce," Davidson answered.

"And what if I had said, 'Yes, I slept with Tom,' would I have gotten a get more quickly?"

"It's not clear," Davidson answered. "If Jonathan did not want the divorce, they may not have believed you."

THREE

The Ping-Pong Agunah

The rule of law requires the government to exercise its
power in accordance with well-established and clearly written rules,
regulations, and legal principles. A distinction is sometimes drawn
between power, will, and force, on the one hand, and law, on the other.
When a government official acts pursuant to an express provision of a
written law, he acts within the rule of law. But when a government official
acts without the imprimatur of any law, he or she does so by the
sheer force of personal will and power.

"Rule of Law," *Free Dictionary*

"This is it," we proclaimed, after perusing Dalia's papers. "This case will bring
down the rabbinic courts."

"Doubt it," Dalia retorted. "I've heard that before. And, see, despite everything, the courts still stand, as powerful as ever. But, *baruch ha'shem* (thank
God), so do I. I was not so sure of that for a while."

Three months into their marriage, Dalia and Ari share the easygoing freshness
of mature newlyweds, smiling and finishing each other's sentences. In their spa-
cious and immaculate rental apartment in an old, leafy suburb of Tel Aviv, the
coffee table is laden with nuts, sweets, and cookies, underscoring the welcom-
ing feeling. A warm and gregarious woman, Dalia, quickly offers the use of her
computer to a visitor who has to check a train schedule. Walls freshly painted,
a beige leather couch in the living room, the new apartment bears no clutter
from earlier traumatic lives. And Ari and Dalia, both Orthodox, had plenty of
trauma to put behind them. Ari nursed an ailing first wife for three years, taking

early retirement from his senior government position to care for her until she died. Reflecting on Ari's devotion and the "blamelessness" of widowerhood, Dalia remarks, "It's no one's fault that she got sick, and the marriage ended." Dalia, on the other hand, was an agunah for nineteen years and is suing her ex-husband and the State of Israel for upending her basic rights to marry and divorce as she saw fit, to have the freedom and autonomy "to write the story of her life," as one civil court judge put it when reviewing another woman's claim for damages for get refusal. Now Dalia has to pause to recall details of her unhappy years. "Who wants to remember what is painful?" she wonders aloud. Her demeanor is relaxed and generous. Wearing a narrow, white bandanna as a nod to the Orthodox precept that married women must cover their hair, Dalia smiles as she says, "I am happy, at last."

Tall and fit with reddish-blonde hair, Ari is the only son of a Holocaust survivor mother and a sabra father, both Ashkenazim, Jews of European descent. Dalia is a petite, olive-skinned Yemenite whose youthful figure and sprightly demeanor belie her sixty-plus years. When she first got married at age nineteen in 1969, her parents would have balked at the idea of an Ashkenazi son-in-law. But these differences are hardly relevant anymore, she says. "What's important is that the person is a decent human being," she says, stressing that Ari had been a good husband and had lived contentedly with his late wife and their two children. After his year of mourning was over, Ari started dating, and he and Dalia met online. Having been burned once by a man who withheld a get, Dalia asked Ari to take a lie detector test. She wanted to make sure that he wasn't married or involved in anything dubious. "I asked this of everybody whom I dated seriously," she says in a matter-of-fact tone. Ari obliged. He understood that Dalia's trust in men had been shattered by a horrific marriage and an inordinately long divorce process. He hoped that, in time, she would be able to trust him without relying on third-party confirmation of his integrity.

Today Ari is home early from his religious studies class to escort Dalia on their weekly fun outing — this time to Tel Aviv's flea market. Though he was raised secular, Ari turned Orthodox many years ago when he was still married to his first wife. Ari never made religious demands on his wife or children, and they remained secular, he says. Their home was not kosher, save what Ari put aside for himself, although his late wife attended the mikveh to accommodate Ari's new lifestyle.

These days, Dalia relates, Ari rubs cream into her feet after she does the housework when the maid doesn't show up. "Ari is wonderful, kind, and generous to me," Dalia laughs. "It's only now, at age sixty-one, that I am experiencing a normal marriage." Indeed, when Dalia was married to a man whom we shall call Yitzhak, there were no foot massages, only beatings, fury, pettiness, and abusive behavior.

"How," we wondered out loud," did such a savvy, cautious woman find herself in this impossible position?"

Born in Yemen, Dalia Ovad was only three months old when she and all the other members of her devout and traditional family were brought to Israel in Operation Magic Carpet, the secret airlift that brought forty-nine thousand Yemenite Jews to the new Jewish State of Israel. Growing up in northern Israel, she was a pretty and inquisitive-looking child with brown, almond-shaped eyes. She met Yitzhak when she was eighteen. He was her older brother's army buddy and visited the house often. He began courting Dalia and once brought her a bouquet of flowers. Yitzhak Carmeli seemed like a good catch to Dalia's father, whose opinion was all-important and who recommended that she pursue the relationship, saying he would handle the marriage negotiations. Yitzhak was a fellow Yemenite Jew, a kohen, and, most important, at age twenty-five Yitzhak had a good position at a bank and was financially independent. Today Dalia bears no grudges against her late parents for encouraging her to marry Yitzhak, the man who robbed her of so many good years. "How were they to know?" she asks. True, an argument erupted while Dalia and Yitzhak were engaged that made Dalia think twice. Having learned that Dalia had been in a short relationship with another man before him, Yitzhak, uncontrollably jealous, went to the old boyfriend and threatened him not to come near Dalia. She was alarmed by his conduct and considered ending the relationship. Domestic violence counselors warn that extreme jealousy is often a precursor of abuse, and future events proved that Dalia's instincts were right. "But the invitations were already printed, and I felt it was too late to break up," she says ruefully. The couple wed in a hall in Rehovot, near Tel Aviv, in 1969. Dalia was nineteen.

Things were bleak from the onset. Yitzhak was irritable and took out his anger on Dalia. He was critical of just about everything about her, including her cooking, mothering, and housekeeping skills, although, by her account at least, she seems to have been a fabulous mother, an adequate cook, and a fanatic about keeping her home clean, as she still is. In the first seven years of their marriage, the couple had four children. Yitzhak, a budding misogynist, was angry that three of them were female. He accused Dalia of "producing only girls." Yitzhak did not visit her in the hospital after the birth of their fourth child when he heard about the sex of the newborn baby. He wanted sons.

Dalia endured verbal insults, which quickly escalated into physical violence. She kept her anguish to herself, but her mother remarked that she "always seemed sad." Dalia recalls that the violence started with a *flick*, using the Hebrew slang for "slap." The situation got worse, and in 1976 she filed her first request for a get in the Ashdod Rabbinic Court, claiming that she was a victim of physical and verbal abuse. Yitzhak denied her allegations. The court ruled that the couple should try to achieve a reconciliation (*shalom bayit* or "peace at home," a term that implies the Jewish religious ideal of domestic tranquility and positive, healthy relations between husband and wife). Rabbinic judges in Israel used to recommend shalom bayit as an initial response to many divorce actions, no matter what grounds were involved, even sexual abuse. But such decisions have become less frequent in recent years, as judges realized that they did not curb the soaring divorce rate, and attorneys strenuously opposed them. Dalia was told by the court that a marriage is not discarded because "a little something goes wrong." A dutiful and religious woman, she took the rabbis' words seriously and decided to try, again, to make her marriage work. Her parents agreed.

Two more daughters were conceived during the so-called shalom bayit phase of the marriage. Dalia cringes when she remembers those intimate encounters but explains that she obeyed the rabbis' directive "to behave like a thoroughly devoted wife." Today she feels blessed by her daughters. "I guess they made it all worthwhile," she tells us. Dalia asked the hospital staff not to reveal to Yitzhak the sexes of the subsequent babies before they were born. "I wanted a few months of peace," she says.

With the passage of years, violence escalated. Intimacy became increasingly impossible for Dalia. At night, she retreated to a separate room. Sometimes, Yitzhak would break in, pull her by her hair, and throw her to the floor, where he would "carry out his evil intent," as the Hebrew phrase for rape goes. Sometimes, Yitzhak would prohibit Dalia from returning to her bed to sleep. Sometimes, in anger over her refusal to meet his needs, he would lock her in the bathroom for an entire night and she would sleep on towels in the bathtub. This sad and awful set of circumstances infuriated Yitzhak, and he threatened to kill her.

1987–1999

In 1987 Dalia was convinced that Yitzhak was unhinged mentally. Besides subjecting her to terrible abuse, he had attempted suicide several times. Dalia decided to flee "with the shirt on my back. That's all. Not even a baby bottle." With six children in tow, she returned to her parents' home. Eventually the older couple would build a second home on their property for Dalia and their grandchildren. On the day she fled, Yitzhak lost no time and filed a lawsuit of his own in Ashdod Rabbinic Court, suing for "reconciliation or, alternatively, for divorce." Specifically, he asked the court to classify Dalia as a *moredet* (rebellious wife) who forfeited her rights under her marriage contract in the event that the court rejected his request for reconciliation. Dalia countersued for divorce, her second official request for a get. She also sued for child support and for the division of the marital property in the district court (the precursor of the family courts), in accordance with standard protocol and the recommendation of her attorney, an honest eager young man named Pinhas (Pinny) Stoleman. Yitzhak hired a rabbinic pleader to represent him in the rabbinic court and an attorney to represent him in the family court. He cut off almost all ties with his children, refused to pay child support, and became a self-taught and self-proclaimed expert on Jewish divorce law and legal procedure. He switched representatives a number of times before he found ones who would take his opinion with the weight and seriousness he felt it deserved and who would not try and convince him to compromise on anything. Yitzhak was determined to beat Dalia in this contest of wills.

What ensued during the next two decades became a hellish ordeal. Dalia was treated like a human ping-pong ball, bounced from one court to another, from one conflicting judicial decision to another. Only in 1991, four years after she had left home for good and filed for divorce for a second time, did the Ashdod court finally reject Yitzhak's petition; it ruled that he "must" (*al ha'baal*) divorce Dalia and give her a get. "The chances that a reconciliation will work are zero," wrote the judges. The court had gotten a good close look at Yitzhak during the "many long and intensive hearings" they held and did not like what they saw. Or perhaps more significantly, neither did the court-appointed expert psychologist who was asked to evaluate the family's chance at reconciliation. After reading his report, the court wrote that Dalia had good reason to be "revolted" by Yitzhak "for whom feelings of love and hate were so mixed up in his mind that [he was] dangerously violent."

But Yitzhak appealed that decision to the High Rabbinic Court, claiming that "zero chances of reconciliation" was not sufficient grounds to order him to divorce Dalia. The higher court, located in Jerusalem, set a date to hear the case a year later. When it finally reached a verdict in April 1993, it held that Yitzhak's appeal was moot and superfluous, since he mistakenly believed that the Ashdod court's ruling "obligated" him to give a divorce, whereas, wrote the appeals court, the ruling said only that he "must" divorce his wife. "Must" did not mean "obligated to" (*hayav*). The lower court decision was, in the words of the higher court, merely a "recommendation," a statement advising that it would be a mitzvah for Yizhak to give a get, an empty ruling with, effectively, no legal consequences attached to it at all.

What Dalia and Stoleman later suspected, but could not know for sure, was that it was quite possible that Yitzhak's latest rabbinic pleader — Shalom Sheinfeld, a tall, handsome man, meticulously dressed, with a full head of blond hair slicked backward like a 1950s movie star — had managed to maneuver the couple's file into a particular rabbinic appeals tribunal known for its formalistic and conservative rulings. Sheinfeld would have been able to do this simply by insisting that the rabbinic court clerks set down the appeal for a certain day of the week on which he claimed he was available and which, just coincidentally, happened to coincide with the day on which the conservative tribunal sat. Such finessing was common practice among the well informed and not at all hard to do for those who were, as was Sheinfeld, chummy with the court clerks in the small appeals office then located in the Old City of Jerusalem and who knew which tribunals sat on what days. It would have been particularly easy for Sheinfeld, who, with his winning smile and charm, had developed a specialty in handling appeals cases and was especially adept at defending the appeals of recalcitrant husbands who had been ordered to divorce their wives.

Based in Bnai Brak, a predominantly ultra-Orthodox suburb of Tel Aviv, he handled these cases at a steep price for men who came to him from all over the country. He knew exactly what halakhic arguments to make and what practical steps to take to be sure that those arguments fell on sympathetic ears. Most run-of-the-mill divorce attorneys lack this type of expertise. Their preconceived tactic is to avoid setting foot in a rabbinic court at all until matters ancillary to the divorce have been either settled out of court or determined by a family court. Creating a fait accompli for their clients, divorce attorneys prefer to arrive in the rabbinic court only for what they see as the mere technicalities of the divorce ritual. They will rarely, if ever, take a divorce case on appeal, something that may require them to draw on what are often confusing and contradictory references to fourth-century Talmudic sources in Aramaic or to dense rabbinic tomes written in the Middle Ages, which are confusing and seem hardly relevant to the facts at hand. But rabbinic pleaders, like Sheinfeld, are mostly male yeshiva graduates and are on home turf in all rabbinic courts. They understand how to talk there, what to look like, how to curry favor with judges and clerks. They have pored over esoteric Talmudic texts since childhood, and, most important, they understand how to position themselves.

A seasoned pleader like Sheinfeld knew that Rabbi T's tribunal would *never* order a man to give a get. Rabbi T's tribunal sat on Tuesdays. On the other hand, Rabbi D's tribunal would *never* let a man get away with not giving a get if they saw that the marriage had broken down — a fact presumed if a case had reached them on appeal and a lower court had actually made a decision against a recalcitrant husband. Rabbi D's tribunal sat on Mondays and Wednesdays. Unlike attorneys who can appear in both rabbinic and family courts, rabbinic pleaders can appear only in rabbinic courts. So hiring a pleader may require a litigant to hire two professionals, one for the rabbinic court and one for the family courts. But if the goal is to torture a spouse into submission, a pleader is probably a good choice. And among pleaders of this sort, Sheinfeld was probably the best choice of all. What appears to have been his clever maneuvering among the High Rabbinic Court tribunals in the early nineties would seal Dalia's fate for the coming decades.

Back in the lower court, Dalia again asked the Ashdod Rabbinic Court to obligate Yitzhak to give her a get, as well as to order him to pay alimony in a high amount until he indeed did so. Incensed at Yitzhak and Sheinfeld and frustrated with the appeals court, the lower court again rallied to Dalia's side, this time making it clear that they were ordering Yitzhak to grant a divorce and not merely recommending that he do so. In February 1994 ten months after the appeals court had said that "must" did not mean "obligated to," the court "obligated" Yitzhak to divorce Dalia, holding that Dalia's claim that she was "revolted by" or "fed up" with Yitzhak was supported by the facts (and, though the tribunal did not say so, it was clear that they were fed up with him too). In July 1994, when Yitzhak still had not given the get, the lower court awarded Dalia the requested punitive alimony. And again, Yitzhak appealed to the same appeals' tribunal, now the designated decisors in Dalia's case. He claimed that the lower court had no new facts before it that would justify its new ruling "obligating" him to divorce Dalia, that he was sincere about wanting a reconciliation, that Dalia did not really mean it when she claimed that he disgusted her, and that even if he did disgust her, this was not grounds to obligate him to divorce her. And if he was not so obligated, he asserted, the court could not order him to pay punitive alimony.

In November 1994 the High Rabbinic Court again set aside the lower court's decree, both the part that had specifically obligated Yitzhak to give a get, as well as the part requiring him to pay alimony (which they vacated retroactively). Rabbi Tufik (his real name), writing for the majority, held,

> We heard the parties and reviewed all the material in the file, and we also read the expert opinion. Even if we were to find that the "wife is revolted by her husband for good reason" — a claim of which we are not convinced — this is not grounds for obligating the husband to divorce his wife, as it is written in the Shulkan Arukh, siman 77, seif. 2. In the case of a woman who makes the argument that her husband is repulsive to her, if her husband wants to, he can divorce her and she will not receive [the money allotted to her in] her marriage contract. But one cannot order him to divorce his wife against his will. See also Rabbinic Court Reporter Vol. 7, page 4. . . . Moreover, even though the husband is a Yemenite, and Yemenites have accepted Rambam's position that it is possible to obligate a husband to divorce his wife on grounds of revulsion, we must accede to the husband's claim that he is from a particular clan that does not accept the rules of Rambam. Moreover, the couple married in Israel, where we must apply the rules of the Shulhan Arukh. . . . And since it is not possible to obligate the husband to deliver a get, it is not possible to obligate him to pay punitive alimony, and we accept both parts of the husband's appeal. (C. v. C., 1994)

Back again at square one, and with no other path open to her if she wanted a divorce, Dalia again asked the Ashdod Rabbinic Court — for the third time — to obligate Yitzhak to give her a get. Stoleman decided to bring additional witnesses who had not been heard before and who testified that Yitzhak had been violent with Dalia and the children. In February 1996 the lower court again held, in a majority opinion, that Yitzhak was obligated to give a get. And again Yitzhak appealed, but this time the appeals court upheld the lower court's decision. But by now it was February 1997. A year had passed since the Ashdod court had reissued its original ruling, and ten whole years had gone by since Yitzhak threatened Dalia and she fled the marital home. With nothing having changed except for the passage of time, and with Rabbi Tufik holding firm to his original position, but this time in the minority, the tribunal held as follows:

[Rabbi Nadav:] It is true that the lower court admitted testimony of family members who normally are not considered under Jewish law to have capacity to testify. But since the purpose is to determine the truth, and since the lower court has been dealing with the parties for a long time now, and they know and understand them and have reached a definite conclusion, we cannot interfere with [that court's] discretion to determine that the parties cannot continue living together because of the husband's behavior. Thus, even if [this court] would not compel a husband to give his wife a get if the wife claimed that he was repulsive to her, that is only the case if the husband is not responsible for the circumstances at hand, and if it were merely [the subjective feelings of] the wife which prevented her from living with him because she was revolted by him. In those circumstances, we would not compel a husband. And this was the case when this court accepted the appeal of the husband [in the past] and dismissed the holding of the lower court. But today, after further investigation, the lower court wrote the decision that is the subject of this appeal. After the lower court has been persuaded by the justice of the wife's claim, we do not see any room for us to interfere with that discretion or with the conclusions of the lower court.

[Rabbi Eliyahu:] I agree with Nadav that the appeal should be denied.

[Rabbi Tufik, dissenting:] It appears from the reasoning of the lower court that it adheres to its original position that it is possible to obligate a get if the [wife] argues [that her husband is] repulsive to her, as it has so held in the past. This court has already decided this matter and rejected that position in its decision of November 1994. Therefore we should vacate the decision of the lower court of February 1996 that is the subject of this appeal in accordance with the reasons set forth in the aforementioned decision [of November 1994]. (C. v. C., 1997)

The lower court began to try to implement its now affirmed decision, slowly. First, in May 1997 it ordered all the sextons of synagogues surrounding Yitzhak's place of residence to refuse to allow him into the synagogue, to be given the honor of reciting the blessing over the Torah portion, or even to ask if he is well. (Yitzhak did not bother to appear for the hearing on this matter.) A few weeks later, it ordered Yitzhak to appear weekly in court "to explain his position and in the hope that with time he will begin to understand that he must stop torturing his wife." The order was open-ended and Yitzhak simply ignored it.

By December 1997 Sheinfeld understood that he and Yitzhak had played their initial card to its end. Sheinfeld decided to change tactics. He directed Yitzhak to declare that he was now willing to give Dalia a get. Yitzhak should no longer insist that there were no grounds under halakha to force him, the ideal husband, to divorce his beloved wife. Now, instead, he should use the Maharashdam ploy, the sixteenth-century rabbi's ruling that a man cannot be compelled to divorce his wife if she refuses to consent to his "easily fulfilled" terms for the divorce (see introduction).

And as his and Sheinfeld's newly formulated conditions for now agreeing to giving a get, Yitzhak would demand that Dalia return the money he had been obligated to pay her under the settlement that had been brokered, signed, and executed in the civil courts in November 1991 and May 1996. After tortuous negotiations Yitzhak had paid Dalia only 24 percent of the value of the marital home in exchange for her waiver of any rights to it, as well as a few thousand dollars for her share in the family's modest cash, investments, and personal property. He wanted the money back. He also wanted Dalia to forgive his child support debt. And he wanted the court to stay any sanctions imposed against him for refusing to give a get. In March 1997 the Ashdod rabbinic judges, long ago fed up, refused to hear any more excuses and held that Yitzhak had to obey its order to give Dalia a get without further ado or conditions. He and Sheinfeld again appealed.

On December 18, 1997, the appeals court, in a majority decision, denied most of Yitzhak's petition. It held that "the husband is obligated to give a get in accordance with the decisions that have already been issued and cannot delay it on the basis of monetary claims that no longer exist." It refused to reopen the civil court property settlements. But it also held that Yitzhak had to pay only 70 percent of the child support debt. Rabbi Tufik again dissented, saying that Yitzhak's request to set conditions for the get had a halakhic basis. He thought that Dalia must allow the rabbinic court to decide if she owed Yitzhak any money and that so long as she did not agree to rehear the marital property issues in accordance with Torah law, Yitzhak was not obligated to divorce her.

With their divorce order more or less in place and thinking they were finally finished with the case, the Ashdod judges set a date for the delivery of the get and summoned Yitzhak to court, but he didn't show up. The court set another date and, this time, directed the police to bring him in. By February 1998 Yitzhak was still refusing to give a get, and the rabbinic court ordered him put in jail for six months or until he did so, explaining that he was "deriding and belittling" its decisions.

But the day that he was to enter prison, Yitzhak — with the help of Sheinfeld, of course — got sympathetic officials at the High Rabbinic Court to arrange an urgent hearing on his request to suspend the order sending him to jail. Incredibly, in March 1998 the higher court complied in an ex parte hearing, without inviting Dalia or Stoleman to respond in any way and voice their objection. A month later Yitzhak, at large and feeling emboldened, directed Sheinfeld to appeal the decision to have him jailed and asked the appeals court to make the temporary stay of execution of that decision permanent. In April 1998 the rabbis agreed, citing the Maharashdam, in direct contradiction of the majority decision of December 1997. Echoing Rabbi Tufik's minority opinion of that date, they held that they would arrange for a get only as soon as Dalia authorized the court to rehear the property matters that had already been resolved between the parties in the civil courts.

Yitzhak could not be penalized in any way possible for not divorcing her until Dalia acceded to his conditions for the get. Dalia and Stoleman were shattered. They had seen the Promised Land but were barred from crossing the Jordan. This decision is ultra vires," Stoleman told Dalia. "Way beyond the court's authority. A rabbinic court has no jurisdiction to order you to waive a settlement approved and authorized by a civil court, just like it had no authority to forgive Yitzhak's child support debt. And it's interfering with your fundamental right to your day in court. We need to petition the Supreme Court sitting as the High Court of Justice (or Bagatz, as it is commonly referred to by its Hebrew acronym). It will vacate the decision."

In their petition, Dalia and Stoleman claimed that in addition to the legal points, the rabbinic court decision "violated the laws of 'natural justice' since it was self-contradictory; not adequately reasoned; discriminated against a woman's right to file for her marital property in the secular courts; placed a woman in a position inferior to, and subject to, her husband; violated her constitutional rights to property and dignity; had no basis in evidence; and had no basis in reason" (*C. v. High Rabbinic Court*, 2001). Satisfied with his pleading, Stoleman felt confident that the court would rally to Dalia's support.

The Attorney General's Office defends the decisions of the rabbinic courts in challenges filed with the Supreme Court. But at a preliminary hearing on Dalia's appeal in the Supreme Court, legal counsel for the rabbinic courts showed up as well. He informed the Supreme Court justices, who are generally reluctant to challenge rabbinic rulings or antagonize the "ultra-Orthodox street," that if they voided the High Rabbinic Court's March 1998 decision, it would not help Dalia. The rabbinic judges would simply refuse to reissue an order putting Yitzhak in jail.

Consequently, the Supreme Court, which in addition to disliking any frontal attack on the rabbinic courts also dislikes issuing ineffectual rulings, withheld judgment. It advised Dalia to compromise. And so it transpired that she agreed, however reluctantly, to her husband's terms. To receive her get, Dalia would ask the different civil courts to vacate the agreements she had entered into and transfer her disputes to the religious courts for rehearing. She informed the High Rabbinic Court that she would agree to those terms in exchange for a get and asked them to arrange it.

Back on his home turf in the High Rabbinic Court, Sheinfeld and Yitzhak regained their bearings and their chutzpah. They now had, in addition to the concessions already achieved, still new conditions for giving a get. It was not enough for the court to rehear the property issue. They wanted to make sure the case would not be heard by the Ashdod Rabbinic Court, where, they felt, the rabbis were too sympathetic to Dalia to begin with. Once again, the High Rabbinic Court granted Yitzhak's wish and in August 1999 it ruled that the case would be heard by the Ashkelon Rabbinic Court. They also ruled that both Yitzhak and Dalia would not have any right to appeal a decision of that court.

On October 19, 1999, after twelve years of separation and wrangling, Yitzhak finally handed Dalia the get, and the couple was divorced in Ashkelon. Dalia asked the Ministry of the Interior to change her status in her government-issued identity card from married to divorced.

But the case was far from over.

1999–2006, 6.5 Years

Two months after he had delivered the get, in January 2000 Yitzhak asked the Supreme Court to dismiss Dalia's petition, which was still outstanding but, in his mind, moot. When Dalia did not immediately agree and the court set a date for a hearing, Sheinfeld and Yitzhak asked the High Rabbinic Court to void the get, claiming that Yitzhak had been tricked into giving it. Taking their accusations seriously, the High Rabbinic Court swiftly issued an ex parte decree barring Dalia and Yitzhak from marrying. A few days later, Dalia withdrew her petition to the Supreme Court. But Yitzhak was still furious and sure that he had been tricked into parting with the get and its precious leverage. He was worried that Dalia would now do whatever she could to breach her agreement to have the rabbinic court review his property demand. He and Sheinfeld insisted that the court now actually void the get, not just bar Dalia and Yitzhak from marrying. They wanted it absolutely clear that the two were still married and needed another get to be free. In a hearing with both parties present, the High Rabbinic Court agreed to suspend the get until all hearings in the rabbinic court were completed.

Frustrated and now again yoked by rabbinic fiat to Yitzhak, Dalia was at the end of a thin tether of sanity. How could they suspend her divorce? Did this mean she was undivorced? Was there any other court in the world that could do such a thing? Were all Jewish women in the world bound forever to the whims of their ex-husbands and rabbinic courts who did not want to lose control over them? She and Stoleman decided to file another petition with the Supreme Court, asking it to reinstate the civil courts' financial settlements, claiming that Dalia had agreed to dismiss them under duress, and to vacate the rabbinic court decision suspending the get, arguing that there was no basis in law or halakha for such suspension.

But again, not surprisingly, the Supreme Court refused. Reluctant as it always is to antagonize the rabbinic courts and the ultra-Orthodox community and its representatives in the government coalition, it particularly does not like to interfere with what rabbinic courts claim is their exclusive realm of halakha. Invoking the halakha — what is tantamount to a set of rules, regulations, and principles known and knowable only to them — the rabbis and their advisors silence the judges and force them into, what is for them, the comfortable and manageable corners of the civil law. With respect to halakha, there is no judi-cial review. It is separate and above the law and subject to the rabbis' interpreta-tion alone. If they say they can suspend a get, so be it. The Supreme Court de-fended and justified its ruling on the basis of contract law — "she agreed" — and ignored the gross imbalance of power that had preceded Dalia's "agreement," even accusing Dalia of "trickery":

> With all due sympathy toward the petitioner's plight, we cannot extend her relief. Her attorney admitted to us that her declarations — before the High Rabbinic Court and the district rabbinic courts — that she agreed to rehear the marital property matters in accordance with the laws of the Torah were a ruse meant to extract the get by trickery. Now she asks this court to excuse her from the con-sequences of her supposed agreement. We cannot lend a hand to this. A party who appears before official courts, and knowingly leads the courts astray, cannot expect the High Court of Justice to help turn back the wheels. We are not oblivi-ous to the unacceptable position taken by the respondent who demanded, as a condition for his agreeing to the get, to exempt him from his agreement and to defer to the discretion of the rabbinic district court in all matters relating to the couple's marital property. The problem is that the petitioner expressly declared to the rabbinic court that she acceded to this demand. If the petitioner wants to claim that her declared agreement was not an agreement at all, she should do so before the court of law in which she made her original declaration of agreement. (C. v. High Rabbinic Court, 2001)

But Dalia was not about to ask the rabbinic courts to declare her agreement void on the basis of duress, which was not only halakhically sanctioned but seemed to be halakhically dictated by the Maharik-Maharashdam rule. Dalia had no choice but to return to the Ashkelon Rabbinic Court to reopen her marital asset agreement and to address the question of her challenged get. It was now 2001. Almost fourteen years had passed since she left the marital home and filed her second petition for divorce. From Dalia's perspective, a veritable lifetime had gone by, and she was far from finished. From the rabbis' perspective, buttressed now by the words of the Supreme Court, Dalia, not Yitzhak, was at fault: she should not have reneged on her promise to give in to extortion. She had only herself to blame.

From 2001 to 2003 the Ashkelon Rabbinic Court proceeded to rehear the couple's entire divorce file and even, at Yitzhak's request and though not relevant at all to the issue at hand, recalled witnesses in the domestic abuse events of some twelve years ago. But on the day scheduled for hearing their testimony, one judge failed to show up and the hearing was canceled. Witnesses who had traveled to distant Ashkelon had done so for naught. Not wanting to bother the witnesses again, the court decided to waive their testimony and instead asked Dalia and Yitzhak to repeat lie detector tests performed for the Ashdod Rabbinic Court many years earlier to affirm, or refute, Dalia's allegations of physical abuse on the part of Yitzhak during the marriage. Once again, Dalia's testimony was found to be truthful.

On November 23, 2003 — two and a half years after the rabbinic court had been authorized to rehear the marital property issues, four years since the get had been handed by Yitzhak to Dalia, and after only two hearings had been conducted on the matter of the couple's marital property — the Ashkelon court finally made two substantive rulings: first, that Dalia had to pay Yitzhak six thousand dollars in legal fees to cover expenses incurred by him as a result of her appeal to the Supreme Court, ignoring the fact that the matter of such expenses was not a question of marital property but rather an issue for the Supreme Court to decide; and second, that "because of her behavior" of having turned to secular courts to wiggle out of her obligations, Dalia was now required to obtain a *get l'humra*, a symbolic "abundantly cautious" get that would serve to dispel any religious doubts that may have arisen about the halakhic validity of her earlier divorce. This meant that Yitzhak had to deliver yet another get to Dalia (*C. v. C.*, 2003).

And so it came to pass that fourteen years after Dalia had left the family home, she was, it seemed, again right back at the beginning. The Ashkelon court decision was a groundbreaking one, and an atrocious one for women, enabling husbands and rabbinic courts to extend the long arm of halakhic patriarchy over women way past the term of the marriage (see chapter 2 for attempts to control women's sexuality after divorce). Until now, Israeli rabbinic courts had condoned, and even encouraged, preget extortion, with Israeli civil courts, including the Supreme Court, turning a consistent blind eye to this practice in the name of contract law and the finality of judgments. Since Dalia's case, postget extortion has also been condoned. Israeli rabbinic courts have in fact penalized women for "bad behavior" if they attempt to challenge their divorce agreements in any way, or even if their husbands merely allege that they have breached them.

In theory at least, questioning the validity of a get is discouraged and disparaged under halakha.Until Dalia's case, revoking a get for bad behavior was unheard of. Rabbinic judges conducting divorce ceremonies repeatedly quiz men to ensure that they are acting of their own free will. They ask husbands to disclaim, again and again, any statement that may have been made regarding their willingness or refusal to give a get, thus supposedly dispelling any future question that may be raised with respect to the validity of the divorce and assuring its finality. The event is watched by at least two independent witnesses. Presumably, Yitzhak was also appropriately quizzed to make sure that the get was final and could not be challenged. Now, rabbinic courts and husbands use the threat of the repealed get to keep women in line and make sure that they keep their promises, however draconian the terms of the divorce agreement or the circumstances that preceded the signing of the agreement.

Her spirit quelled, Dalia was reconciled to receiving a get l'humra from Yitzhak but wondered if perhaps there was something else she could do. She consulted with rabbinic pleader Rivkah Lubitch on how she should proceed. Rivkah thought Dalia should appeal the Ashkelon Rabbinic Court's decision to the High Rabbinic Court and then perhaps back to the Supreme Court. She did not think the High Rabbinic Court would approve of a decision that questioned the validity of a get given in an authorized rabbinic court. Suspending a get was one thing; effectively revoking it was quite another. But Dalia had no strength left for appeals, and she wanted to make sure that no one, anywhere, on any grounds, could claim that she was in any way still connected to Yitzhak. She wanted that to be very clear. If that meant she needed to receive another get, so be it.

Rivkah agreed to accompany Dalia on her odyssey for a second get. Relying on court assurances that should Yitzhak fail to show up to deliver the second get he would be subject to an immediate, court-issued "compelled divorce decree," Rivkah and Dalia hoped that this time the rabbinic court would act on their promise and have mercy on Dalia. Indeed, as Dalia suspected, Yitzhak did not show up to the first hearing set for the get. He said he was ill. Nor did he show to a second hearing. Instead he filed still another appeal against the Ashkelon court's decision in 2003 regarding the money he claimed Dalia owed him. He wanted more. But to Dalia's horror, though Yitzhak was flagrantly in contempt of the court's order to deliver a second get and though he was in breach of the agreement that the couple had signed in August 1999, which stated that neither side would have the right to appeal, not only did the Ashkelon court fail to issue a decision compelling him to give a second abundantly cautious get, but in March 2004 it also agreed to his request to postpone the delivery of the get, pending his appeal. Though seventeen years had passed since Dalia had left Yitzhak for good, she was still tied to him and the rabbinic courts were still tied to its policy of appeasing recalcitrant get withholders. No exit was in sight. Again in the High Rabbinic Court against her will, Dalia counterappealed, claiming that the first get was valid and that there was no need for an abundantly cautious second get and asking the court to declare that Yitzhak had to pay her linkage to the cost of living on his outstanding child support debt.

It was now October 2004. New rabbinic judges sat on the High Rabbinic Court. They did not know Dalia and Yitzhak and seemed unmoved by the long ordeal or their complex divorce file. Despite Dalia's argument that the couple had agreed in 1999 that there would be no right of appeal of any decision regarding their marital property, the senior court agreed to hear Yitzhak's petition, again yielding to the demands of the (reinstated) husband. Almost a year after he appealed the financial awards made by the Ashkelon Rabbinic Court that he himself had designated to hear his case, the appeals court ruled that the original decision would stand. But they relieved Yitzhak of paying Dalia any interest on his debt for child support, and they returned the case to the Ashkelon court to determine if Yitzhak's owed any linkage to the cost of living index for that same debt. With regard to Dalia's appeal concerning the need for a second get, they withheld any determination until all the husband's financial claims were finished and settled in the lower court.

Spring 2005. The Ashkelon court turned down Dalia's request to determine that Yitzhak owed her linkage of the outstanding debt to the cost of living index, declaring simply and obtusely that their previous decision, as well as that of the appeals court, was clear on the matter. They did, however, set down hearings for the delivery of the second get. Yitzhak failed to show up for the next three hearings. (When Dalia requested compensation for the days she missed at work when Yitzhak failed to show for scheduled hearings, the court denied her request.) At all three failed hearings, Rivkah reiterated her claim that the original get from 1999 was valid and that there was no reason to demand a second get.

Seeing that Yitzhak was not going to be cooperative, the Ashkelon court took the initiative to send the file back up to the High Rabbinic Court to decide how to move forward. Rivkah pleaded with the court to validate the original get from 1999, insisting again that a second divorce was indeed unnecessary and to have pity, finally, on Dalia. On January 22, 2006, the High Rabbinic Court of Appeals agreed and at last declared that the get issued six years earlier in 1999, suspended two months later, and effectively invalidated in 2003 by the district rabbinic court, was nonetheless still valid and that a second get was indeed not needed (C. v. C., 2006).

In the meantime nineteen years had gone by.

2007–2011

In 2007, with the help of Center for Women's Justice (CWJ), Dalia sued her ex-husband and the Ministry of Justice for damages in the amount of 4.5 million shekels (about $1.2 million). She asked that her husband compensate her for the intentional infliction of emotional distress that she endured because he refused to give her a get and then spurned the one he actually gave her, placing Dalia in limbo for a total of nineteen years. She charged the ministry with failing to oversee the rabbinic courts, which, she claimed, botched her case and with willful disregard — if not actively and intentionally — contributed to that emotional distress. She cited the multitude of needless hearings, of repeated decisions made and unmade, and the unnecessary six years during which the original get was suspended. The Center for Women's Justice filed her case with the family courts and was given a waiver by the court clerk for her filing fee.

The Ministry of Justice did not like this lawsuit, which would have opened it up to a floodgate of litigation, and challenged it, citing the principle of judicial immunity. It fought back hard and vigorously. As its first rung of attack, it claimed that Dalia owed a 1 percent filing fee for the lawsuit (something that was not at all clear from the family court regulations) and that she was not entitled to a waiver of those fees, since she owned a house registered in her name (the one her parents built for her). Until she paid the full filing fee of forty-five thousand shekels (about twelve thousand dollars), the court would not hear her case. CWJ fought the case of the filing fee all the way up to the Supreme Court and lost. The Supreme Court held that the case did not fall under the rubric of "personal injury" (distinguishing emotional from bodily harm), which would have lowered the filing fee, and that although the case was for nonpecuniary damages (estimated damages that could not be calculated exactly), the lawsuit was for a set amount, and therefore payment had to be a percentage of the amount sued for — the full forty-five thousand shekels.

Obtaining a donation from a private individual for the filing fee, Dalia refiled her claim for a lower amount in the family court. Adhering closely to that court's regulations, CWJ filed a motion asking to include the Ministry of Justice as a respondent in the lawsuit. This time the ministry moved to dismiss the motion, stating that it was not necessary to hear the case against it in the family court along with the case against Yitzhak, since the claims were based on two separate causes of action — one, against Yitzhak, for the intentional infliction of emotional distress, and the other, against the state, for the negligent supervision of the rabbinic courts. The family court judge agreed, claiming that the cases were indeed distinguishable and ruled that Dalia must file her suit against the state in the civil court, where the filing fee for such cases was 2 percent of the amount sued for.

Dalia is girding herself for a third attempt to sue the state. For personal reasons, she has dropped her claim against Yitzhak.

Dalia Ovad married Yitzhak Carmeli when she was nineteen. She sued him for divorce when she was twenty-seven, and then again when she was thirty-seven. She was forty-nine when Yitzhak finally gave her a get and then obstructed it, and fifty-six when the state finally declared her free to remarry. During the time that that her divorce status was suspended, she had two offers of marriage.

FOUR

The Accidental Agunah

———

Every woman, every person, is entitled to write the story
of their life as he or she wishes and in accordance with their choice —
as long as he or she does not trespass into the domain of others — and this
is the autonomy of free will. If a person is compelled to follow a path that
he or she did not choose, the autonomy of free will is infringed. Indeed, it
is our fate, human fate, that we constantly act and refrain from acting
not of our free will, and in this way autonomy of our will is found
lacking. But when autonomy of free will is profoundly infringed,
the law will intervene and speak

Jerusalem Family Court judge Ben-Zion Greenberger

———

Friendly, feisty, and quick to laugh, our "accidental" agunah gently rejects our
suggested pseudonym. "It's too plain," she grimaces from the confines of her
orange swivel chair in her Holon office. With amused defiance, she announces
that she wants to choose a name for herself. We are pleasantly surprised. "The
glory of a king's daughter is [her] inwardness" wrote the psalmist (45:14) — according to one interpretation of the Hebrew verse — and ultra-Orthodox women
are encouraged to be reticent and subservient, but this one seems to be neither.
And though she wears a brown shoulder-length wig in keeping with the customs
of her *haredi* (ultra-Orthodox) community, it has blond streaks in it, and she has
a mischievous glint in her eye. A pharmacist who supervises a state-subsidized
pharmacy near the home where she lives with her only son, she has had much
taken away from her over the years, and we are not about to take away her choice

Judge Greenberger (S. v. S., 2001), applying to get refusal a quote from Mishael Cheshin in *Taib v. State of Israel*, 2000.

98

of a name, even a phony one, so we instantly agree to her request. She proposes Tikvah, or "hope" in Hebrew.

It is an ironic choice, and it's both apt and inapt at the same time. On the one hand, Tikvah is indeed full of hope and promise, and she is eager to co-operate with us. She is currently working on her second degree, and when we suggest the possibility of her doing a doctorate, she smiles, suggesting that it is not out of the question. On the other hand, while thirty-nine-year-old Tikvah has at least half of her life ahead of her, in the society to which she belongs, we observe, she is considered old and without much hope for the future. Sadly and reluctantly, she agrees with this harsh assessment. The mother of only one son and separated from but "anchored" to the man she accidentally married, she does not anticipate that she will be able to have more children, or even attract a youthful second husband and experience a loving marital relationship. And she isn't interested in "becoming a nurse-maid" to an older man. She explains, "In the *haredi* community, single men my age want women in their twenties who can have a dozen children. The men who would want me are old, fat, bald, and sick." So Tikvah is resigned to concentrating her domestic energies on her son Yair, now thirteen years old, who, she hopes, will have a happy marriage and many children of his own. "There were years that I dreamed of having more kids, but it's not my fate," she laments. "My son doesn't even bother to ask me for brothers and sisters anymore. He understands what happened."

What happened is fairly simple. Tikvah cannot marry and have more children, or even go out for coffee with a man, because she does not have a get. Her husband, Ze'ev, a man with whom she lived for just three months, has refused to give her a divorce for the last fourteen years. She believes she will die his wife or his widow. After all, Ze'ev has said more than once, she recalls, that he will withhold the get "forever." Rabbinic judges have told Ze'ev it would be a mitzvah for him to give Tikvah a get, but they have refused to order or compel him to do so, although they have the power to put him in jail until he agrees. Though aware that Tikvah's situation is untenable, the rabbis have disturbingly blamed her for the stalemate and have expressed annoyance with her almost from the beginning of the case. In their litany of complaints: she filed suit in the family court for child support instead of letting the rabbis decide, she left the marriage after only three months, she had been reluctant to tell Ze'ev where their son's circumcision ceremony would be held, she caused trouble over the visitation arrangement, and, most recently, she filed for damages in civil court. "She's anchoring herself," the judges wrote with indifference to her suffering in one of the many decisions they have handed down in the case. This is what they and their colleagues tend to say when a woman does not accede to what they think are her husband's and their reasonable demands.

Tikvah says that although she remains ultra-Orthodox, she has lost faith in the rabbinic courts altogether. "They're motivated by politics, not halakha," she says without elaboration. The truth about Tikvah and Ze'ev's complicated marriage, and the even more complex attempts at dissolving it, are clear for all to see, she argues. Ze'ev is unstable and dangerous. "Being around him was a living nightmare. He's crazy. No one could have stayed with him," says Tikvah.

Tikvah Hamami was a new immigrant from Iran who arrived in Israel in a hush-hush operation in 1994. Together with her parents, sister, and paternal grandmother, she settled on the outskirts of the town of Yavneh, south of Tel Aviv, where many Persian Jews reside. They all lived in a small, boxy apartment in an ultra-Orthodox area, short on greenery but long on children. Two older brothers who had been in Israel for many years and were themselves no longer ultra-Orthodox helped the family navigate Israeli bureaucracy and softened the shock of the move. A few months after they arrived, her father, a businessman who traded in scrap metal, made the mistake of returning to Iran for what was meant to be a brief visit that would allow him to somehow transfer family assets abroad. Accused of spying for Israel, he was jailed and tortured and kept in prison for years. The incarceration became the center of the family's life, and his release was all they lived for. When he was finally freed and came back to Israel, his mother collapsed and died.

Tikvah had hoped to pursue her dream of becoming a physician, but not only was she distracted by the drama of her father's imprisonment, but a nosy neighbor had warned her that "a free lifestyle was not acceptable among the ultra-Orthodox in Israel. . . . You have to marry first." She suggested that Tikvah meet Ze'ev Nuriani, a thirty-one-year-old "God-fearing" yeshiva student. Feeling lonely, out-of-sorts, and hoping for happiness, or at least some sense of grounding, Tikvah agreed to the meeting.

Two Dates and a "Vort"

On their first date, the couple chatted as they ambled aimlessly around the streets of Meah Shearim in Jerusalem. Ze'ev seemed modest and quiet. He had grand claims, she told us, which turned out to be at odds with the facts. He said that in addition to studying at yeshiva he was working in the afternoons as an architect, but he was not. Another time, he told Tikvah he was giving classes in kabbala at the yeshiva; he wasn't. He also promised that once wed, he'd buy an apartment for himself and Tikvah, but he never did. Other aspects of Ze'ev's behavior were particularly irksome to Tikvah. For instance, he tried to sneak her onto buses and into other places that required payment for admission. "I was embarrassed and upset," she recalls today. She also didn't care for his unusually close bond with his mother, a small, untidy, tightfisted woman she did not like or trust. Despite all this, and feeling caught in the constrictions of her pious surroundings, Tikvah believed that at age twenty-four she should already be married. She imagined it would somehow hasten her father's return. She also felt her family deserved some happiness and hoped a wedding would cheer things up.

Tikvah's brothers were not convinced of the worthiness of the match. To say that they disliked Ze'ev is an understatement. They wanted to end the relationship, fast. Their instincts were alerted the minute they set eyes on Ze'ev, whose lack of direction and definition of character, as well as of money, were not what they wanted for their little sister. But there was almost no time for deliberation. Before she knew it, friends had arranged for an engagement party and Tikvah and Ze'ev, though both were Sephardic, celebrated their intended marriage with an Ashkenazi *vort* ceremony. Yiddish for "word," a vort is a premarriage rite popular in *haredi* communities, with the couple giving their word to one another and committing to marriage. The mothers of the future bride and groom break a plate wrapped in cloth. This is meant to symbolize the seriousness of the occasion. Just as breaking the plate is final, so the engagement is not easily terminated. And like other seemingly innocent rituals, the vort has social consequences. It's much more than a party. If a side wants to back out of the union after a vort, some community protocols demand that a document be signed to indicate that a promise has been broken. Sometimes the jilted party insists on some form of compensation for lost time, wedding expenses, or the return of costly gifts the couple may have exchanged. Theoretically, one side can make the argument, though this is rare, that the couple had a binding oral agreement. In disputes involving compensation resulting from a broken vort, a rabbinic court may be consulted to determine the amount owed to the faithful party. So after the vort, Tikvah felt stuck. She had, quite literally, given her word.

"How did you feel?" we asked her. "At the vort. At your wedding? After you were married? Were you happy? Was there any moment when you smiled or had any hope for a happy future?"

"How did I feel?" Tikvah responded rhetorically. "I felt as if the earth was opening up, and I was slipping into a big hole. I was falling fast, and nothing could stop my fall. It was my destiny."

At the vort, Tikvah refused to eat. She couldn't. At the wedding, which took place two months later in a windowless hall in the basement of a tatty hotel in Yavneh, she tried not to interact with Ze'ev. Men and women sat and danced separately, with a big divider between them that prevented one sex from watching the revelries of the other. Occasionally, the men would pull Tikvah into the men's section, where she sat on a chair next to Ze'ev as the men entertained them by juggling or standing on their hands. Most of the time Tikvah was on the women's side, with her mother and girlfriends. The music and dancing numbed her, and she managed to laugh as the single girls pranced around her in their flowing, long skirts and the older married women with their incongruous wigs and tired eyes encircled her with their slow hora. But her jittery nerves quickly returned as soon as the music and dancing stopped, everybody was gone, and all that was left was Ze'ev. He had appropriated as many gift checks as he could for himself and given them to his mother for safekeeping. After the wedding they went to an apartment Ze'ev had rented. It was sparsely furnished, dimly lit, and oddly ominous. Tikvah hated it. It was a far cry from the luxurious accommodations he had promised to buy for their private use.

She hated every minute from that moment onward, until she left him. The evenings of *sheva brakhot*, the seven-day parties that religious Jews consider obligatory, drained her energies. Each day, she dragged herself to a different hosting home, trying her best to eat something and not to cry when the participants spontaneously erupted in loud song in praise of God, who had created "joy and happiness, groom and bride." She did not want those generous women who had cooked and prepared in celebration of her new marriage to get a glimpse of her deep sadness, her ever-growing sense of revulsion, and the gnawing feeling that her new husband was not "normal." The dark nights of *sheva brakhot* were even worse than the evenings. If Tikvah had not been taught that the Torah obligated her to make all of herself available to her new husband, she would not have been able to endure a moment in bed with Ze'ev.

And it was already during *sheva brakhot* that Ze'ev began his acts of violence against Tikvah. On the third night he burst out in anger over some minor infraction and hit her. To try and remove the mark from her forehead, he forced her to the sink, where he washed her face with floor cleanser. In the coming months, Ze'ev would subject Tikvah to a series of unending threats and violent, erratic physical attacks that included beatings, strangulation, and shoving her against doors and walls. Once he locked her in the bathroom. On another occasion, he locked her out of the house. Tikvah had no understanding of what triggered these outbursts of violence and cruelty, and she found it impossible to negotiate them or to placate Ze'ev. His sense of humor was no more understandable to her than his aggression. "His idea of fun was to wrestle me to the floor, rest his foot on my chest, and then wave his hands as if he just climbed the highest mountain," she told us.

Tikvah became pregnant, but the violence only worsened. Ze'ev would hit her in the stomach and rant that he did not want the baby or the financial burden that it would bring. He threatened that she would find herself in a pool of blood. She lived in fear and loathing. During that period, if someone said a nice word to her, she burst into tears. And to make matters even worse, if this were possible, Tikvah was hungry. Ze'ev hid money from her, so, he explained, she would not waste it. Once she drew some money from a small joint account that they had set up, and Ze'ev yelled at her. He would bring home leftover food from the yeshiva for their meals. Why squander money on food? They would often eat at his mother's or her sister's home.

It took less than three months of marriage for all of Ze'ev's demons to come out, and Tikvah began to wonder how she would be able quit the marital home with her life and sanity intact. She also had some hesitation. Perhaps she was being rash? Maybe Ze'ev could change with some help? But her life was intolerable, and she decided to leave on a day that Ze'ev was at the yeshiva. But before she could plan exactly when and how to make her getaway, one day while she was out Ze'ev changed the locks and her decision, like the apartment, was sealed. Perhaps things had been bad enough that even Ze'ev anticipated she might bolt. Or perhaps he also wanted out. She went to her mother's apartment, and there she stayed, having left with only the clothes on her back, except for a few pieces of gold jewelry that she had managed to remove from the apartment a few days before.

Tikvah considered filing a complaint with the police about the brutality she endured at Ze'ev's hands, but her mother and rabbi objected, preferring that she keep things quiet, in keeping with the ultra-Orthodox preference of not involving the secular authorities in the affairs of the community. Later on Ze'ev would dispute Tikvah's claims of mistreatment when she raised them in court. Yet though she did not report the abuse to the police, Tikvah did divulge her horrible story to a community social worker and to her rabbi, Rav Roubini, as well as to a few friends, her mother, and the matchmaker who introduced them. "He often said he wished that the marriage would last 120 years," says Tikvah with a bitter laugh. "I couldn't survive 120 days!"

Safe in her mother's home (her father was still in an Iranian jail), Tikvah felt she was beginning to climb out of the deep hole that her destiny had made her slide into. Her mother, a round warm woman with a deep laugh and innocent trust of people, felt guilty that she had let her daughter marry without carrying out an adequate investigation of the groom and his family and sorry that she had not listened to her sons. She could not do enough for Tikvah. She cooked her favorite dish of lentil soup with lemon and cumin, which Tikvah liked to eat with dates. She gave her daughter her own bedroom, which she decorated with white lace homemade curtains. It was not going to be easy to recover from those three awful months, but Tikvah, heavily pregnant, was optimistic that her divorce would be soon. So was her attorney, David Yashar, an eager-to-please man with a close-cropped beard, who was a friend of a friend, a fellow Iranian, and a licensed rabbinic pleader as well as a lawyer.

Days after Tikvah left the marital apartment, Yashar filed a petition in Tikvah's name for alimony in the Tel Aviv Rabbinic Court. Yashar had several reasons for filing with a rabbinic court rather than the family court, even though Rabbi Roubini had given him and Tikvah religious dispensation to file in whatever court was best for her and the yet-to-be born baby. "We need to get her out of this marriage as fast as possible," the rabbi told Yashar. "Tikvah's life is in danger, and so is the baby's. And the halakha allows you to do whatever you have to do under those circumstances."

"So why are we suing in rabbinic court?" asked Tikvah after Yashar had explained that civil courts might give her a tactical advantage. "And if we are already in rabbinic court, why aren't we suing for divorce?"

Yashar outlined his strategy: "One, because I want to lure Ze'ev into the rabbinic court and force him to ask for a get himself. According to halakha," he went on, "Ze'ev has an obligation to support you if he wants to stay married. And since it's clear he doesn't want to pay for your support, I think he'll give you a get out of his own initiative. After divorce, a husband has no more obligation to support his former wife. He's free to start over. Ze'ev needs a real wife, who sleeps in a real bed next to him and who makes him real meals, not one on paper. I want him to think that the idea for divorce was his. Two, I want the rabbis to be on your side. If you sue in civil court they will immediately be antagonistic. This way, they will want to help you. And since what you really want is a get and not alimony, we don't really lose anything by going to rabbinic court. And three," he continued, "if we sue for a get, this would automatically give the rabbinic court jurisdiction over the question of custody and visitation of your unborn child. And, while I am not really worried about this issue, I'm going to try and make sure the family courts have jurisdiction over these matters."

"So when will we sue for custody and child support for the baby?" Tikvah wondered. "Can't we sue now, before the baby is born? And what if it's a boy? I'm worried if we end up in a rabbinic court. Doesn't the halakha say that a boy goes with his father? If they take this baby away, I will kill myself. I don't even want him to visit with the baby. I'm afraid of him."

Yashar had it under control. "First," he told her, "we sue for wife support and force Ze'ev into rabbinic court. Then, if he doesn't give a get on the spot, right after the baby's born, we'll sue for custody and child support in the family court. Ze'ev can't prevent you from suing for child support in a family court, because Israeli case law has ruled that a child has a separate claim for support that has nothing to do with divorce. Theoretically, Ze'ev could beat you to the courthouse and have the rabbis decide on custody of your child, if he sues for divorce, but this will be good since we will simply say, 'Okay, we accept the get.' And trust me, if worse comes to worst, and he does win the race, there is no rabbinic court in the world that will give custody to Ze'ev. He won't even ask for custody. I don't imagine the issue will be raised. I think he'll give a get even before the baby is born. Moreover, there's no property to divide."

Money is often the reason couples cannot reach an agreement to divorce.

The Ispahanis had nothing except some small change left from the wedding, which Ze'ev held in a separate account, and some gold jewelry that Ze'ev's mother had given Tikvah as part of the customary exchange of gifts. Tikvah was willing to give up on the wedding money and to make do with minimal child support. She had already sold the jewelry. All this indicated a rapid divorce. What was there to fight over? Yashar was satisfied that the papers were in order, that the strategy was well mapped out, and that all that was needed was to sign an agreement. He even prepared a draft for signature. The rabbinic court set a hearing on the matter of Tikvah's request for support immediately after receiving her papers. Ze'ev did not show up.

Ten months after Tikvah and Ze'ev married and six and a half months after Tikvah was locked out of the marital home, Yair was born. One week *before* the birth, Ze'ev filed a one-page petition in the rabbinic court, in which he sued for "divorce, and ancillary matters such as custody, child support, alimony." He also asked the court to order Tikvah to "divorce, return home, and return the things she had taken from the apartment." The petition was a standard form, available in 1997 at all rabbinic courts. Someone had filled in the blanks for Ze'ev (probably a friendly clerk) in a way meant to make sure that he won the race to the courthouse and that the rabbinic court would have jurisdiction over all ensuing matters. Ze'ev added in his requests and signed at the bottom. "Good," Yashar noted complacently when he saw the papers. "See, he wants a get. Now he will have to give one."

Tikvah did not invite Ze'ev to the circumcision ceremony, the *brit milah*, which celebrated the child entering into the covenant of the Jewish people with the God of Israel eight days after he was born. But a month after the birth, at the intervention of Rabbi Roubini, who tried to broker some sort of very temporary truce between the warring parties, Tikvah agreed that Roubini could inform Ze'ev of when and where the ceremony marking the redemption of the first born was taking place. The ceremony commemorates the special status given under biblical lore to a first-born male child who, according to custom, must be "redeemed" by a member of the priestly sect from his preordained obligation to devote his life in some way to God. Not every religious family is obligated to conduct such a ceremony, and those who are — plebian Jews ("Israelites") who cannot trace their ancestry to the priestly or Levite sects and whose first child is a son born naturally, not by caesarian section, and not preceded by a miscarriage — consider it to be a special honor. Ze'ev felt particularly proud to have fathered a son. At the celebrations, Roubini asked him to say a few words to consecrate the moment. Tikvah ignored Ze'ev, who blessed Yair "that he should grow up to be a Torah scholar and bring much joy to his parents."

Two weeks later after the redemption ceremony Tikvah sued for child support in the family court, and Ze'ev sued for visitation rights, this time with a pleader who filed formal papers, in the rabbinic court. The family court set a date for a hearing, and the rabbinic court, as a matter of course when a visitation claim is made, appointed a city social worker to meet with the parents and prepare a report about the family. The court noted in its directives to the social worker that it would set a date for a hearing for Tikvah's alimony claim and for Ze'ev's divorce suit immediately after the report was ready. These reports give the rabbis information from a neutral source about the parties, untainted by the hyperbolic exaggerations of divorce attorneys and pleaders and their clients.

After describing Ze'ev's deteriorated mental state and setting forth in detail the violence that Tikvah had endured at his hand, the social worker wrote,

We have here a couple that was separated and who became parents almost as soon as they married. The husband depicts his marriage as excellent and denies all allegations of violence. However, the impression of the social worker who spoke with him is that his description of a very difficult situation lacked any emotional affect, and she surmises that his behavior and his feelings are not in sync. Perhaps this is in order to impress us that his circumstances are grave or perhaps to cover up the aggression bottled up within him. Nonetheless, it is necessary to enable the father to visit with his son.

From discussions with the wife, it is our impression that we are dealing with a woman who experienced severe physical and verbal abuse even before she was able to experience a period of courtship or honeymoon. The pain that has formed within her is very great. She is having trouble understanding the right of the husband to meet with his son after he cursed her and hit her and put the fetus in danger. With all this, she understands the husband's right to have a relationship with his son.

It is my feeling that it would be best for the father to meet with his son only in the city's family visitation center and to forbid him from being in the vicinity of the minor and his mother's residence.

Recommendations:

It is recommended that the parties end their marital relationship as soon as possible and that the minor stay in the custody of his mother.

Despite Yashar's planning, things did not simply fall into place in the rabbinic court. Most irritatingly, Ze'ev would often refuse to appear when summoned. And the first hearing at which he did appear, a year and a few months after the wedding, was a disaster from Tikvah's perspective. Ze'ev, at his pleader's advice, withdrew his divorce suit and asked for a reconciliation, declaring that he loved Tikvah and could not bear to divorce her. "It's something deep within me," he said in court. Tikvah's reaction was succinct. "I want a divorce. Reconciliation is out of the question. I would rather die than go back to him. He put me through hell," she declared. The court refused to rule on her petition for alimony since she had, by her own admission, abandoned the marital home. Even if Ze'ev had changed the locks, he regretted his actions, was repentant, and willing to take her back. Halakha, they explained, absolves a man of having to support his wife if she has left him and is not meeting her wifely obligations. To justify marital support, Tikvah had the burden of proving that she had left Ze'ev for a good reason. A date was set for a further hearing, at which she could try to prove her allegations of violence as a justification for her leaving.

Yashar was beginning to worry. He had already sued for child support in the family court in Yair's name, as planned, and at least that issue was in place. But the situation was not as he'd anticipated in the religious courts. Ze'ev had done a tricky about-face, to snatch the tactical advantage of litigating in the rabbinic courts. Yashar had represented, and even advised, men who had acted deviously, like Ze'ev, but he had not foreseen this in the Nuriani case. He'd been sure Ze'ev wanted a divorce, otherwise he may have tried to outrun him to the family court earlier with a claim for custody and visitation. But how much earlier could he have sued? He didn't think that a family court would hear such a case before the baby was born. And Ze'ev had filed for all ancillary matters in rabbinic court before the birth.

Annoyed with himself, but resigned to the unique circumstances of the case, Yashar advised Tikvah to file a separate petition for divorce. If they had to go back to rabbinic court to prove Ze'ev was violent in order to win their claim for wife support, they might as well piggyback the divorce suit. Though nervous,

Yashar was still confident that there was enough proof of Ze'ev's violent behavior that the rabbinic court would be quick to order him to divorce Tikvah and pay her support until he did so. Tikvah was young and had lived with Ze'ev for only three months. Anyone with eyes in their head could see that the marriage was over and that Ze'ev was, in Yashar's words, "cracked."

A few months after she sued for child support, the family court awarded Tikvah 1,800 shekels (about $500) a month in child support. Since Tikvah was not working, she was able to collect the money directly from the National Insurance Institute instead of having to run after Ze'ev. The institute began to pursue Ze'ev for the money he owed. Ze'ev ignored them. Years later, when Tikvah started working, Ze'ev was receiving a disability allowance — he has refused, despite a family court order, to disclose what his disability is — and the institute simply started docking part of his stipend.

Still Hopeful in the Rabbinic Court, 2000

It was not so easy to get Ze'ev back into the rabbinic court after the initial hearing, where he'd managed to avoid being ordered to pay alimony. The tribunal would set a date, and he would not bother to appear, claiming he was sick or had not been properly informed. Rabbinic courts never issue a default judgment under such circumstances. Finally, a little less than three years after Tikvah left home, when the court threatened to send police to bring Ze'ev if he did not show up for the next hearing, he did come, and the court finally heard testimony regarding the alleged violence that Tikvah had cited as her justification for leaving home and her right to alimony. Ze'ev declared that he had not tried to choke Tikvah and, at most, "came close to her and caught hold of her and squeezed her tight so I could kiss her." He begged sympathy since, as he claimed, he suffered from mental illness.

Tikvah's first witness was a friend who testified that he had heard Ze'ev threaten Tikvah that if she did not listen to him there would be "pools of blood." Next, the couple's rent collector said Ze'ev had admitted to punching Tikvah and had demonstrated with his fist to show him how he did so. Ze'ev denied knowing him. Then, an upstairs neighbor described how she had heard Tikvah screaming and shouting from the apartment on several occasions and had seen her crying and sad.

At the end of the hearing, Yashar asked the court to award temporary alimony, because Tikva's leaving home had been justified. For the past three years, he argued, the husband had not supported his wife, who was now an agunah and was "going through a nightmare." He claimed to have met the burden of proof and shown that Tikvah had good reason to leave the house. "In my opinion," he declared, "there are also grounds to order a get. They have not been living together for a very long time. This is turning into a terrifying ordeal that is taking up much too much time."

Not happy with the turn of events, Ze'ev asked to bring witnesses on his behalf. The court agreed and to quiet Yashar's protests that the trial had ended and that Ze'ev had already "had his day in court," told him he could also bring more witnesses. Ze'ev promised to show up. At the next hearing, Tikvah brought another neighbor, a rabbi, to testify that he'd heard Tikvah screaming and crying hysterically and how he'd been afraid to interfere because he wanted to protect himself. Ze'ev brought yet another neighbor who claimed that he had not heard anything and neither had his wife. On cross-examination, that neighbor admitted that he thought it could be permissible for a man to slap his wife. "It depends on the couple and the circumstances."

At the end of the hearing Rabbi Roubini himself testified on Tikvah's behalf, imploring the court with great drama to accept that it was a commandment from God himself that the couple divorce. "I am begging him to give a get. . . . I am willing to abstain from eating and drinking so that he give a get. . . . If there had been one chance in a thousand for reconciliation, I would not make this recommendation."

Tikvah then again asked the court to order Ze'ev to divorce her. The following is the dialogue as recorded by the court scribe summarizing each party's position at that point:

Husband: "Put me in jail for five hundred years, and I won't divorce her."
Wife: "Kill me, but I won't go back to him."
Husband: "I am willing to give a get on [the] condition that I have custody of my son so that I can raise him. Her brothers are apostates. I cannot let him . . . grow up in such an environment."

Two months later, the court issued a decision denying Tikvah's petitions for alimony and for an order obligating Ze'ev to divorce her. It held that she had left home without sufficient reason and that the court did not recognize a claim of revulsion as grounds for divorce (see chapter 3). Regarding the alleged violence, the court ruled that Tikvah had not met the burden of proof; the court required actual eyewitnesses to the acts described: "The court cannot determine with certainty whether the husband behaved violently toward the wife since we have conflicting witnesses. Furthermore, the wife appeared before this court very agitated, particularly with respect to her husband. So long as no witness saw *explicitly* what happened inside their home, it is difficult to determine with certainty what happened there. Especially since the parties lived together for only three months" (*N. v. N.*, 2000).

Regarding the get, the judges ruled, "With respect to the . . . question of whether we should order a man to give his wife a get if she claims that her husband is repulsive to her, there is a difference of opinion among the rabbinic authorities. . . . [We hold] that we do not so order a husband in the circumstances before us, when his wife claims that her husband is repulsive to her." Nonetheless, they did decide that "the wife has the right to live apart from her husband" and that it would be a mitzvah if the husband were to divorce his wife. Two months later, they awarded custody of Yair to Tikvah, whom the social workers had recommended as the obvious choice as custodial parent. They gave limited visitation rights for Ze'ev for one hour a week at the local visitation center. Both Tikvah and Ze'ev appealed to the High Rabbinic Court, but it upheld the decisions, beseeching him to "listen to the words of wise men" and divorce Tikvah and urging Tikvah, in response to Ze'ev's complaints that he was not seeing Yair, to let Ze'ev visit with Yair in accordance with the terms set forth by the lower court. They gave the couple two weeks to reach an agreement.

The Five-Year Fortnight, 2000–2005

The "two weeks" lasted for the next five years, from 2000 to 2005, with Tikvah constantly trying to convince Ze'ev — through various rabbis, friends of the family, and well-meaning ultra-Orthodox individuals — to either reach an agreement or to return to court. At one time, in 2004, it looked as if they were about to agree that Ze'ev would give a get in exchange for Tikvah's waiving all child support and his waiving visitation rights, except for minimal contact, with

Yair. Tikvah felt that Ze'ev caused harm to Yair and used his limited visitation rights as a way to take revenge on her for leaving him. In the first few years, she would bring Yair to the visitation center, and Ze'ev would either not show up or do something that would make the child cry. Eventually, she stopped bringing him. The rabbinic court approved the waiver of child support but refused, on principle, to allow the waiver of regular visitation, though Ze'ev had initially agreed to this. At intermittent hearings, judge after judge, court after court, rabbis and social workers, all urged the couple to end their sham of a marriage. Tikvah was only too willing, but Ze'ev was consistently recalcitrant.

Sometimes Ze'ev would say "Yes, but . . ." He wanted Tikvah to make sure he saw Yair on a regular basis, to return his property (the nature of which he did not specify) and the jewelry he gave her on their engagement, to transfer jurisdiction over child support to the rabbinic court, to cancel his debt to the National Insurance Institute for the child support it had paid in his stead (something that the rabbinic court can arrange in certain difficult cases), to waive her right to collect any unpaid child support, to provide guarantors for all these promises and commitments, and more. Tikvah agreed to everything, except when it came to Yair. She was not willing to make him part of the negotiations over the get. Conversely, with time, Ze'ev understood that Yair was his perfect shield for not giving one. Tikvah filed another petition with the court asking them to replace their ruling that stated it would be a good deed if Ze'ev agreed to divorce her, with one that obligated him to do so. Ze'ev continued to say "Yes, but . . ."

Eight full years after Tikvah had left the marital home, in 2005, the rabbinic judges, despite their exhortations urging a divorce, denied Tikvah's request to obligate Ze'ev to divorce her and compel him if he refused to do so. They found that Ze'ev's demand that the court retain jurisdiction over all issues reasonable, in particular with regard to child support and custody. The judges wrote, "It was agreed that the rabbinic court would ask the opinion [regarding these demands] of the rabbinic court's legal advisor, who confirmed that the husband was right [in making them]." Moreover, they added, it seems that "the wife is not willing for the husband to see the child or have any contact with him."

Ignoring both the fact that the couple had lived together for only three months and Tikvah's claim that Ze'ev was not really interested in seeing Yair except just before hearings, the court reviewed the rabbinic literature regarding grounds for divorce and held that under halakha "additional time passed" did not constitute sufficient grounds for obliging Ze'ev to divorce Tikvah. The rabbis acknowledged that in light of the passage of time it might be possible to make the claim that reconciliation was unfeasible and that Tikvah, therefore, had the right not to be anchored to a failed marriage. Nonetheless, they were not even willing to put pressure on Ze'ev by calling on the community to refuse to give him, for example, certain religious privileges in the synagogue. Ze'ev's claims were reasonable according to Torah law, and so long as Tikvah did not accede to them, it was not possible to issue any ruling in her favor. In a marriage that had been over before it began, they ruled as follows:

If the mother is not willing to cooperate and to honestly facilitate an examination of the best interest of the son with respect to visitation with his father, and is even willing to anchor herself to a failed marriage in order to prevent any connection between father and son, she has no one to complain to except herself. The husband should not be seen as someone who is anchoring his wife. She is anchoring herself. . . .

Similarly with respect to child support, the father is requesting that jurisdiction be transferred to this rabbinic court, as is required by the halakha (the parties are both ultra-Orthodox); and he claims that he is willing to divorce immediately after all the legal issues are straightened out. The wife's attorneys are postponing matters and engaging in all sorts of shenanigans to ensure that jurisdiction is not with this rabbinic court, thus the husband is not deemed by the halakha as anchoring his wife and it is not possible to order him to give his wife a get. (N. v. N., 2005)

At the end of their decision, the court added,

So much for what we have written from the perspective of the halakha.

This court cannot ignore the great suffering endured by the parties. . . . This court turns to the attorneys on both sides: The ability is in your hands to end this painful matter. Please, reach an agreement with respect to those issues that are outstanding between you in order to bring this file to an end, the sooner the better. (N. v. N., 2005)

Disgruntled, disappointed, frustrated, tired, empty-handed, poorer, older, and not closer to any type of resolution, Tikvah refused, despite legal advice, to appeal this decision to the High Rabbinic Court. At the very least, she wanted some peace of mind and quiet to pursue her personal goals. She had decided to go back to school now that Yair was seven, and she vowed never to set foot again, at least at her initiative, in a rabbinic court.

A young reporter on an ultra-Orthodox newspaper who had been following Tikvah's case closely, and had even accompanied her with permission of the court to the hearings held for the year prior to the 2005 decision, encouraged Tikvah to look for justice elsewhere. "If I had not seen this for myself, I would not have believed it. How can a Jewish court act with such indifference? This is not Torah law," he proclaimed. Thanks to the reporter's efforts and encouragement, Tikvah found her way to the Center for Women's Justice (CWJ), one of whose goals is to file damages suits for get refusal in Israeli family courts. Shortly after the rabbinic court refused to issue any injunction against Ze'ev, Tikvah decided to sue for damages, becoming part of an ever-increasing number of women who have turned to family courts in the attempt to find relief from what had until now seemed to be their inevitable plight.

"More than 50 percent of our clients receive a get within one year and two months of filing these claims," a CWJ attorney told Tikvah. Damages suits seemed to tip the scales of power, and husbands, more often than not, agreed to swap the get for withdrawal of the suit. "But you can never tell what will happen," the lawyer added. "In the worst case, the family court would award damages and, with respect to the get, you will be no worse off than you were before. It is really a win-win situation — get, damages, or sometimes even both." Tikvah replied, "Even if he does not give me a get, and even if he does not pay the money awarded, this lawsuit will get Ze'ev off my back. He will be afraid to bother me if he thinks that the family court is watching him. Do it."

Eleven Years into the "Marriage," 2008

With the help of CWJ, Tikvah sued, and Ze'ev did, in fact, leave her alone for the period during which the case made its way through the family court. He apparently did not feel quite as confident as he did when his contact with Tikvah involved the rabbinic courts. The ultra-Orthodox community funded Ze'ev's attorney, who assured his backers that a claim for damages could be made only if a rabbinic court had ordered a husband to give a get, citing a 2004 decision of Judge Menahem HaCohen of the Jerusalem Family Court, who had awarded actual damages in one of the first cases of this kind. (HaCohen has since retreated from this position, ruling in another case that damages can be awarded without reference to a rabbinic court order.) In the Nuriani case, the rabbinic court had told Ze'ev only that it would be a good deed to give his wife a divorce. It had not ordered him to do so. Ze'ev's attorney, a newly admitted member of the Bar but a seasoned rabbinic pleader, was certain of his position and of the unequivocal righteousness of his client's withholding the get, because of Tikvah's alleged recalcitrance on other matters — she, after all, in the words of the rabbinic court, was "anchoring herself." In his response to the suit, he argued that Ze'ev was not a get refuser, citing the 2001 and 2005 decisions of the rabbinic court, and, as such, he owed no "duty of care" to his wife and certainly no obligation to give her a get.

In December 2008, eleven years and eight months after Tikvah married, and eleven years and five months after she left the marital home, Judge Tova Sivan of the Tel Aviv Family Court awarded Tikvah seven hundred thousand shekels (about two hundred thousand dollars), because Ze'ev had refused to grant her request to free her from her failed marriage. Get refusal, Judge Sivan ruled, was *not* a question of legal status but one of fact: did he, or did he not, give a get to Tikvah after being requested to do so? The court must determine the facts of the case on the basis of the evidence brought before it, and here, it held, it was clear that Ze'ev was a get withholder. Tikvah had asked for a get, and Ze'ev had refused, not even bothering to show up to most of the hearings in the rabbinic court to which he was summoned. Sivan wrote,

There is no dispute that the parties lived together, under one roof, for barely *three months*. There is also no dispute that a large number of hearings were scheduled for the parties before the rabbinic court, the majority of which (and this is not denied) the defendant did not bother to come to, and the minority of which he attended only after he was dragged by court order or arrest warrant, and that the rabbinic court proceedings continued for many years.

Regarding this, I refer to the cross-examination of the defendant set forth in the transcript dated March 11, 2008, p. 17 . . .

Q. Is it true that from 1997 until 2005 you were summoned to at least twenty-one hearings?

A. I don't remember and can't verify this. These questions are irrelevant to the issue. I don't remember.

Q. Is it correct that out of twenty-one hearings to which you received summons, you did not appear for seventeen hearings?

A. I don't remember.

Q. Is it true that on these dates the court issued at least five orders to have you brought to court?

A. I didn't appear at the hearings for medical reasons or because the mail in the absorption center [didn't get to me because the distribution] is really something horrible. I did not get all the dates on which I was summoned by mail and that's why I did not appear. If they notified me, and I felt good, I appeared, and if I did not feel good, I did not appear.

While Tikvah's case was being heard in Tel Aviv, the notion that get withholding should be viewed as a civil wrong and not a religious right was catching on and gaining legal credence in other courts. In a separate decision in which another client of CWJ was awarded 550,000 shekels (about $150,000), Judge Ben-Zion Greenberger, a family court judge in Jerusalem (and incidentally an ordained Orthodox rabbi), confirmed that get refusal is a question of fact independent of any rabbinic court ruling:

Divorce in the State of Israel is based on Jewish law, and as such, two separate routes are available to a couple interested in divorce. One route is the route of ordering or coercing the delivery of a get, and in order for a wife to succeed in such a lawsuit, she must convince a rabbinic court that a cause of action exists from among those recognized by halakha that warrants obligating the delivery of the get. So long as a rabbinic court is not convinced that such a cause of action exists, the court will not obligate the husband to grant his wife a get. However, a second, independent route exists, which has no connection whatsoever to causes of action that exist under the halakha for ordering the delivery of the get, and this is the route of granting a get by agreement. At the moment that the husband agrees to grant the get, the rabbinic court will not investigate whether or not there is a halakhic basis for divorce. The only thing the court will investigate in this type of situation is whether the get was given with the agreement of the husband of his own free will, that and nothing else.

Therefore, if a wife asks her husband to grant her a get, it is within the husband's power to agree to this request even if there are no halakhic grounds accord-ing to which the rabbinic court would order him to grant a get. And if a husband for whatever reasons he may have refuses to agree the fact of his refusal — as a result of which, and only as a result of which, the divorce is not implemented at the wife's request — is behavior that is tantamount to negligence, with all its ramifications, if it is foreseeable that this aforementioned refusal would cause harm to his wife. (*K. v. K.*, 2008)

Benjamin Shmueli, a lecturer at Sha'arei Mishpat College, expressed a similar opinion in a law review article reviewing these tort cases, pointing out that by refusing to give a get a husband inflicts emotional harm, without regard to whether or not there is a rabbinic order: "If indeed the source of the harm caused to the plaintiff [i.e., the wife] is emotional harm as stated, the date on which the rabbinic court orders the husband to grant his wife a get will not always be of any significance. . . . The plaintiff should not be denied the op-portunity to argue and prove that the emotional harm began earlier (and even much earlier) than the official date on which the husband was declared a get recalcitrant. . . . The laws of tort obligate this conclusion!" (Shmueli, 2007, p. 310–311).

After losing in the Tel Aviv Family Court, Ze'ev lost the support of his haredi backers, who refused to pay for his attorney to appeal. Ze'ev applied to the Ministry of Justice's Legal Aid Office. He was allocated an attorney who appealed the family court ruling to the Tel Aviv District Court, and lost. At the preliminary hearing held before a tribunal of three secular female judges, the court was visibly upset by the case.

"Too bad you did not countersue for higher damages," one judge told the CWJ attorneys. "The damages here are incalculable."

"She won't let me see my son," Ze'ev yelled at the tribunal.

"Visitation has nothing to do with the get," they answered him. "There is no contributory negligence here," meaning that Ze'ev cannot excuse his malfea-sance with allegations of Tikvah's wrongdoings, if they were even true, since the one had nothing to do with, and did not contribute to, the other. "The divorce is an issue that is separate and apart from visitation. If you want visita-tion, sue for visitation, and we will hear your claim."

Here too the tribunal tried to convince Tikvah to exchange her rights for her freedom, though admittedly this time at a much, much lower price than heretofore suggested to her. In exchange for the get, they wanted Tikvah to waive the trial costs of thirty thousand shekels (about eight thousand dollars) that she was entitled to because they were about to deny Ze'ev's appeal. Tikvah agreed. Ze'ev, however, stood firm, and the tribunal upheld the lower court's opinion and the costs for the appeal, stating, "The respondent had the right to a get from the moment she wanted one, and all the more so when she married the appellant at the age of twenty-four, was with him for all of three months, and never knew any comfort from him. Today, almost forty years old, she continues to suffer from his cruelty toward her. He prevents, and prevented, her from experiencing life's joys, establishing a family, and especially from having children. . . . We are talking about immeasurable damage that increases by the day. . . . These actions are immoral and go against the Basic Law of Human Dignity and Liberty" (N. v. N., 2010).

Neither the family court award, nor the loss on appeal, nor the suggestion that the court would waive Tikvah's costs in exchange for the get, prompted Ze'ev to give the get. Ze'ev had his principles. He applied again to Legal Aid for a lawyer to appeal the district court's decision. Because of the importance of this case, the likes of which had never before been decided by the Supreme Court, they agreed and managed to convince an attorney with a prominent Jerusalem family firm to take the case.

Ze'ev's new attorney filed a preliminary motion with the Supreme Court, asking for special permission to file a second appeal with the court after having lost the first appeal that he was entitled to by right of law at the district court level. CWJ has filed to dismiss the motion, but at the time of writing the Supreme Court's decision on this was still pending. Ze'ev's attorney also requested that the court allow him to submit the rabbinate's opinion on the matter. Though CWJ objected, the Supreme Court agreed, and attorney Rabbi Shimon Yaakobi, legal advisor to the rabbinic courts, submitted his "response," stating that the court should give Ze'ev the requisite special permission to appeal to the Supreme Court since the matter at hand is, in his opinion, of "world war" proportions (here he was citing a rabbinic court judge in another case — see chapter 5). In a lengthy written argument, Yaakobi drew on the language of equality, autonomy, free will, and freedom of religion to support his position, thus attempting a dialogue with Judge Greenberger's arguments, cited earlier, or perhaps more accurately, attempting to dissimulate by means of doublespeak the infringements on right to equality, autonomy, and freedom of religion so characteristic of these cases (see chapter 7). Regarding the interplay of religious law and civil law, Yaakobi asked the court to defer to religion in cases of conflict, writing, "Religious law [Yaakobi does not use the term "halakha" but *ha-din hadati*] and civil law must intertwine together in a harmonious manner. And there is an irrefutable presumption that civil law cannot interfere with religious law, this would be in direct conflict with the principles of freedom of religion. Any conflict that would present itself between civil law and religious law must be resolved in such a way that will not result in the interference, or even the possibility of interference, with religious law" (*N. v. N.*, 2011).

Yaakobi is wrong. We must begin to unravel the increasingly problematic intertwining of religion and state that is choking Jewish women in Israel (see introduction) and understand that harmony is not possible. Where there is a clash between religious and civil laws, the state must make its priorities clear: it cannot let the human rights of its citizens be trampled on in the name of religious freedom. Ze'ev, by misusing religious laws backed by the state, has pummeled the rights of Tikvah to equality, liberty, due process, and property. She is entitled to be compensated for those violations of her rights. To defend those violations in the name of religious freedom and, more so, to impose those violations in the name of religious freedom, makes a mockery of the state, as well as of those freedoms themselves.

Meanwhile, fourteen years after their very short-lived, accidental and ill-advised attempt at achieving marital bliss came to an end, Tikvah and Ze'ev are not divorced under either the laws of the State of Israel or of Orthodox Judaism. Yair, their son, has just celebrated his bar mitzvah. His father was not invited.

Tikvah would like to have had more children but knows this is unlikely, and getting more unlikely with each passing day. She has wasted her fertile years in pursuit of a get. She cannot have children with another man so long as she still is officially married to Ze'ev. If she did, those children would be stigmatized as mamzerim and barred from marrying other Jews not similarly stigmatized or would be registered as Ze'ev's children even though she has not been with him for fourteen years. Perhaps Ze'ev will divorce her one day when she can no longer bear children and is no longer at risk of giving birth to mamzerim.

The Israeli rabbinate has a blacklist of children and adults suspected of this status whose lives are thus monitored by the state.

A few years ago, the Knesset Committee on the Status of Women held one of its periodic hearings on the problems of obtaining a Jewish divorce in Israel. Several women sitting in the audience angrily admitted that they had given birth to children whose fathers were not their husbands because their husbands had refused to give them a get, and as a result the children were mamzerim. Knesset members who were rabbis responded by putting their hands over their ears, evoking the tradition that one must not sully one's soul by even hearing of another's transgression.

Postscript: On February 3, 2012, Justice Handel of the Supreme Court denied Ze'ev's request to hear his appeal, stating that it was not appropriate for review and then rebuking Ze'ev's behavior. He continued, "I will allow myself to add that any actions taken by the wife do not in any way justify the petitioner's resolve to keep his wife chained as an agunah — not from a legal perspective and not from a halachik perspective" (N. v. N., 2012). The court did, however, leave room for a similar case to be brought before them in the future.

FIVE

The Agunah Pawn

This court will do everything in its power not to injure the
"vineyard of Israel" as a result of the delivery of a forced divorce
that is void, and whose consequences lead to mamzerut and the
destruction of the family unit. . . . This is the opinion of this court and
the opinion of our Holy Torah. The court is not looking to
any outside source for guidance on this matter

Michael Amos, Rabbinic Judge

Now in her early fifties, Nava Levi, a mother of four from the port city of Haifa,
is a senior nurse who administers the emergency room of a busy government
hospital. Her poise in confronting life and death issues, her professional aplomb,
and her well-honed and intuitive nursing skills ("I have to listen to people and
sort out their worries") do not reflect the chaotic state of her own personal life.
It took Nava ten years to get divorced, or more, depending from when you start
counting. And "things are still not 100 percent in order," she tells us. Her colleagues, she says, don't easily think of her as a victim. It's not in keeping with
her strong demeanor and upbeat personality. They find the helplessness she
experiences with regard to her divorce, and its aftershock, to be quite baffling.
"Honestly? I am embarrassed by how I live," Nava confides.

Weary of explaining why she stayed with Avner for almost twenty-five years
in a violent and destructive relationship and bore him four children before
she ultimately decided to press for a divorce, Nava responds sadly that many
women quietly remain in turbulent relationships despite knowing better.

"Why do educated women stay in bad relationships?" she asks rhetorically.
"I could write a book about it," and in fact she did. It's all in longhand, and

she keeps promising herself to type it up and get it professionally edited, but she hasn't gotten around to it. She takes comfort in lugging the manuscript everywhere and often adds and makes changes to it. "Sometimes it's hard for women to break up their homes," she says. " Sometimes there are complicating circumstances — kids, for example. And Israel is hardly a hospitable environment for divorce. It's not easy to get out of a bad marriage, as you know."

Nava knows what she is talking about. Ten years after she formally requested a divorce, and a veritable lifetime after she informally did so, Avner was still refusing to give her a get. It took many lawyers, much fancy legal footwork, and sophisticated positioning to extract her from her failed marriage. A nonobservant Jew, Nava had several relationships with men after the couple split, but all her boyfriends left her when they understood that her status as a married woman was not about to end soon.

Almost despairing of ever getting her divorce, Nava sued Avner in the Haifa Family Court for damages she sustained through his refusal. Avner, in response, asked the Haifa Rabbinic Court to issue a declaratory judgment that he was not a "get withholder." The rabbinic court, flying in the face of the facts, complied. And in a lengthy decision, one member of the tribunal called the phenomenon of suing for damages a scourge on the system, declaring that the strife between Israeli rabbinic and civil courts was no less than a "world war."

What makes Nava's story so unusual is the zealousness with which the rabbis took up Avner's cause, making her a mere pawn in the power struggle and culture war being waged between Israeli rabbinic courts and its family courts. (For more about how the two court systems have parallel jurisdiction and how clients push and pull to get their cases heard in the tribunal of their choice, see introduction.) Attorneys who function in both systems can readily affirm that there has always been a strong undercurrent of judicial frustration and mutual criticism in the relations between the two, to say the least. Civil court judges refuse to interfere with the length of time rabbinic courts drag out cases and their reluctance to take action against recalcitrant husbands. Rabbinic judges can't tolerate what they see as the civil courts' lack of knowledge of, and respect for, halakha and tradition.

But for the most part, until recently the two systems tried to give at least the appearance of not treading on each other's toes. Neither court wanted to be seen as directly antagonizing the other or instigating a battle that would spill into the streets. Civil courts have historically tried to preserve the symbolic value of religious marriage while developing various means of circumventing its harmful aspects. Rabbinic courts have counterattacked, adopting strict minority views of halakha. But any gentle tiptoeing went out the window in the case of Nava Batzri Levi versus Avner Levi. And matters just got worse after Nava filed for damages in family court. Once she did that, Nava was persona non grata in the rabbinic courts. The facts of her case became irrelevant. Her suffering was collateral damage in the rabbinic judges' battle to defend their pride, power, and boundaries. All that mattered to them was to stop this insidious practice that was threatening their control over jurisdictional borders and over definitions of who was divorced and who was not, of mamzer and non-mamzer, of the God-fearing and the damned, of who was in and who was out — of the purity of the Jewish people.

Hitchhiking

Nava was born in Migdal Ha'emek, a small town located between Nazareth and Haifa, to parents of Iraqi origin and into a home she refers to as "traditional." Her father was a police officer who rose through the ranks until he was appointed superintendent of a police station. Nava recalls how her parsimonious father was always fighting with her mother about money, even about basics like groceries. His family had been wealthy in Iraq, but they had been forced to forfeit all their wealth when they came to Israel in the 1950s, shortly before Nava was born. Nava's father was irate at the idea that he had to budget at all, and he would unfailingly accuse Nava's mother each month of wasting his salary. The second of four children, Nava was always trying to negotiate a cold peace between her parents. She credits her mother with safeguarding the family's basic needs. "My mother always made sure that there was plenty of food," she says.

Nava was twenty when she met Avner in 1975 while hitchhiking, because she didn't have the money to purchase a bus ticket. Avner, who was then twenty-four, had a steady job as a civilian employed by the military engineering corps. He had a good laugh; big, strong arms; and an open heart for the downtrodden, and Nava was certain he would take care of her. She didn't necessarily connect the dots, but clearly her plan was to escape the rigors of her childhood home and its deprivations. She mentions in passing that she moved to a kibbutz at age fourteen for several years, something municipal authorities used to encourage for the welfare of children in disadvantaged or dysfunctional families. The wedding took place in 1977, about two years after the couple met and immediately after Nava had finished her first degree in nursing. It was a stark affair held in a modest hall located in the basement of the building that houses the Haifa rabbinate. This was all the couple could afford. They served cold sandwiches and soft drinks and invited just a few friends and close family. There were no flowers, no photographers, and no music, but Nava, a very young and pregnant twenty-two-year-old, insisted on wearing a long, white gown. And Avner, as gracious as he could be with his limited funds, paid for it.

But leaving her parent's home for Avner's in Kiryat Ata, a mainly working-class suburb of Haifa and about a half-hour drive from her parents, didn't work out the way Nava had hoped. Avner is a large man with a big heart, but with a matching explosive temper. He turned out to be a "walking volcano," in Nava's words, whose internal turmoil and rumblings unsettle and intimidate people all around him. The first flare-up Nava remembers occurred when she was about four months pregnant with their first child. Angry about something completely insignificant, Avner shattered several items within his close reach — a lamp and a picture, she recalls. Later he broke windows and even walls. Occasionally he struck Nava, and once he threatened to choke her with a telephone cord. "I was constantly terrorized," she says. After each outburst, Nava would ask for a divorce and Avner would promise to get help and swear there would be no more violent episodes. Nava believed him and did not believe him, on and off, for about twenty-five years. It was in this manner that she managed to have four children.

But like many angry and abusive men, Avner did not get help or change. Instead, he forced his wife and four children to endure a reign of terror that each relives with great emotion when asked to tell their story. When testifying in court in 2002 after the state initiated a criminal prosecution against Avner for alleged assault, the couple's oldest son, at age twenty-four, described domestic life with his father: "There was always this feeling that nobody was free, that we could not do what we wanted. We all lived in fear. As I grew up, I felt less threatened. I felt strong. I felt that I could be more supportive and help. But my mother was scared, I knew that. She was terrified. He threatened suicide, to put a bullet in his head right in front of us little kids, cursing, horrible things. My mother would gather up her things, leave, and then come back. Terror and fear ruled the house." The court would eventually acquit

Avner of actually assaulting his wife and children for lack of evidence, but convicted him of threatening behavior and issued a suspended sentence and community service.

In 1999, after an incident in which Avner slapped Nava for some minor transgression she cannot recall and threatened to burn the house down with her and the children inside, Nava gathered all her strength and money and went to see an attorney. Swift on her feet, the attorney filed papers in the family court, asking for child support, custody, a division of the marital assets, and, most important, a restraining order to keep Avner away from the house. The court issued a temporary order for a week and referred the couple to a family therapist to see if he could help them resolve their differences and give the court some insight as to what was happening between them. After she filed papers with the family court, Nava's attorney petitioned for a get in the rabbinic court. Buttressed by attorney, therapist, and multiple court papers, this time Nava's demand for divorce was clear and vigorous. But Avner remained obtuse and unyielding. The therapist, summoned later to testify on Nava's request for an extension of the restraining order, summed up the feud this way: "Avner is preoccupied with his refusal to divorce Nava. He knows that he cannot prevent it, but he is still fighting. Today he is taking the tactical position of 'sitting and doing nothing.' The sooner the couple is separated physically, the better off each of them will be."

The family court, however, did not feel it had a legal basis to extend the restraining orders beyond the week that had elapsed. There is no legal separation under Israeli law and all restraining orders are, by law, limited in duration. When it lapsed, Nava withdrew her other petitions. She explains, "What I wanted was a divorce. I didn't have the emotional strength to deal with an extended court case after I saw how adamant Avner was about not giving me a get, and his indifference to my needs and requests." Her attorney told her, quite presciently as it would turn out, that if Avner did not give a divorce of his free will, she would have to get ready for a long battle. "I did not have the strength to fight for a divorce with him back in the house," she adds. "And I had nowhere to go with four kids."

For a short while things were almost tolerable. However, at the end of 2001, Avner's temper got the best of him once again and this time he hit the couple's nine-year-old hard on her backside, causing her to fall down steps and sustain severe bruises. This was the "straw that broke the camel's back," Nava tells us.

She again petitioned the family court for help, this time without an attorney. Avner too was unrepresented. A judge assigned to hear emergency petitions issued a temporary restraining order and asked the municipal family services to intervene, interview the sides, and write up a recommendation. The social worker's report was unequivocal: Avner should be referred to a rehabilitation center and the couple should not live under one roof during the period it would take them to get divorced.

Family court judge Ofra Biton, appointed to oversee the family's case, encouraged Nava to hire an attorney. She chose Frieda Ohrbach, a soft-spoken, graceful woman who provided a refreshing contrast of calm and deliberation to Nava's increasing agitation. Ohrbach advised Nava to sue immediately for child support and custody in the family court, and she did so. So long as Nava was in the house with the children, Ohrbach suggested that they hold off for the time being from suing for the sale of the family home, the couple's chief asset.

Judge Biton was a down-to-earth, no-frills woman in her midforties, who had just been appointed to the bench. She had spent many years as an attorney in the trenches, representing women whose husbands battered and beat them. A mother, wife, and feminist, Biton had helped draft Israel's 1991 Law against Family Violence, as a volunteer member of the Women's Network's Committee on Matters of Personal Status. She, better than most judges, knew a dangerous situation when she saw one. She was not about to take risks with the safety of the women and children who appeared before her and she managed to convince Avner, for the sake of himself and the family, to "agree" to a renewal of the restraining order so that she would not be bound by the time limitation with the law. (Four years later, in 2005, when Avner's good will ran out, Biton would take the unprecedented step of extending the order for yet another year or "until the couple divorced," whichever came first.)

From that moment onward, Avner never returned to live with his family. Nava remained alone with the couple's four children, who at the time of separation were nine, fourteen, eighteen, and twenty-four. "I was relieved. But even though he was not allowed to come close to the house, I was still petrified of him, scared to death. He could go crazy and out of control at any time and at any place," she recalls.

In the beginning, Biton ordered Avner, who no longer worked for the army and took occasional day jobs in construction, to pay a nominal amount in temporary child support. And, to help him out, she also ruled that all money collected as rent for a small unit attached to the family home should be paid to Avner so that he could take a room for himself. Not impressed, Avner refused to pay even the minimal child support, pocketed the money from the rental, and insisted on living in his car. When asked by Biton why he wasn't working regularly, he admitted that it was out of choice: "When I can live with respect, the respect that is owed me, the right that I have to live like a human being in my own house, with my own clothes, and my own property, then I can think about rehabilitating myself. I am not a cripple." When asked about his unusual sleeping arrangements, he retorted, "I prefer to sleep in the car. Why should I rent a place when I have a house that is mine, and I have never been found guilty of anything?" He refused an offer from his oldest son to live with him. When Avner decided to park his car in front of the social services offices, the social workers, feeling threatened, filed a petition with the magistrate's court asking them to order him to move: "He isn't directly threatening us but his presence is an act of defiance and . . . harassment that raises the suspicions and fears of both the office workers and clients." The magistrate's court judge concurred and, like Biton, convinced Avner to "agree" to move his car and not to enter the site. He moved it but did not find alternative housing, despite the encouragement of family, friends, and attorney.

Avner's attorney also encouraged him to petition the family court for a declaratory judgment that the house was all his, claiming it was a gift from his mother. But Avner did not want to pay the required filing fee, and, instead, his attorney sent the draft of the lawsuit, which included a request for half of Nava's pension, to Ohrbach. With the threat of the new lawsuit hovering in the background, the two attorneys started negotiating a settlement that would include the sale of the house, the division of Nava's pension benefits, and a get. At pretrial hearings scheduled with respect to visitation, custody, and child support, Biton supported those efforts. Trying to broker an agreement for divorce between the agitated Nava and the disgruntled Avner and to balance between the needs of a woman and her four children for a roof over their heads and the idiosyncrasies of their rancorous, unemployed father, Judge Biton delayed making any final decisions on the matters formally before her. She wanted to keep things calm, for the sake of the children, if nothing else. And she hoped a comprehensive agreement, including a divorce, would be quick in coming. The couple needed closure.

Twists and Turns in the Rabbinic Court

Meanwhile, in late 2001, at about the same time that Nava sued in family court for child support and custody of the children, Ohrbach suggested that she also sue for divorce in the rabbinic court. Ohrbach wanted to apply pressure on Avner from every possible direction. Like Biton and the therapists who had met the couple, Ohrbach understood that their relationship needed to be terminated. To save Nava some money, the two decided, after much deliberation and hesitation, that Nava would represent herself in the rabbinic court hearing. "I can't predict what will happen there," Ohrbach told Nava, in all honesty. "Or how long it will take. And you might be better off alone, if you can muster the sympathy of the tribunal." Avner, also unrepresented, countersued for a reconciliation.

At first it seemed as if the rabbinic court was moving in the right direction from Nava's perspective. In early 2002, a month or so after she filed for divorce, the judges sized up the situation quite succinctly and dismissed Avner's request for a reconciliation and closed his file: "The wife wants a divorce and that's an understatement," they said. "The court cannot compel a woman to agree to shalom bayit."

But in Jewish law, no hope for reconciliation is not necessarily grounds for divorce. Nine months after throwing out Avner's request for reconciliation, the rabbinic court held a hearing on Nava's request for a get. In a truncated court protocol, the court stenographer recorded the opening statements of the couple as follows: "The wife informs the tribunal that the couple has been living apart for a year. The husband informs the court that he wants to rebuild their life together and that, before he had been forced out of the house, he had engaged in sexual relations on a regular basis with his wife in the early hours of the morning. The wife responds, 'Sex with him was not with my consent or pleasure. It was rape every morning.'"

Nava's allegations of rape were not well received by the three rabbinic judges. Under Jewish law it is a wife's duty to be sexually available to her husband. A woman who is not is deemed "a rebellious wife" (Mishna Ketuboth 5:7). The rabbis' indignation at Nava's claims of rape unnerved her. Her twenty-five-year-old failed marriage had in effect, if not by law, been over long ago, and she did not understand why she had to discuss her sex life with three Orthodox Jewish men even after they themselves had dismissed Avner's request for reconciliation. Frustrated and without counsel to restrain her, Nava burst out in desperation, demanding that the rabbis set her free. "I want a divorce, is that so difficult for you to understand?" she beseeched the court, ignoring their challenges to her rape allegations. The court reproached her and when she did not acquiesce, they ended the hearing, noting laconically, "The wife has interfered with the smooth operation of this hearing and has spoken out of line four times. We reprimanded her, and she continued to act impudently. We set a date for another hearing."

Nava did not show up for that next session, in February 2003. She claims to have made a mistake regarding the date. Perhaps she had subliminally given up hope for a fair hearing. Or perhaps she thought matters would resolve themselves in family court. But when she did not appear, the rabbinic judges promptly closed her divorce file. When Nava realized what happened, she petitioned the court to reopen her case and set a new hearing. The court refused, informing her that she must file a new claim for divorce and pay yet another filing fee. She balked indignantly at this, but at Ohrbach's gentle insistence, relented. "It's cheaper and faster than fighting the decision to close the case," she told Nava. "And I think I should come with you next time," she suggested, despite Nava's grumblings that had become something of a mantra: she had no money for all this nonsense, and she did not understand why she was still married, with four children to take care of by herself.

At a hearing in June 2004, with her lawyer at her side to calm her down, Nava reiterated her tales of terror and marital rape. On the basis of Nava's testimony, Ohrbach asked the court to rule that Avner was obligated to divorce Nava since he abused her physically and emotionally. To support her claim, Ohrbach also submitted all the protocols and decisions in the criminal proceeding that had by then been brought against Avner, including the incriminating testimony of the couple's oldest son, mentioned earlier. The criminal court had held that "the wife and children were victims of ongoing emotional violence" and convicted Avner of "threatening them with physical violence." It also held that while it believed that Avner had been physically violent with their daughter, it could not convict him of the specific act alleged because of the lack of corroborating evidence required by law.

One month later, in July 2004, the rabbinic judges arrived at three split decisions. They couldn't even agree about whether Nava had proved that Avner was physically violent. Two asserted that she "lied," and a third stated that there appeared to be a basis for her claims. And it was far from clear what Nava would have had to do to prove her claims in a manner that would satisfy the rabbis. Why wasn't Nava's testimony enough? Must she meet the same burden of proof in a rabbinic trial as a criminal one? (For more on the burden of proof in a rabbinic court, see chapter 4.) They also seemed to disagree about whether emotional abuse or separation was grounds for issuing any type of directive against Avner with regard to the get. One stated that those were not sufficient grounds, another argued that separation was grounds to "recommend" a divorce, and still a third asserted that emotional violence was a reason that a husband "must" (al-habaal) give a get. The following is a translation of the different decisions, practically in their entirety:

July 20, 2004

JUDGMENT

It appears that the [criminal] court has acquitted the husband of the criminal charges brought against him for physical violence. Similarly, the police have, twice, rejected complaints that the wife brought before them, claiming that there were insufficient grounds for bringing criminal charges.

The wife does not allege physical violence, instead she bases her request [for a get] on the fact that her husband was ordered to leave the marital home because of threats. The husband claims that because of a legal error, there was no substantive finding regarding those allegations.

The wife also claims that she was raped, a claim which is not true. If she had been raped, it is clear that she would have filed a complaint [with the police] since she filed complaints on much more trivial matters. Certainly, she would not have kept silent on big matters.

Therefore, this court holds: We reject the wife's petition since we do not find any grounds upon which to order a husband to give a get, and there is no clear reason that [the husband is repulsive to his wife], certainly not one that this court can see. However, we do not order the wife to return to her husband. Moreover, it has been determined that the wife lied to both this court and the [criminal] court.

Rabbi Haim Shlomo Shaanan

Upon review of this file, it appears that the parties have been living apart for more than two years — and the wife accuses the husband of having raped her each morning. This claim has not been proven. She also raised claims with regard to physical violence, but those claims have been deemed lies by the civil court. Though it is clear that the husband's anger does not contribute to any possibility of reconciliation, to say the very least.

The parties were referred to a marital counselor by the civil court [in 1999] and his conclusions were "Before us is a couple who, with respect to their marriage and relationship, can be deemed to be emotionally divorced. And it is my opinion that it is not in our power to rehabilitate the relationship between them."

Because of all this, I must recommend divorce.

Rabbi Michael Amos

After we heard the parties and upon review of the file, it appears to me that even though there are no grounds for divorce, we have before us a woman who claims that her husband is "repulsive to her for good reason." See Beer Heitev [a brief commentary on the Shulhan Arukh by German Rabbi Yehudah ben Shimon Ashkenazi, 1730-1770] 77:32: "If she says he is 'repulsive to me' because of his bad deeds . . . and in his anger threatens to mortgage, burn, commit suicide and sell [property], there is nothing more repulsive than this."

With respect to the file at hand, the wife makes such claims, stating that her husband, when he is angry, threatens to burn down the marital home and to commit suicide, and that he inflicts terror on the household. Even the children feel it and experience it. And even if she did not prove her other claims (like those about how he relates to her in the early morning, etc.), it does appear that there is a basis to her claims, especially after we read the material from the civil court, including the testimony of the son. It appears that there is a good reason for her revulsion.

. . . Yet the Rema, in his commentary on Shulhan Arukh (Even HaEzer 77, no. 3, gloss), states that under such circumstance we cannot compel him to divorce her, nor her to be with him. . . .

Therefore, so long as there was no proof of grounds upon which we can justify compelling him to divorce his wife, the conclusion must be that we cannot compel a reconciliation or a get. Nonetheless [I hold that] the husband must divorce his wife.

Rabbi David Bardugo

In summation, before us are three decisions. One rejects the wife's petition. Another recommends divorce. And still another orders the husband to give a get, but does not compel him to do so. We therefore, by majority opinion, recommend that the couple divorce.

Rabbis Shaanan, Amos, and Bardugo (*L. v. L.*, 2004)

Ohrbach did not like the decision. Nava was not a liar. And the criminal court had clearly convicted Avner of threatening Nava and the children. But since the bottom-line, compromise position of the district rabbinic court was to "recommend" that Avner and Nava get divorced, and since the court had already set a date to take care of the preliminary technicalities to that end, there was no reason for an appeal. Nava would simply appear at the stated date, two months hence, ready and willing to receive the get. If Avner did not show or balked, they could always ask for another hearing. In fact, Avner did fail to show up and the rabbinic judges, annoyed, warned that if he did not come to the next hearing, they would order the police to bring him.

Two weeks later, Avner appeared as summoned. Nava was certain she was going to make progress toward the get and felt confident that she could risk going to court without counsel. Avner also appeared unrepresented, but well prepped, it seems, on how to maneuver. He stood before the rabbinic court and said, "Yes, but . . ." agreeing to give the get, but on the condition that the court hear and decide all his demands relating to the couple's marital property. But neither Avner nor Nava had submitted any formal petition to the rabbinic court asking them to adjudicate those matters. Moreover, they were already being dealt with, de facto, in family court, where Judge Biton had been trying to help the parties negotiate a comprehensive settlement, including a get. She had even appointed a receiver for the sale of the marital home.

To Nava's great astonishment and consternation, the rabbinic court did not insist that Avner deliver the get, as they had recommended. Neither did they follow correct procedure and end the hearing that had been scheduled for a delivery of a get. Instead, they changed course and insisted on conducting an impromptu hearing, right then and there, on Avner's (still inchoate) property claims. Nava was completely nonplussed after the hearing. What had happened? She wanted a divorce. The marriage was over. Even the rabbis said so. What was so complicated?

"Outrageous," Frieda Ohrbach commented after reviewing the transcript, which was as truncated and disjointed as usual. "If I interpret this in the most favorable light possible, it seems to me that the court wanted to placate Avner so that he would have no more excuses to refuse to give you a get. So they held a hearing, albeit without your knowing what it was about and without your ability to introduce any documents as evidence, so as to take the position that they have jurisdiction over the house, as per Avner's request. If I interpret this in the worst possible light, it is a naked grab for jurisdiction. A rabbinic court has no authority to decide how to dispose of marital assets unless a party has sued for divorce and attached those matters to their claim "in good faith." Or if the parties agree. Avner has not sued for a divorce at all. And you did not ask, or agree, for the rabbinic court to decide these issues. And these matters are being handled by the family court. This is a complete violation of due process [see chapter 7]. But I don't think it pays to appeal this. If the rabbinic court issues any substantive decision, then we'll appeal."

At the rabbinic court's initiative, another hearing was held March 30, 2005, for the delivery of a get. Nava appeared, without counsel, ready and willing to accept one. Avner appeared, without counsel, and refused to give one, saying again that he wanted the court to take jurisdiction over the property matters, without mentioning what was happening over at family court. He was trying to convince the family court to pressure Nava into selling the house as part of a comprehensive agreement and, at the same time, persuade the rabbinic court to stop bothering him about a get.

With respect to the rabbinic court, his ploy worked. The rabbinic court ruled that since it already had held a hearing with respect to the couple's property matters, it had jurisdiction, and thus it was now possible to complete the get process — as soon, of course, as Avner was ready to do so. With respect to the family court, his ploy hit a temporary snag. On July 11, 2005, Biton issued a final decision giving Nava formal custody over the couple's minor children and ordering Avner to pay retroactive child support in the amount of 3,200 shekels (about $900) a month from 2003. Biton also imposed a formal restraining order on Avner for an additional year, stating that "a clear picture has been established of the atmosphere of terror and fear that the defendant has inflicted on his family from the beginning of the parties' marriage" and that, despite the passage of time, "the danger to his family has not passed, but increased." With the custody and child support case closed, Biton stopped pressing for a comprehensive agreement regarding the marital property. Nava remained in the house with the children.

After the family court ruling, Attorney Ohrbach wanted the rabbinic court to "order," not just "recommend," that Avner give a get. She also wanted it on record, in no uncertain terms, that Nava had asserted that the court had no jurisdiction over the distribution of the couple's marital property.

At the next hearing, on September 9, 2005, Avner did not appear. When Ohrbach tried to explain why the court lacked jurisdiction over the couple's marital property, it refused to hear any of her arguments. When she implied that the court had taken advantage of Nava's being unrepresented to conduct a hearing that had material implications that Nava was unable to understand, the tribunal asked Orhbach "where it was written" that they had the responsibility of disclosure to the parties of the legal consequences of the proceedings? And when Ohrbach persisted, they suggested that rather than concern herself with the couple's property, she should proceed with the get, otherwise, "with such an attitude," the case "will continue for many years." They set another date for the delivery of the get, two months later.

"What happened?" Nava asked Ohrbach. "Did the rabbis threaten us that if we continued to insist that they don't have jurisdiction over the house, they won't go forward with the get?"

"Yes," Ohrbach answered. "That's exactly what they did. But as I originally suggested, I don't think there is anything for us to do unless the court makes a substantive decision, which I doubt it will do. Let's just keep pressing for the get."

In November 2005 another get delivery hearing came and went. Avner accused Nava of being responsible for the failure to reach an agreement and stated that he did not want to give Nava a get until all the property matters were resolved. When Nava complained that Avner was not paying child support, the tribunal, with manifest cynicism, asked Nava if she had filed a petition with the rabbinic court asking for such support, fully aware that she hadn't. When Nava asked again for a get, they answered, "With respect to a get, *we* have already made a decision," and there was nothing more that they would do for her.

Damages

In December 2004 Frieda Ohrbach had seen *Sentenced to Marry*, an Israeli documentary about agunot, directed by Anat Zuria, produced by Amir Brauer, and screened at the Sha'arei Mishpat College in Hod HaSharon. There she heard a lecture by Susan Weiss discussing the possibility of anchored women suing their recalcitrant husbands for damages. Seeing the Levi case come to a standstill, she thought a tort claim might speed the process along for Nava, and she referred her client to the Center for Women's Justice (CWJ), the NGO that specializes in these claims.

In June 2006 CWJ lawyers filed suit for Nava in the Haifa Family Court. They asked the court to award Nava 1.4 million shekels [about $450,000] to compensate for the pain and suffering that she had endured because Avner had been refusing to give her a get since February 2002, the date the rabbinic court held that there was no chance of reconciliation. CWJ's goal in filing the lawsuit was not necessarily the same as Ohrbach's or Nava's. It did not do it just to "move Nava's case forward" or to simply obtain a get. The members of CWJ believe that their clients deserve both their get and damages, and they do not want to sacrifice one for the other, although their clients often would. And they are interested in setting precedents that will help all Jewish women whose husbands hold the unfair leverage of the get, not only individual clients. By 2004 CWJ had succeed in convincing Israeli family courts that a cause of action for damages for get refusal exists when a rabbinic court has "ordered" a husband to give a get. Now CWJ wanted to expand that precedent to include cases in which no such order had been given. The NGO also wanted to expand the grounds on which courts were basing their damages awards and to declare that get refusal was a form of abuse under the Law against Family Violence, and not just unreasonable behavior that fell under the general rubric of the "negligence" statute. They believe that get refusal is never reasonable. Nava's case was a perfect opportunity to advance CWJ's goals. Nava's marriage was over. Even the rabbis had said so, though they had refused to order a divorce. And the case was being heard by Biton, a judge who would be receptive to a creative interpretation of what constitutes family violence.

At first, things seemed to be turning around for Nava. Judge Biton was back in the picture both because of the tort claim and because the restraining order was coming to an end and Avner wanted to go home. Biton called an informal hearing of the parties' attorneys who, once again, lobbied for a comprehensive solution. Avner showed signs of softening. In September 2006 the couple signed an agreement in the family court providing for the sale of the house and for the money to be held in escrow until Biton determined the value of the parties' pension benefits. Avner promised to deliver the get immediately, and the couple agreed that the court would have the authority to delay the sale of the house and the division of assets until the divorce was finalized. Nava agreed to withdraw her tort claim.

Judge Biton was happy, but Nava wasn't. She didn't know where she could move to and didn't trust Avner to give her a get. Avner was not so happy either, since he claimed the house belonged to him in its entirety and what's more, he did not trust Nava to sell it. CWJ lawyers were not so happy, but as is the organization's policy and professional responsibility, they deferred to their client's wishes. Ohrbach and Avner's attorney encouraged the couple to move matters along. Avner's attorney explained to him that if he gave a get, the court would order Nava and the children to vacate the house, if need be. Ohrbach explained to Nava that if Avner refused to give a get, the court would delay the sale of the house. Despite the reassurance, Avner refused to go ahead with the divorce and after a few months Ohrbach requested the court to stay the sale of the house, as had been agreed. Judge Biton summoned the parties and reminded Avner that he needed to go to the rabbinic court and give his wife her get.

Subsequently, on January 29, 2007, Nava, Avner, and both their attorneys appeared in the rabbinic court in accordance with the September 2006 agreement. And again, at first it all seemed to be going as planned. Both sides announced their desire to live up to the September agreement. But, when asked again by the court if he was giving the get of his free will and desire, Avner expressed apprehensions, summed up by the court scribe as follows:

> Husband: Yes, I want to divorce. But I do not want to go to family court. I have not "tied up all the loose ends." The wife lives in the house, and I live in the street. I am not sure that she will honor the agreement. I obligated myself to what I am obligated. I have no choice but to get divorced.
>
> Court: Is there duress being placed on you?

Husband: The family court is forcing me to divorce. My wife filed a tort claim against me for refusing to give her a get.

Court: If there is a damages claim against the husband for 1.5 million shekels for get refusal . . . even if the husband were to plead before us that he wants to give the get, we will not allow the ceremony to take place. And even if we were to allow it, the get would be invalid according to all opinions, and if the wife would remarry any child born to her would be a mamzer.

JUDGMENT

Only after it has been proven to this court that the tort claim against the husband has been dismissed with prejudice and cannot be reopened, will this court hear a request to arrange a divorce.

Rabbi Haim Shlomo Shaanan, Head of Tribunal (*L. v. L.*, 2007[1])

In other words, according to the rabbinic judges, the damages claim itself was tantamount to invalid pressure on a husband (see introduction). While rabbinic courts consider it valid to demand that women relinquish homes, and in rare cases even custody of children, in exchange for a get, men cannot be pressured, especially if not "obliged" by the court to give a get. The court wanted the tort claim dismissed for good and in a way that it could not be reopened. Only after it was dismissed and Avner did not have it hovering over his head would the court allow the get ceremony to take place.

With the sale of the home now on hold until the delivery of a get, Judge Biton set a preliminary hearing on Nava's tort claim on April 22, 2007. CWJ attorneys asked her to set a date for trial, but Biton had another agenda. She wanted to know why a get had not been arranged. Convinced by Avner and his attorneys that the rabbinic court, and not Avner, was the problem — Avner really wanted to give a get, but the court would not let him because of the tort claim, Biton insisted that the parties figure out how to resolve what she felt was a technical dilemma. CWJ attorneys suggested that they draft two short, separate papers, one asking the rabbinic court to arrange for the get, the other providing for the dismissal of the tort claim with prejudice *after* the delivery of a get. All the attorneys agreed that if the parties really agreed to the divorce, the rabbis could not dictate its terms. All that was necessary was to arrive at the rabbinic court and insist that it conduct the get ceremony in accordance with the couple's wishes.

Two weeks later, Nava and Avner, without their attorneys, asked the rabbinic court to proceed with the get. It is unclear what exactly was said, since there is no transcript of what transpired that day, but it is clear that there was no get. Avner apparently presented the rabbis with both papers, the request to arrange the get, as well as the agreement that the dismissal of the damages claim was to occur subsequent to the get. The head of the tribunal wrote simply, "Only when this court is satisfied that the damages claim against the husband for get refusal has been dismissed with prejudice will it consider the parties' motion to arrange for a get."

"The problem lies with Avner, not the rabbinic court," the CWJ people told Nava's attorney, Frieda Ohrbach. More than half of CWJ's clients received a get in exchange for waivers of their tort claims. None of those clients agreed to drop their tort claims *before* a get was given. All previous agreements drafted for CWJ clients had unambiguously linked the get to the waiver and stated that it was subject to the delivery of the get. It was clear to them that while the rabbis were certainly being problematic, Avner was fanning the fires and pushing all the right buttons. CWJ asked for another pretrial hearing in the family court to insist on a date for trial. In May 2007 CWJ attorney Yifat Frankenburg appeared in court, ready to stand firm. But Judge Biton was not interested in setting a date. She still thought that the problem lay with the rabbinic court and not with Avner, who had, after all, expressed his willingness to grant the divorce. It was almost five years that she had been dealing with the case, and she wanted to see the couple divorced and the proceeding finished. "Why is the couple still married?" she wanted to know. "Why has the get ceremony not taken place?"

Avner, who should have been the very last person to listen to in this matter, offered an explanation: "I wanted to give the get. But the rabbinic court insisted that the family court first dismiss the suit for damages, and only then would it agree to arrange for the get. It's a halakhic issue. First, close the tort file."

Attorney Frankenburg didn't buy it. She suggested a penalty if Nava agreed to withdraw her claim, and Avner reneged on his promise to give a get. "We will dismiss the case," Yifat agreed. "But if Avner does not show up to give the get, or refuses to give the get, we want his rights in the house transferred completely to Nava."

"What if Nava does not appear or fails to agree to accept the get?" Avner and his attorney wondered.

"We will agree that the same penalty be imposed on her," Yifat countered.

"No," Avner responded. "It won't work."

After much deliberation, heavy pressure from Biton, and Avner's adamant refusal to agree to do anything in exchange for dismissal of the tort claim except promise to give a get, Nava and Yifat caved. They agreed that they would authorize the court to dismiss the case on the spot so long as, at the same time, the parties signed a separate statement before the court asserting that Avner's agreement to give the get and Nava's agreement to dismiss the case were "dependent" on each other. The statement could not undo the dismissal if Avner failed to give a get, but it was more than nothing. And if Avner reneged, the statement was clear proof of his bad faith and fraud, which could serve as a basis for a new suit by Nava. The parties signed, and their attorneys authorized the signatures of their clients. Satisfied that it was over and that Avner would finally deliver the get, and that the rabbinic courts would be satisfied that the tort claim no longer hung ominously over Anver's head, Judge Biton dismissed the case with prejudice and deposited the parties' statement into the court's safe. The parties would present the family court's dismissal of Nava's damages claim, signed, sealed, and completed, to the rabbis.

Two weeks later the parties, and Ohrbach, arrived again at the rabbinic court. Avner's attorney stayed away, but Avner, once again, appeared to have been well coached for the hearing. He quickly told the rabbinic court about what had transpired in the family court to undermine him, and them, intimating that he was being "forced" and not acting of his own "free will." He also claimed that he would even be put in jail if he did not agree to the get — a statement with no basis in reality or law. At this point it became obvious, if it had not been before, that Avner was blatantly stoking up the rabbinic judges against the family court. The following is an excerpt from the protocol:

June 10, 2007
Protocol

Husband: I want to show the court the protocol from the family court. . . .
    Court: The claim was dismissed.
    Husband: In the document that I have attached, paragraph 3 states that all

conditions of this agreement are contingent one on the other. The court forced me to sign this agreement. The other document submitted to this court has no such clause. It is "shady" legal maneuvering. . . .

Wife's attorney: . . . The husband is looking for another way to delay.

Court: We want to know in no uncertain terms. Was the damages claim dismissed with prejudice, and unconditionally? Or is this a misrepresentation and an attempt to defraud this court by presenting an agreement to dismiss with prejudice, while at the same time there is another agreement stating that the dismissal is void if the get is not given? . . . On the face of things, it looks as if there was an attempt to deceive this court. . . . There are two agreements, one that was authorized [by the court] and one that was not. . . . Too bad. If not for the shady legal maneuvering the get would have been given a long time ago.

Wife's attorney: This is not accurate. This court is not letting the wife divorce, and the husband has been out of the marital home for five years.

Court: There is no divorce petition outstanding before us . . . since the court had already made a decision recommending divorce back in 2004. . . . Has the tort claim been dismissed, or not?

Husband: It hangs over me like a sword. The judge forced [the agreement] on me.

Court: Why did you sign?

Husband: If I didn't, I would have been put in jail for contempt.

The court will deliver its opinion on this later. (*L. v. L.*, 2007[2])

Not a Get Recalcitrant

Avner reneged three times on his promise to divorce Nava in exchange for waiver of her tort claim — in January, April, and June 2007. After Nava withdrew her suit in May 2007, she spent the next three years trying to reinstate it, as well as to sue for still more. She wanted damages for get refusal not only from 2002 to 2006, as in her original suit, but also from 2007 to 2010. She had to file an entirely new lawsuit, claim that she had been fraudulently induced to withdraw her old one, and conduct a new trial to prove it. During those three years, Avner replaced his attorney with a young, eager law school graduate, Amnon Lalouz, who did everything in his power to drag things out and delay proceedings.

Lalouz sued for summary dismissal of the new lawsuit and appealed to the district court when he lost. He moved to recuse Biton, claiming she was prejudiced against Avner. He delayed filing his pleadings way beyond the allotted time, taking advantage of the fact that the family court usually will turn a blind eye to such delays. He even convinced the rabbinic court's legal advisor to file an astonishing complaint with the state ombudsman against Biton for taking part in an attempt to "defraud" the rabbinic court into arranging a get. The ombudsman rejected the complaint.

Finally, after delay, appeals, and complaints had abated, Biton set the trial for Nava's new expanded claim for September 2010. Biton directed attorneys to submit direct testimony of their witnesses by affidavit. She ordered the trial taped and transcribed, rather than typed by a court reporter, as was standard procedure. She knew that whatever ruling she made would be appealed and wanted full transparency.

The trial took only one day. Nava and her brother testified that she was suffering and that Avner was aware of such suffering. They were cross-examined by Lalouz, mostly about Nava's relationship with other men and the fact that she had done repairs on the house without Avner's approval. Lalouz wanted to show that not being divorced was not hurting Nava. Avner was cross-examined to show that he was well aware that Nava had been asking for a divorce since 1999 and that, despite this knowledge, refused, intentionally, willfully, and maliciously. In summation, CWJ attorney Susan Weiss argued that the facts proved that Avner was a get refuser and that Nava suffered from such refusal. She asked the court to base the charge of emotional distress for get abuse on the Law against Family Violence, as well as on the basis of the Basic Law of Human Dignity and Liberty, not on the "negligence" statute. Citing cases won by CWJ in Jerusalem and Tel Aviv in July and December 2008 (see chapter 4), Weiss argued that it was not necessary to hang a claim for damages for get refusal on a rabbinic court order "obligating" a husband to give a get. Lalouz argued that the negligence standard applied and that since the rabbinic court had never held that Avner was obligated to divorce Nava, only "recommended" that he do so, he owed no "duty of care" to her and, as such, by definition, was not a get refuser, referring to the Jerusalem Family Court decision rendered by Judge Menahem HaCohen in CWJ's original 2004 suit (C. S. v. C. P., 2004).

At the end of the trial and oral summation, Biton permitted both sides to submit additional concluding remarks in writing once they received the transcript of the trial. Lalouz characteristically delayed filing his remarks, and Biton was characteristically slow in writing her decision. But meanwhile, Lalouz was quick to hire a seasoned rabbinic pleader to sue in rabbinic court for a declaratory judgment that Avner was not a get refuser. Lalouz erroneously thought that if the rabbinic court decided that Avner was not a get refuser, the family court could not rule that he was responsible for damages for get refusal.

In January 2011 the Haifa Rabbinic Court issued a fourteen-page judgment that in effect complied with Avner's request. Proclaiming that a "world war" was upon them, it held that it was Nava's fault that she was not divorced and that she was "anchoring herself." Excerpts of the judgment follow:

January 23, 2011

JUDGMENT

Before us is a sad story of a wife who has been anchoring herself for many years even though there have been many opportunities to divide the property equally [and] to dismiss the frivolous tort claim brought despite a rabbinic court decision [in 2004] in which the husband was not ordered to grant a divorce. According to the decision, the wife lied repeatedly when she complained about the husband. The husband was acquitted of physical violence, and the police twice rejected the wife's complaints. The decision of this rabbinic court speaks for itself, and we do not have to add to it.

We need not declare that the husband is a not a get recalcitrant with respect to legal proceedings being conducted in a different jurisdiction, when it is unavoidable, to our great dismay, that such court will not accept our determination. However, the decisions of this court, together with all that accompanies it, speak for themselves. Perhaps the wife should awaken from her deep slumber and stubbornness and learn and understand, that she is the get recalcitrant in this case and that she is anchoring herself!

This is the place to express dissatisfaction with regard to legal proceedings in the form of "damages claims," whose purpose is to force husbands to divorce against the laws of the Torah, indirectly and "through the back door," actions that lead to invalid forced divorces and the surge of mamzerim. These legal proceedings are the direct cause of the woman's anxiety and inability to extract herself from her failed marriage, the exact opposite of their purpose and goals.

Let us note that in this case the husband was never ordered to deliver a get. And it must be understood, that even in those circumstances in which a husband was ordered to deliver a get, any petition brought for damages would invalidate a subsequent get, all the more so in a case such as this one in which the husband was never ordered to give one; in a case like this there is no doubt that the divorce is forced in a way that does not accord with [Jewish] law and is invalid. [The court quotes extensively from an article by a Rabbi Lavie, head of the Tiberias Rabbinic Court, who writes that filing petitions for damages invalidates any subsequent get (Lavie, 2006).]

. . . This court appeals from the bottom of its heart to those who carry weight within the legal community in Israel to refrain from dealing with these damages claims. Their purpose is to help those who bring these claims, but in fact they cause them direct harm and anguish. Such proceedings lead divorce cases to a dead end, and they themselves are the cause of foiled divorces for many years to come. I hope that my words will be internalized, for the good of the matter.

Shniur Pardes, Rabbinic Judge

My colleague is correct that, from a halakhic perspective, the relatively new phenomenon of filing for "damages for get refusal" between parties who are in the midst of divorce proceedings carries with it serious halakhic problems of the "improperly forced divorce," a matter that leads to a void get and mamzerut.

To my dismay, the trend in the last few years to file these types of damages claims has become very popular. The High Rabbinic Court related to this phenomenon in two key decisions . . . and raised all the halakhic problems that can occur . . . with respect to get refusal. The clear and precise directions given by the High Rabbinic Court to the district rabbinic courts in these matters are — not to arrange a get under such circumstance until the tort claim is dismissed. . . .

I must note that the solution of having the complaint [dismissed by the family court] does not resolve the problem completely. What happens if a woman withdraws her petition in the family court and declares to the rabbinic court that she has no claims against her husband and then, subsequently, she sues for damages after the get for the years that she was anchored? This raises anew a different question, this time the halakhic question of the "fraudulently induced get"! . . .

It appeared that after the High Court of Justice's decision in the Matter of Felman (written by the current president of that court), the jurisdictional battle between the rabbinic courts and its fellow civil courts has quieted down. The rules of reciprocity in jurisdictional matters were defined and framed in such ways that were clear and fixed, and thus resolved and settled, in most circumstances, the trials and tribulations that had been the lot of the judicial system that dealt with family laws, in general.

But to my regret, with the proliferation of the phenomenon of damages claims with regard to personal status we are reverting to the "Dark Ages" of jurisdictional struggles and wars. Only this time, the war has taken on a more severe shape. We are no longer dealing with preliminary matters regarding *judicial authority to decide questions that are ancillary to divorce*, but with something much worse. We are dealing here with a struggle over the *authority to adjudicate*, and over the very existence and validity of rulings that were made, or will be made, by a rabbinic court in matters of divorce.

Unfortunately, this is not just any battle, but, on the contrary, it is a "world war." From a pure halakhic perspective, we are dealing here with the most serious and substantive issues of personal status — the validity of the get and the fear of mamzerut. If this difficult phenomenon of damages suits proliferates and expands without clear barriers, who can foresee where all this will end?

The old legal debate with respect to the battle over jurisdiction affected only the issue of reciprocity between the different courts with respect to matters ancillary to the divorce, and nothing else. The current debate regarding these damages claims will, first and foremost, cause irreversible damage precisely to women. Such a woman who thinks her salvation will come from a particular step that will help release her from her husband brings upon herself, with her own hands, just the complete opposite result, like a boomerang that flies back at her and completely closes off any solution in the way of divorce.

It is like the proverb of two persons who grasp at one prayer shawl: one person says it's all mine; the other claims it's all mine. One pulls from this side, and the other pulls from that side until the prayer shawl tears. . . . One court grabs the get and its antagonist grabs damages claims, and the woman is torn between them. She may win damages, but not the get. Money instead of freedom.

It would be appropriate if the Supreme Court would make a determination in this matter, as it did in the past with regard to [the race to] jurisdiction. And it would seem to be proper that this be done in coordination with the High Rabbinic Court, since we are dealing here with an issue that, at its core, is of a purely halakhic nature.

Ariel Yanai, Rabbinic Judge

The husband was never ordered to give a get, and he certainly does not have the status of a get refuser. With regard to tort claims [for get refusal] filed outside the rabbinic courts, this court has twice issued its opinion in two decisions rendered by the High Rabbinic Court, case 7041-21-1 and 8455-64-1, in which it sets forth the halakhic problems and mishaps that such cases can cause.

The instruction is clear and the halakha is clear, and there is no other apart from it, that a get will not be arranged until the complaint is dismissed.

The giving of a get is in the sole jurisdiction of this rabbinic court. Any person who supports this type of activity [filing of tort claims] chains a woman with such actions.

This court will do everything in its power not to injure the "vineyard of Israel" [a metaphor for the wholeness and purity of the Jewish people] as a result of the delivery of a forced divorce that is void, and whose consequences lead to mamzerut and the destruction of the family unit and, by itself, causes damage to the vineyard of Israel. This is the opinion of this court and the opinion of our Holy Torah. The court is not looking to any outside source for guidance on this matter. There is a presumption that anyone who is involved in this matter is aware of its consequences. May God circumscribe the infractions of Israel. The above is my humble opinion on the matter, and may God save me from any errors. Amen.

Michael Amos, Head of the Tribunal

In summary, the husband is not anchoring his wife. The wife's request to order her husband to give a get was denied, and this court recommended that the couple divorce by agreement. To our regret, the defendant has not shown any flexibility that will allow for the final disposition of the [marital] property and prefers to continue the legal fight and to even file a new claim in the guise of a petition for damages against the husband.

Given on this day, the 18th day of Shevat 5771 (23.1.2011):

Rabbi Michael Amos (Head);
Rabbi Shnuer Pardes; and
Rabbi Areil Yanai (*L. v. L.*, 2011)

Armed with this decision declaring that he is not a get refuser, incredible as it may appear to any objective observer, Avner filed it with the family court as a defense against Nava's claim that he owes her damages for get refusal. In addition, he used it, at the recommendation of his attorney, to support a claim against Nava (!) for damages in the amount of 1.4 million shekels (the same amount that Nava sued for in the family court) for get refusal, which he filed in April 2011 in the rabbinic court. Quoting the rabbinic court decision stating that Nava is anchoring herself, Avner claimed that Nava is the one responsible for the stymied divorce proceedings and should pay *him* for the ensuing damages. Since Avner had never filed for divorce, the rabbinic court informed him that he needed to open a file asking Nava to accept a get so that the court could claim jurisdiction over his damages suit as a matter "ancillary" to the divorce. Nava moved to dismiss the case for lack of jurisdiction. She informed the court that she was willing and ready to accept the get.

CWJ agreed to represent Nava in her defense against Avner's damages suit and on June 29, 2011, the entire legal staff — Susan Weiss, Yifat Frankenburg, and Rivkah Lubitch — drove to Haifa. They had prepared extensive arguments for the court and felt that Nava needed all of them there. The tribunal opened the hearing with a statement to the effect that the parties should waive each other's claims for damages and get divorced. Not about to see their second claim go the way of the first one, the CWJ attorneys were not inclined to agree. But Nava was willing to give it one more try. She really did want a get. After deliberation, CWJ staff told the court that Nava would agree, but only if the get was delivered there and then and only if a document was signed that stated clearly that the agreement to dismiss the damages claim was contingent on the giving of the get on that very day. Avner asked that Judge Biton authorize the agreement before he underwent the ceremony.

Rivkah and Nava ran back and forth from the family court to the rabbinic court to put all the pieces in place. The agreement read as follows: "The parties are honored to inform this honorable court that they have reached an agreement that [Nava's damages suit] will be dismissed with prejudice, subject to the arrangement of a get today. The honorable court is asked to authorize this agreement and give it the status of a legal judgment."

Judge Biton was flabbergasted at what she saw. Using exactly the same language that the rabbinic court had disallowed in 2006 and had ruled in 2011 was halakhically improper, the new agreement clearly linked the divorce to the dismissal of the tort claim and stated in no uncertain terms that the dismissal would *not* be effective until *after* the delivery of the get. "Did the rabbinic court confirm this language?" Biton asked. Yes, Rivkah told her, and so Biton complied with the request. It took one more day. But Avner Levi and Nava Levi were now finally divorced.

CWJ attorneys were disappointed that more than five years of work did not end in an important legal decision. They had hoped that the case would reiterate that damages for get abuse were not dependent on a rabbinic court decision obligating a husband to give a divorce, a proposition accepted by family court judges Greenberger, HaCohen, and Felix of the Jerusalem Family Court (*K. v. K.*, 2008; *T. v. T.*, 2007; *Plonit v. Ploni (HaCohen)*, 2010; *K. S. v. K. S.*, 2011), as well as by Judge Sivan of the Tel Aviv Family Court in 2008 (*N. v. N.*, 2008). They had hoped that the court would award significant damages to Nava, including exemplary damages, because of Avner's gross bad faith in breaching three promises to give a get, a record even for CWJ cases. And, most important, they had wanted to make it clear that get abuse was never reasonable or justifiable, or an act of mere "negligence," but intentional, violent and emotionally distressful, in direct violation of the Law against Family Violence, as well as the Basic Law of Human Dignity and Liberty. And, perhaps, they thought, this case might indeed initiate the inevitable, direct confrontation between civil and religious courts that would lead to the necessary reforms that would protect women. CWJ attorneys felt that they had exchanged a treasure for a sack of potatoes. Nava, however, was thrilled. "I really did not want him to be left with nothing," she told us. "He is the father of my children, after all."

SIX

The Reluctant Agunah

I had a civil marriage and I had a choice back then, so
How come I have none now, when I want it all to end?
How come I have no choice? It makes no sense to me!
Why am I on the steps of the beit din rabbani?!
I don't care about the dayanim,
'cuz I have my haverim
Who will dance and sing with me
And remind me that there's life outside the beit din rabbani
Outside the beit din rabbani
And who'll dance and sing with me,
On the steps of the beit din, on the steps of the beit din, rabbaniiiiiiiiiiii

Vered Shavit, YouTube video

What's astonishing about Efrat's case is that even though she didn't marry through the rabbinate, she nonetheless became an agunah. However briefly, reluctantly, and inadvertently, she had put herself at the mercy of the rabbis by getting married — albeit in a civil ceremony — instead of just living with the man she eventually had to divorce.

Efrat Ben-David and Yoav Kaplan are both kosher Israeli Jews who could have married in an Orthodox ceremony in Israel. Their Jewishness was not in question. They were not converts. Neither was a child of a mother's extramari-

---

The epigraph, translated roughly from Hebrew, is from a YouTube clip with Vered Shavit and her friends on the steps of the Tel Aviv Rabbinic Court, reworking the Israeli oldie, "I'll Dance on the Steps of the Rabbinate," by Amnon Dankner.

tal affair, a mamzer. And even if Yoav were a kohen, a member of the priestly caste, which he is not, Efrat was not a divorcee, another of the unions forbidden under halakha. But instead of standing under a chuppah and being married by an Orthodox rabbi, they chose, of their own free will and conscience, to marry in Cyprus in a civil ceremony devoid of any religious aspects or allusions and to later have a Reform wedding in Israel, just so friends and family could celebrate with them. And they didn't even bother to register either marriage with the Ministry of the Interior.

Still, when it came to ending her marriage, Efrat could not avoid finding herself, like Vered Shavit (see epigraph) on the steps of the rabbinic courts — the beit din rabbani. And, although at a certain point both she and Yoav asked the court to dissolve their marriage with a judicial pronouncement rather than require them to undergo a get ceremony, the court refused. The rabbis ruled that the rite was required under halakha and that halakha is the law of the land when it comes to divorce in the State of Israel. And when Yoav balked, they showed him very clearly who is in control.

While she was going through the mandatory motions of the divorce, Efrat related to the process as if she had been caught up in some medieval play, rather than as a serious, contemporary, legal event. Today, with the episode behind her and thinking back to her university political science classes, she has grasped the implications of the act in which she was forced to take part. Beyond the gross infringement on her personal freedom of conscience, what happened to her and Yoav is an example of how a state, guided by the word of God (as interpreted by the rabbis) can use its almost unlimited power to invade the private lives of its citizens and force them to perform religious acts for the purpose of the routine regulation of their private lives; what is more, it appropriates public funds to pay judges, police, and petty bureaucrats to that end.

"I can't believe this is happening in modern Israel," says Efrat. "I'm horrified."

Born in Tel Aviv, Efrat, a gregarious, dark-haired amateur pastry chef who collects gourmet cookbooks, grew up in a dusty small town in the heart of the Negev Desert. Her parents ran a llama farm, where vacationers on the way to the Red Sea resort of Eilat were encouraged to stop and watch the "curious and amazing life habits" of the llamas. But besides the llamas, Efrat tells us, nothing much happened. Eventually, her parents would separate. "My father was active outside the marriage," she explains. Her mother moved with Efrat and her little brother to Eilat, where she worked as special education teacher. Her father stayed on the farm, enjoying the company of other women, in particular those of tourists who sought temporary employment with him. Her parents were separated for five years before her father agreed to give her mother a get.

At eighteen, Efrat, like most Israeli youth, was drafted into the army. She became a communications officer in an intelligence unit. She met Yoav, a party and event planner, who sported an impressive set of dreadlocks and an engaging case of attention deficit disorder, at a five-year reunion celebration he organized for her army unit. At the time, she was twenty-five and completing her first degree in political science at Ben-Gurion University of the Negev in Beersheba. He was thirty and had no college education. They came from completely different backgrounds — he was the son of German-Polish Ashkenazim, and she was the daughter of Sephardim from Turkey and Bukhara — but they hit it off and moved in together a few months after they met. It was an impetuous mistake, Efrat now admits, eight years later. "Yes, I loved him," she concedes, "his ready laugh, his guitar, and his almost childlike enthusiasm. Most of all, I loved that he was, well, unconventional."

In 2003 Efrat thought that marriage was an unnecessary, outdated, and bureaucratic institution. With her mother's experience looming somewhere in the background of her consciousness, she also knew that she wanted nothing to do with the rabbinate. She and Yoav were living together happily in a small rented apartment in Beersheba. Why get married? But two people were pressuring her to cement their relationship — Yoav, who was becoming more "spiritual," in the New Age sense of the word and, curiously enough, her mother, who despite her own less-than-successful marriage and divorce was, according to Efrat, "conservative and conventional." She wanted to see her daughter's relationship with Yoav consolidated and formalized in a Jewish way.

With time Efrat relented and agreed to a ceremony conducted by a Reform rabbi in Israel (which has no legal validity in the Jewish state) and a civil marriage in Cyprus (which does). She would have happily forgone the Cypriot ceremony altogether and made do with the Reform one, but at that time the civil marriage was an express prerequisite of the rabbi, designated by the Movement for Progressive Judaism, to officiate at the wedding. He explained if they were married in a civil ceremony registered by the Ministry of the Interior, this act alone would give them the rights afforded married couples by the social security services, tax authorities, the Ministry of Housing, and all the health care organizations (Center for Pluralistic Judaism, n.d., p. 4). Such rights are not automatic for people in common-law partnerships, who must somehow prove their status to the authorities rather than just simply produce a marriage certificate. Yoav arranged for the civil wedding in Cyprus by himself and, together with Efrat's mother, organized the religious ceremony, as well as the details of the celebrations. "I had nothing to do with the planning of either," Efrat says proudly.

Cyprus is a popular destination for Israelis and citizens of other countries who want to marry in quick, civil ceremonies. Interfaith marriages are routinely performed in that eastern Mediterranean island, only 260 miles and an hour's flight away from Israel. Thousands of Israelis go there to get married, some go because halakha (and thus Israeli law) prohibits their marriage in their own land, while others, like Efrat and Yoav, simply cannot tolerate the idea of having anything to do with the rabbinate. Still others go because they belong to different faiths and intermarriages of any kind cannot be performed in Israel (see introduction). In late June 2011 the *Jerusalem Post* reported that 154 Israeli couples were married in a mass ceremony in a medieval fortress in Lanarca, Cyrpus, in an attempt to get into the Guinness Book of World Records category for mass marriages (*Jerusalem Post*, 2011).

Efrat's mother's father and his father before him were rabbis in Turkey. She wanted her daughter to have a Jewish ceremony, though she was willing to forgo it being Orthodox. It just had to look Orthodox. "God only knows why. To appease her elderly aunts, I think," says Efrat with a laugh. The wedding took place in the spring of 2003 on the llama farm, with music supplied by two D.J.'s and Yoav's favorite jazz band, and organic cuisine conjured up by a Tel Aviv caterer and served by Beduin youth from the vicinity. Her mother, despite her initial hesitation, agreed to walk Efrat to the chuppah with her ex-husband. Only two hundred guests attended, a small wedding by Israeli standards. Probably only a few guests, if any, realized that the marriage was considered invalid. "Most of the guests had no idea they were even at a Reform wedding," says Efrat. "The ceremonies are very similar. Only the rabbi had no beard. Also, I left out a few customs. I refused to have Yoav break the glass [to commemorate the destruction of the Temple], and I didn't circle him [to indicate that I was now entering into his domain]. Nobody noticed," she told us. "Otherwise, it looked and felt the same as an Orthodox wedding. And of course, we danced the hora."

By contrast, Efrat's "valid" Cypriot wedding was a sterile, lonely affair, wanting for friends and family. It took place in a local municipal building, she thinks. Efrat wore a white blouse and a skirt, but cannot remember too many details. "We each read texts in English in front of a Cypriot marriage officer," she recalls blandly. "I didn't pay much attention to what we were saying. There was no great emotion. We exchanged rings. The whole thing took five minutes." While they were waiting to be summoned by the officer, five Israeli couples were wed. Four more were waiting in line when they left.

Efrat and Yoav returned to Israel and to what they then thought was an enchanted, fluid lifestyle — Yoav to his random parties and Efrat to her freelance work editing academic articles. But the allure of their carefree years soon dissolved. Quarreling all the time and with a baby on the way, Efrat began to question the life strategies and values of the man with whom she shared her bed. She needed some more order and predictability. What had appeared carefree and flexible now seemed immature and reckless. When their son was born in 2004, Yoav was happy to embrace fatherhood but was still "finding himself," spiritually and professionally. Efrat did not work during the pregnancy and money was tight. Disgruntled that Yoav was not taking more responsibility and worried that they may not be able to meet their bills, Efrat says that the marriage unraveled further when the couple argued over issues such as whether the baby should be allowed to sleep in the parental bed (Efrat, yes; Yoav, no) or placed in a day care center when he was six months old (Efrat, yes; Yoav, no). When Efrat decided to take steady work as an executive secretary in a local high-tech company, Yoav, she says, took this as a sign for him to work less. "We had a lot of expenses and very little income. I became embittered, angry, neglectful of my physical appearance and a terrible mother." Worse, Yoav was straying from his secular roots and becoming religious. "I couldn't relate," she says.

Like many couples whose marriages were in trouble, Efrat and Yoav decided that another child might bring them closer and cure their troubles. A strategy of despair, it failed. They couldn't even agree on their most basic hopes: Yoav wanted another son, and Efrat hoped for a daughter. The baby girl's arrival in 2007, however blessed, didn't save the marriage. By the time she was two, the couple had moved to a bigger home, taken on more debt, and become irrevocably estranged. Eight months of couple's therapy didn't change a thing.

One day, in January 2009 Efrat came home to find Yoav stretched out on the couch watching a reality show on T.V., dirty baby clothes strewn all over the living room floor. Almost without raising his head from the television set, he asked her what was for dinner, and she told him, rather ungently, that if he wanted to eat, he could "pick up his lazy, fat, indulgent ass off the couch and make something for himself." Or better yet, something for the two of them. Infuriated and humiliated, he grabbed her cell phone, car keys, and her personal diary and threw them out the living room window. In shock, she retreated into the bedroom. It was raining outside and, in what she interpreted as an act of remorse, Yoav went to retrieve the items. When he came back up to the apartment, he called her to come out of the room. She thought he wanted to apologize and hand back her things, but instead, she tells us, he head butted her, bent her fingers back, and slapped her face, acts he later denied. Stunned and in pain, Efrat filed a police complaint. Yoav filed a countercomplaint. In the end, the police believed her and Efrat received a court order directing Yoav to leave the house. And like the other unhappy couples of whose crumbling marriages and woeful lives we have told, Efrat and Yoav now communicated through the courts and third parties.

In Court

With Yoav out of the house, Efrat started thinking about putting her life back together and retrieving some sense of peace and personal happiness. But first she needed to define the borders that would separate her life from Yoav's, especially insofar as the children were concerned; she realized she needed an attorney. She hired Tanya Greenfield, a vocal young women's rights activist who used no makeup and had a liking for silver jewelry — she wore bangles that covered most of her left forearm and Efrat wondered if she slept with them on — who had been recommended by Naamat, one of Israel's leading women's organizations. In February 2009 they filed for custody and child support in the Beersheba Family Court, located in a modern government complex that houses all of the city's courts, including the rabbinic courts.

The Ben-David versus Kaplan case was assigned to Judge Tamara Weisenfeld, a no-nonsense, well-coiffed, sharp-tongued woman who had a successful private practice before being appointed to the bench. Sick of running after her clients for her fees and wrangling with other divorce attorneys, Weisenfeld was happy to be in a position where she could make decisions. She knew what she was doing and understood that in this case she was dealing with a man whose hurt pride would not allow him to be reasonable about anything. She appointed a social worker to take a close look at the family, awarded temporary custody and temporary child support to Efrat, and gave Yoav generous visitation rights that he nonetheless found wanting. In protest, he stopped visiting the children altogether and discontinued all child support.

At a hearing for child support, the designated social worker testified that it was her opinion that, among other things, the couple needed to end their marriage with a divorce, for their sake and for the sake of the children. Over Yoav's protests that he would never divorce Efrat, Weisenfeld asked the parties if steps had been taken to advance that end. When they said no, she recommended that the couple file for divorce in the Beersheba Rabbinic Court. "But no one knows that I'm even married," Efrat objected to Tanya. "My I.D. card states that I am single, and I got married in a Reform ceremony in Israel and a civil one in Cyprus. Not an Orthodox one. Why do I need to get divorced at all? And if I must go to court, why do I have to go to a rabbinic one? Can't the family court decide this?"

"No," Tanya told her. "Family courts have nothing to say in this matter. Only the rabbinic courts have jurisdiction over divorce. It doesn't matter how you married. And just because you neglected to register your Cypriot marriage doesn't mean that it did not happen. It just means that it wasn't recorded. If you want to marry someone else, whether here or outside of Israel, you cannot declare that you are single and free to marry, and if you did, you would be lying and any marriage you entered into would be bigamous, or polyandrous, to be more exact, and illegal. You need a divorce."

"What if I don't want to marry anyone else?" Efrat wondered.

"You need a divorce, Efrat." Tanya told her. "Like Judge Weisenfeld said. For your sake. The kids' sake. And for the sake of any man you might meet who, like most persons, would not want to start up with a married woman. Also, so long as you are married, Yoav and you are connected. You need to separate. But I'm hoping it will go pretty quickly for you. The rabbinic courts don't like Jewish Israelis who go to Cyprus to get married. The rabbis will just say that you are not married and that will be the end of it."

On December 1, 2009, less than a year after Yoav left their apartment and with the ancillary suits regarding custody and child support neatly filed and under way in the family court, Efrat sued for a get in the rabbinic court, claiming physical and emotional violence as the basis for her petition.

In the Rabbinic Court

On February 2, 2010, two short months after Tanya filed Efrat's papers, the rabbinic court held a hearing on her request for a get. Yoav appeared, represented by a novice attorney who apparently had no nuanced understanding of halakha or of the rabbinic court. Thinking that he would impress the tribunal of his client's good will and turn them against Efrat, he informed the court that Yoav wanted a reconciliation, but that Efrat had told him, "Go look for other women. I've already been with other men." But rather than endear Yoav to the court, this pronouncement affirmed what it seems the rabbis already presumed when they were presented with a Jewish couple who had willfully and purposefully violated halakha and married in a civil ceremony abroad—that this was a couple with no fear of God or sense of faithfulness to each other, who would, if the marriage did not end quickly, fornicate and might produce illegitimate, mamzer children. Not impressed that the marriage had a future, the court, on the spot, recommended that the couple get divorced "and the sooner the better."

In addition, the rabbis told Yoav at that first hearing that he could not, as he requested in writing and orally, predicate his agreement to divorce on the resolution of whatever financial claims he may have or on any custody demands he may have with respect to the children. "One has nothing to do with the other," they told him emphatically. And, they added, although the court would give him more time to file a defense to Efrat's petition, this would not stay their decision that he must give a get immediately. They set a date for the delivery of the bill of divorce for one month hence and warned Yoav and his attorney that they had better show up.

At the hearing held on March 11, 2010, three short months after Efrat filed for divorce, Yoav came and said, "Yes, but . . ." *Yes*, I will give a get, but I want to wait until after the family court cases have ended. In stark contrast to how the court responded to such procrastination and excuses in all the other cases described in this book, the rabbinic court was not moved. Incensed, the judges saw this as a rejection of their recommendation. They wrote, "The goal of the husband is to gain time in order to improve the financial terms he anticipates receiving from the family court. So it doesn't matter to him if he anchors his wife for an indefinite period of time (since everybody knows these things take a long time in family court and don't finish in a matter of days). This court will take no part in this." The tribunal then issued a ruling "obligating" Yoav to divorce Efrat. In support of its decision it cited a responsum of Rabbeinu Yerucham ben Meshulam (1290–1350) regarding the obligation to divorce when both parties have rejected each other. It also expressed the opinion of the court that there was absolutely no possibility of restoring peace and harmony between the couple and added, "The parties are not married to each other in accordance with the laws of Moses and Israel, only civilly. And the opinion of the authorities regarding obliging (and even compelling) a get on parties who were married in civil ceremonies is well known. There are no obstacles to obligating a get, as this has been set forth in rabbinic court decisions. Though in the above case, there is reason for obligating a get even without this fact" (B. v. K. [1], 2010).

In a later decision, the court would quote this decision and expand on the reasons for compelling a husband to give a get in cases in which a couple had married civilly, citing a number of hoary authorities and ignoring more modern contrary ones (see introduction and *Plonit v. Ploni [Benai Noah]*, 2003). The judges quoted extensively from the Rema, a sixteenth-century commentary on the authoritative codex of Jewish law known as the Shulkhan Aruch, written in 1563 (see introduction). One such circumstance was if a man divorces his wife with a kosher get and then questions its validity (at Even Haezer, 154, no. 21). (But in the case in chapter 3, where the husband did exactly this, the court did not so compel him.) Other examples include the following: if a man says, "I betrothed you," and the woman says, "I was not betrothed" (Even Ha'ezer, 48, no. 6); if a halakhic betrothal might have occurred but it is not certain that it did (*safek*) (Even Ha'ezer, 42, no. 8); and if a man betroths a woman prohibited to him and to other men (Even Ha'ezer, 154, at the end of no. 7 in the name of the Rosh), referring also to the Bet Shmuel, a seventeenth-century commentary on Shulkan Aruch, written by Rabbi Shmuel Ben Ari Schraga Feibush (at Even Ha'ezer, 42, no. 18). And, the court added, this was the position taken in numerous Israeli rabbinic court decisions that deal specifically with cases in which couples married in civil ceremonies and there was the possibility that halakhic betrothals might have occurred (*safeq kiddushin*) (see, e.g., IsrRabCt 3:374; B. v. K. [2], 2010).

What's more, added the court, if Yoav continued to refuse to deliver a get, it would impose penalties on him, subject, of course, to the filing of a motion requesting the same. A month later when Efrat had not yet filed such a motion, the court specifically ordered her to do so. The problem was that Efrat did not want to file such a motion. "I hated Yoav's guts more than anything else in the world and thought his religious posturing was pathetic. But the last thing I wanted to do was to put him in jail," she tells us. "He is, after all, the father of my children."

Tanya suggested that they consult with the Center for Women's Justice rabbinic pleader Rivkah Lubitch to see what options they might have. Tanya herself had taken care of a few clients who married abroad and then divorced, but in their cases the rabbinic court had simply declared that they were never married. Tanya was not sure she understood what was happening. Together they took the two-and-a-half-hour train ride from Beersheba to Haifa, where Rivkah shared an office with the Emil Touma Institute for Palestinian and Israeli Studies in a beautiful but deteriorating building in Haifa's German Colony.

Rivkah explained to them that prior to 2006 the status of Israeli Jewish couples who chose to marry in a civil ceremony abroad had been unclear. Questions abounded. Though the Ministry of the Interior would register such marriages for statistical purposes, were they otherwise valid? Who had jurisdiction over such marriages if a couple sought divorce? What cause of action would justify such divorces? What obligations did spouses who married in a civil ceremony have to each other? Prior to 2006 Jewish couples who married abroad in civil ceremonies, or even in non-Orthodox religious ceremonies, and who appeared in rabbinic court to get divorced had a number of options. Those who had married in countries where religious marriages were banned, like in the former Soviet Union, were often told that they needed to undergo the get ceremony. Those, who could have married in an Orthodox ceremony and chose not to, like Efrat and Yoav, or who had married in Reform (and sometimes even Conservative) ceremonies, were often told that they were not married halakhically and that therefore they did not need a get. It was as if their marriages were void ab initio and had never occurred at all.

In 2006 former chief justice Aharon Barak was presented with the opportunity to force the rabbinic court system to put its house in legal order with respect to the problem of civil marriages and divorce. A woman whose Cyprus marriage had been declared void in an Israeli rabbinic court appealed to the Supreme Court to vacate the rabbinic court judgment. She was, she argued, married. The rabbinic court could not simply say it never happened, relegating her marriage in Cyprus, not to mention her subsequent Reform ceremony, to legal dust. Her argument resonated with Barak. After all, from Barak's perspective, it cannot be that a judicial arm of a modern Western democratic state would refuse to acknowledge marriages entered into in accordance with the laws of a foreign jurisdiction. Just as Israel would expect a foreign county (the United States, for example) to recognize the marriages entered into in Israel in accordance with its laws, the foreign jurisdiction has every reason to expect Israel to recognize the marriages of couples entered into in accordance with its laws. Reciprocity is, at the very least, good legal manners.

But before Barak settled matters, which would probably have required him to declare that Israeli family courts take jurisdiction over civil marriages entered into between persons of the same faith, he sent the case back to the rabbinic court for further review. Senior rabbinic judge Shlomo Dichovsky saved the day, at least for the rabbinic courts. He declared that halakha recognizes the validity of civil marriages, which he said were marriages "*k'bnai noah*," like the Sons of Noah. Such Noahide marriages are not void ab initio, and, he added, it is the rabbinic courts that have jurisdiction to determine under what circumstances they would be dissolved. Interestingly, and coincidentally, he decided that a court could dissolve a Noahide marriage when it had "irretrievably broken down." Such dissolution would occur by court decision and did not (necessarily) require a get. This satisfied Barak, for the moment at least. It also satisfied the Attorney General's Office, which had been asked by Barak to join the case, since it "raised important and significant issues." They embraced the idea as a way for Israeli citizens married in civil ceremonies to get divorced "without one side holding up the other" (*Plonit v. Tel Aviv Rabbinic Court (civil marriage)*, 2006, p. 19). And it certainly satisfied the rabbis, because it kept the issue of civil marriages between Jews within the walls of the rabbinic courts.

Relying on the Barak/Dichovsky decisions, Rivkah suggested to Tanya and Efrat that they return to the court and refuse to undergo the get ceremony. "Just ask for a declaration of the court that your marriage has irretrievably broken down and that it is therefore dissolved by court order," Rivkah told them. "In fact, this is exactly what the court decided in its March decision. There is no reason whatsoever that you need to go through a get ceremony. Here, take this decision of the High Rabbinic Court and show it to the tribunal." With that, she handed her Rabbi Dichovsky's decision, referred to in the parlance of those in the divorce business as the "Benai Noah" decision (*Plonit v. Ploni [Benai Noah]*, 2003).

In a hearing held on September 6, 2010, Tanya presented Efrat's request that she divorce by decree and not by get. The rabbinic court rejected her request, emphatically saying, "It is the opinion of this court that it is still possible to arrange a get between the parties and not to go the route of dissolution. Open a file for punitive orders," they declared, "including incarceration." Yoav, who did not quite understand what Efrat was asking for, having appeared in court without counsel, was still speaking like a man who had married his wife in an Orthodox ceremony and was holding all the cards. He demanded his "rights" and told the court that he was being "forced" to give a get. He also told the court, in a not very endearing fashion, that he was willing to sit in jail and appeal any decision made to that end. The court ignored him and ruled, "This court heard the arguments and responses of the sides and has decided that there is no room to give a decision declaring the dissolution of this marriage. We must go the route of restrictive orders."

In December 2010, one year after Efrat had sued for divorce in the rabbinic court, Yoav still had not yet delivered the get. But by this time both he and Efrat agreed that a declaration of the court stating that the marriage had irretrievably broken down and was therefore dissolved would be enough. In a hearing held on December 16, he informed the court that although he was not willing to deliver a get to Efrat, he was now willing for the court to declare his marriage over. He told the court, "I cannot divorce a woman that I am not married to." (Or, in other words, what Yoav was saying to the rabbis was, "I do not have to divorce my wife with a get if I did not marry her halakhically and she is not bound to me under the religious notion of *kiddushin*.")

Not impressed, the tribunal issued a ruling declaring that Yoav was "compelled" to give his wife a get and should be immediately arrested until he is willing to do so. They added, "He is to be imprisoned for periods that are measured and limited, in accordance with the discretion of his court, so that we can examine, at the end of each period, if there has been a change in his position." Repeating its holding of March 2010, in its expanded version, the court explained that, even in cases of civil marriage, it is their opinion that a get must be given. Following is an excerpt from the judgment:

In the hearing held on December 16, 2010, the husband's attorney argued that [the husband] was not willing to give a get but was willing that his marriage be dissolved. In her opinion, "A husband cannot divorce a wife that he is not married to," and [she] even repeated this argument a number of times. This court made it clear to the husband's attorney that his personal conscience and motivations are irrelevant, and he must give his wife a get. This court recommended that his attorney try to persuade him outside the courtroom to give his wife the desired get, but he stated immediately, "It's a waste of your time. There is no chance that I will give a get." The wife's attorney repeated her old request to annul and dissolve the marriage. The husband's attorney added, "The husband states — there is no chance that I will give a get, even if one day I may have to sit in jail. So long as I am alive I will not give a get. It's better to dissolve the marriage so that the wife is not an agunah. The wife also wants a dissolution."

. . . It is possible that the husband wants to anchor his wife, but when he adds that he is willing for the court to dissolve his marriage and not to compel him to divorce, it is possible that he has alternative motivations, motivations that are not entirely clear to this court. . . .

. . . And now that the husband is willing to free his wife of the bonds of her anchorage through the dissolution of her marriage, we cannot let him "hide" behind emotional considerations of one kind or another so that he does not deliver a get to his wife. The court cannot let a man "control matters" in a file, without a court being able to assess the nature of his argument and his motivation.

When we have to decide between the two possibilities before us, compelling a get or dissolving a marriage, this court prefers compulsion, for this reason: quite a few authorities think that civil marriage has halakhic validity, in one way or another. Rabbinic courts have taken the position that a get must be given in cases of civil marriage and have not left the matter to the will of the parties that this court declare their marriage over.

Though we are aware that in the case that a woman is anchored, it is possible to dissolve civil marriages without a get, but it is our opinion that in the case before us it is not yet a "situation of anchorage."

The court then proceeded to explain why a prison sentence was not so bad, more the equivalent of the ostracism condoned by Rabbeinu Tam (see introduction) than beating a man with whips or chaining him so he cannot move around, as he may have been so compelled to give a get in days of yore:

Though he cannot walk around freely in Israeli prisons, his bread and water is provided, consistently and with certainty (*B. v. K.* [2], 2010).

Yoav was imprisoned on Wednesday, December 22, 2010. He sat in jail over Shabbat and gave a get to Efrat on Sunday, December 26, 2010, four days later. A full get ceremony was conducted.

And although Efrat's story ended more quickly and swiftly than all our others, its implications reverberate in new and ominous directions that expand the jurisdiction of the rabbinic court and its religious laws beyond its current purview.

By insisting that Efrat needed a get, the rabbinic court caused harm to Efrat, Yoav, and Israeli Jewish men and women who choose to marry in civil ceremonies and, perhaps even worse, to Jewish men and women in the Diaspora who have married in civil ceremonies for decades. Though Diaspora rabbinic courts need not, and do not necessarily, follow Israeli rabbinic court rulings, there is a lot of cross-fertilization, with Israeli rabbinic courts and chief rabbis demanding and commanding the upper hand and final word in deference to the status and power extended them by the Israeli state. This dynamic has been well documented with respect to conversion (Newhouse, 2010). The only interests served by this rabbinic court decision were its own.

It harmed Efrat because she remained married to Yoav for twelve months after she sued for divorce and seven months after the court had held, in March 2010, that her marriage had "irretrievably broken down" and that there was no chance of reconciliation. It was at that point that the court, drawing on the Barak-Dichovsky decisions, could have declared the Ben-David–Kaplan marriage over. Instead, blaming Yoav for buying time to better his financial position, the court declared that he was "obligated" to give Efrat a get. Though Yoav gave the get shortly after he was imprisoned, there is no assurance that he would have done so or how long it would have taken. Nor is it at all clear if and when the court would have decided that no get was needed and that the marriage was dissolved. Efrat could have remained, like our agunah in chapter 5, anchored forever by state decree. By insisting that Efrat need a get, the court also infringed on her freedom of conscience to marry and divorce in the way she saw fit, without religious connotations, far away from the steps of the rabbinic court.

It harmed Yoav because he was put in jail and his most basic liberty was curtailed simply because the state had the power to do so. It could have declared
in a straightforward and uncomplicated manner that his marriage to Efrat was
over and dissolved, leaving Yoav free to plan parties or lounge around to his
heart's content and saving money that the state spent instead on numerous
court hearings, police, and prison wardens who have better things to do with
their time.

It harmed Israeli Jewish couples who, like Efrat and Yoav, and our You
Tube star, Vered Shavit, and her ex-husband, did not want to find themselves
on the steps of the beit din rabbani, subject to the dictates of halakha and the
one-sided veto of a recalcitrant spouse who could anchor the other.

And it has harmed Jewish men and women in the Diaspora who for decades
have been marrying and divorcing without the interference of a Jewish court
and without thinking that they might need to worry about a get, or the possible implications of the lack of one on their children. Thus, the decision of
the rabbinic court to incarcerate Yoav rather than declare his civil marriage
dissolved seems to have raised unnecessary questions regarding the capacity
of Jews worldwide to marry one another without worrying about whether one's
future spouse's agnostic grandmother did, or did not, obtain a Jewish divorce
before remarrying and giving birth to her or his mother.

Moreover, this unfortunate decision has served only the rabbinic courts in
their quest to strengthen their jurisdictional grip on the marital status of all
Israeli Jews, wherever performed, with all the concomitant jobs required; to
expound and apply the fundamentals of Jewish law as set forth by its tenets
throughout the land and beyond (in its newfound "churchlike" status); and to
have the ultimate say on who is in and who is out of the Jewish people (see
introduction).

When Chief Justice Barak sent the rabbinic court decision declaring the
Cypriot/Reform marriage void back to the rabbinic court in 2003, he did so in
an attempt to find a way to prevent a rift between the civil and religious courts
(*Plonit v. Tel Aviv Rabbinic Court [civil marriage]*, 2006, p. 30). He sighed with
relief when Rabbi Dichovsky presented him with the Benai Noah decision.
Here was a way to save face. Secular Israelis could have their civil marriage and
civil divorce too, and the rabbinic courts would not have their power usurped
or threatened but rather enlarged to embrace a new, modern, liberal halakha
reflective of the modern world and changing times. What happened instead

was that the rabbinic court readily took jurisdiction over these cases, thus serving its political interest to impose its laws and will over the largest number of people, but it refused to apply modern terms for divorce, as suggested by Dichovsky and applauded by Barak and the Attorney General's Office — and as understood as well by academics and activists who read the groundbreaking decisions (Lifshitz, 2009). As a result of decisions like the one given in this case, the Center for Pluralistic Judaism (Reform Movement) is currently reevaluating its recommendations regarding getting married in civil ceremonies abroad. Instead, quoting authorities who literally lived in the Middle Ages, long before civil marriages were ever instituted, the rabbinic court left the ultimate say over the dissolution of the marriage in the patriarchal hands of recalcitrant husbands, over whom, it seems, the court may be all the more willing to impose its political police power.

SEVEN

Human Rights Violations in Israeli Rabbinic Courts

_____

After nearly sixty years of statehood, the rift between Israel's religious
and secular publics has never been more intense. The policy of giving
the Orthodox control over non-Orthodox Jew's marriages, divorces
and burials may have had some success in maintaining ethno-racial
unity . . . but this success pales in comparison to the policy's utter failure
to consolidate the Israeli Jewish nation into a people that sees itself as
a unified whole. Racial unity is a tenuous glue for religious groups. It
purchases nominal unity — the ability of a particular group of people to
be considered "Jewish" in the eyes of Orthodox Jewish law — at the cost
of embitterment, antipathy, and, even, the risk of civil war.

Steven V. Mazie, _Israel's Higher Law_

_____

The stories told in this book show that what happens in Israeli rabbinic courts
consistently violates basic human rights and the rule of law. The conduct and
judgments of these courts infringe on the right to freedom of conscience, the
right to equality before the law, the right to privacy, the right to due process,
the right to property, the right to liberty, and, perhaps above all, the right to
marry and have a family. To put an end to these transgressions the state-backed
Orthodox rabbinic court monopoly must be disbanded and replaced by a rich
and vibrant mosaic of voluntary rabbinic courts that will stand alongside a trans-
parent, secular, unified, and unabashedly liberal civil system of marriage and
divorce that protects the human rights of all citizens. Even allowing the existing religious courts to continue serving as a parallel divorce regime would be a

mistake. Apart from their detachment from modern sensibilities and inherent miscarriages of justice, they carry no edifying symbolic significance, they do not minimize the number of mamzerim (and may even increase it), and they hinder rather than enhance the unity of the Jewish people. Rabbinic infringements on human rights take on various forms. On the following pages, the manner in which rabbinic courts violate specific basic rights is discussed, with references to the stories of the agunot that we have told in the previous chapters.

The Right to Freedom of Conscience

Everyone has the right to freedom of thought, conscience and religion.
Article 18 of the Universal Declaration of Human Rights

Except for the Reluctant Aguna, all the women whose stories are told in this book and who married in Israel were married in religious, Orthodox ceremonies. Not only were these women given no choice in the matter, but the legal consequences were not explained to them. Quite the opposite. Marriage in accordance with the laws of Moses and Israel, and all preparations for such weddings, are venerated, sanitized, and introduced as the way to express one's patriotic and Jewish duty. For example, on a rabbinate site explaining how to get married in Tel Aviv, it is written, "Establishing a Jewish home is the most firm and secure way of guarantying the existence of the Jewish People. Maintaining the unique Jewish character of the house is the way to guarantee a successful and happy married life" (Department of Marriage, n.d.). Certainly, none of our heroines were told that should their marriages fail, Torah law, which is the law of the state in this respect, binds them to their husbands' will, indefinitely.

We purposely began with the story of Clueless. This bride represents Everywoman, caught up with the pomp and ceremony and authenticity of her "Great Big Fat Jewish Wedding" and clueless as to the very legal and public consequences of the act of marrying in accordance with the laws of Moses and Israel. Nor was she aware of the fact that by being required to marry in this fashion, her freedom of conscience had been effectively appropriated by the state regarding a decision that was, or should have been, one of her most important.

We purposely ended with the story of the Reluctant Agunah, the one bride who intentionally chose to express her freedom of conscience and to avoid a religious ceremony by flying to Cyprus for a quick civil marriage. This agunah was forced to undergo a not-so-quick religious divorce against both her and her husband's will. Even though the couple specifically requested that the court dissolve their marriage with a court declaration, rather than insist that they undergo a get ceremony, the rabbis used the violent power given to them by the state to put the husband in jail, summarily and without mercy, to gain his acquiescence to a religious act that the rabbis had decided, with state backing, was his obligation to undertake, despite rabbinic opinions stating that a get is not necessary in these circumstances (*Ploni v. Plonit [infidelity]*, 2006; see also introduction and chapter 6).

Insofar as marriage and divorce in Israel are concerned, there is no freedom of conscience. All persons must marry and, most significantly, divorce, in accordance with religious laws. No one can opt out of this arrangement as they could in 1947. And it is to protect this freedom of conscience, in particular, that any solution to the current unendurable circumstances must not allow for the possibility of a state-backed religious system of law to operate alongside a secular civil one. Under the divinely inspired rules of the Israeli rabbinate, for Jews there is no room for belief in, or even the mere tolerance of, other gods except the Orthodox Jewish one.

The Right to Equal Treatment

All are equal before the law and are entitled without any
discrimination to equal protection of the law.
Men and women . . . are entitled to equal rights as to marriage,
during marriage and at its dissolution.
Articles 7 and 16 of the Universal Declaration of Human Rights

Expanding on these principles, CEDAW maintains that parties to the convention "shall take all appropriate measures to eliminate discrimination against women in the political and public life of the country" (Cooke & Cusack, 2010, p. 184). In Israeli rabbinic courts, women are not represented at all on the judicial level. No woman presided over any case described in this book. No woman has presided over any case at all in any Orthodox rabbinic court, whether in Israel or the Diaspora. No woman sits on the bench or holds an important executive position in the Israeli rabbinate. A woman who acted as spokesperson for the rabbinic courts for a short period of time no longer works for them. It certainly can be pondered whether it would ever be possible to command the "equal protection of the law" from a subgroup of persons (such as Orthodox Jewish men) that systematically, intentionally, and arbitrarily bars another subgroup of persons (such as women) from acting as judges or jury. (Think: black persons on trial before an all-white jury and judge in the Jim Crow South in the 1940s.) In two recent situations, the rabbinic court administration attempted to issue tenders for legal assistants to rabbinic judges that would have, in the first instance, precluded the participation of women and, in the second instance, given express preference to men. Only significant legal efforts by the Center for Women's Justice stopped them (*CWJ v. Rabbinic Court Administrative Offices*, 2008). New tenders have been issued, but no woman has been hired.

In rabbinic courts and in Jewish law, women and men are not equal, and they have very different rights during marriage, especially at its dissolution. As described in the introduction, only a man can give a divorce and this must be of his own free will.

All the women in this book were locked into failed marriages until their husbands either reappeared after going into hiding (chapter 1), relented (chapter 2), or were put in jail (chapters 3 and 6) and agreed to give them a get. Until the husbands said, "I do," all these wives were stuck. Had their husbands not agreed, the wives would have remained in their liminal status, forever bound (like the agunah in chapter 4). Should they have dared to get on with their lives and lived with another man, any child they bore him would have been treated as an outcast, or to prevent that would have been falsely registered under the official laws of the state as the child of the recalcitrant husband (Population Registration Law of 1965, §22). In the reverse situation, where a wife refuses to accept a get, a man can, by law, receive rabbinic dispensation to take a second wife, thus thumbing his nose at his wife's recalcitrance and, by state fiat, bypassing Israel's bigamy laws (Penal Code of Israel, 1977, §179). Any child born to him and another women, so long as that woman is not married to another man, would not be cast out or discriminated against in any way.

Grounds for divorce are different for men and for women (if they exist at all for women). The most blatant example is when marital infidelity occurs. A woman's adultery is unequivocal grounds for a husband to divorce her, if he so wishes. Some rabbinic authorities have ruled that he can keep her as his maidservant (see chapter 2). Reconciliation is out of the question — adultery on the part of a wife is unforgivable, however remorseful she may be. It is far from clear that a man's adultery can even be claimed as grounds for divorce by his wife; after all, under biblical law a man can have more than one wife. Husbands' dalliances are frowned on as infringing on rabbinic values but do not violate any divine law (Halperin, 1989).

Halakhic laws are biased in favor of men. Rabbis responsible for vigilantly upholding those biased laws enforce them in ways that cannot, by definition, "equally protect" women, and that can sometimes make the rabbis seem outright hostile to women (chapter 5), by blaming them for anchoring themselves (chapters 1, 3, 4, and 5). This is most clear in those cases in which a husband invokes the Maharashdam-Maharik rules (see introduction). Those fifteenth- and sixteenth-century Talmudic authorities are cited in support of the proposition that a husband cannot in any way be ordered or compelled to divorce his wife, even if theoretical grounds exist for so doing, if he claims that he is willing to give a get so long as his wife meets his demands that are, in the opinion of the rabbis, either justified (Maharik) or easy to fulfill (Maharashdam). In almost all the cases described in this book, the husbands used the Maharik-Maharashdam card as a delaying tactic, successfully undermining their wives' demands for a get and effectively dealing the men all the cards they need to end the marriage on their terms.

In chapter 1 the husband demanded, through his endless stream of representatives, that the wife agree to repeatedly lower his child support payments and that she provide guarantees that she would not sue to raise that sum, ever. These "reasonable" demands succeeded in stymieing all attempts by the wife to obtain any ruling whatsoever from the rabbinic courts against her husband for eleven years.

In chapter 2 the husband insisted that the court hear his adultery claims, even though those allegations were not relevant to the case at hand and both parties had already agreed to the get. This demand was easy enough to fulfill, and the rabbis complied and ordered a hearing on this matter, despite objections by the wife and her attorney.

In chapter 3 the husband "reasonably" demanded that the rabbinic court rehear all of the marital issues that had already been adjudicated and decided by civil courts. He also "reasonably" demanded that the get he gave be suspended (for six years) while such readjudication took place to ensure his wife's compliance with the unconscionable contract entered into so that he would agree to divorce her.

In chapter 4 the husband had, and still has, various demands regarding visitation with his son and the transfer of all matters relating to the couple's case from civil courts to the rabbinic courts. Though having lived with his wife for only three months, he succeeded in garnering rabbinic support for his get refusal for nearly fourteen years, effectively decimating his wife's life, because, in the rabbinic courts' determination, his demands were reasonable and easy to fulfill.

In chapter 5 the husband wanted to make sure that all his demands, though unclear and undefined, regarding marital property were met before he gave the get and that the rabbinic court take jurisdiction over those matters. The court, of course, agreed, even though the husband had not filed for divorce, and they initiated an impromptu hearing with regard to the couple's property to snag jurisdiction. And when the wife stood up for herself and sued for damages, the rabbinic court declared that a "world war" was underway between the two court systems.

In chapter 6 the rabbis interestingly did *not* let the husband set any terms for the divorce, probably because they were in doubt whether the couple, who had wed in a civil ceremony in Cyprus, were really married at all under Jewish law. Thus, they felt more free to pressure the husband to divorce his wife without worrying about the Maharik-Maharashdam rule prohibiting a forced divorce.

The problem of inequality in rabbinic courts is not about people not being treated in the same way. To justify what goes on in the rabbinic court, supporters of the system often point out that men are equally harmed and that they too are denied closure by wives who refuse to accept a get. In 2007 the rabbinic court announced with great fanfare that there are even more *agunim* (men anchored to failed marriages) than agunot (Ben-Hayyim, 2007). The halakha of divorce, its defenders will say, is neutral, and what is more, recalcitrant men can be put in jail, while recalcitrant women cannot.

But, as feminist scholar and activist Catherine MacKinnon (1987) points out, the problem of equality is not about difference; it is about dominance. What happens in the rabbinic court is a problem of Jewish men dominating Jewish women by keeping them in relationships in which men have the final word, and then justifying that act of force by pointing to the unequal rule inscribed in the Mishnah (ca. 200 CE): "A man who wishes to divorce his wife is not like a woman who seeks divorce from her husband" (Yev. 14:1). This power that Jewish men have over their women is part of a greater body of unequal law that justifies the exclusion of women from the judiciary, from learning key cultural legal texts, from authoritative communal positions, and from being counted in a public prayer quorum, making them "peripheral Jews" (Adler, 1973).

The fact that some Jewish men can also be hurt by the rules of divorce, or that others may be jailed for years on end for not obeying a rabbinic order to give a get, does not change the underlying power structure and its insidiousness. Worse, such manifestations are subtle adjustments of male hegemony (Genovese, 1976), a type of camouflage or inoculation that obfuscates the fact that Jewish women are, by law, subordinate to men and that men have power over them. Some men may find themselves behind bars, but their wives will be stuck forever if their husband refuses to give a get. The men have the final word. Some men may be hurt for years if their wives refuse a get, but the requirement that women must agree to accept the get is "rabbinic" in origin and not "biblical," and consequently there are halakhic loopholes to extract men out of bad marriages should the rabbis want to make use of those loopholes. There is no way out for Jewish women.

Jewish law is unequal because it facilitates the unequal power arrangement by which men dominate their wives. *All* Jewish women, without exception, could find themselves, like the wives in chapters 1, 3, 4, and 5, anchored and powerless for a protracted time, even forever.

Moreover, the millet system by definition results in situations where Israeli citizens are not treated equally. Israeli Jews can get divorced without problems if the couple agrees, since halakha allows for consensual divorce. Israeli Catholics cannot get divorced at all, since canon law does not permit it. Muslim men can divorce their wives unilaterally because shariya law lets them. (The fact that Israeli law declares such unilateral divorce a crime [Penal Code, §181] does not mean that actual divorces do not occur under Muslim *shariya* law, which, insofar as Muslims living in Israel are concerned, is the law of the land.) Different rules apply to different millets. There is simply no equality in Israeli divorce laws.

The Right to Privacy

No one shall be subjected to arbitrary interference with his privacy, family,
home or correspondence, nor to attacks upon his honor and reputation.

Article 12 of the Universal Declaration of Human Rights

The "right to privacy" is a term coined in 1890 by Louis D. Brandeis, who later
became a justice of the U.S. Supreme Court, and his friend and future law partner, Samuel D. Warren, in an article that the two wrote, titled "The Right to
Privacy." There, the authors noted the "beautiful capacity" of the common law
to develop in such ways as to recognize that "only a part of the pain, pleasure,
and profit of life lay in physical things" (p. 195), and they called on courts to
recognize and protect not only the physical property of persons from unwar-
ranted invasion, but also the "thoughts, emotions, and sensations" of persons.
Brandies and Warren summed up the right to privacy as the "right to be let
alone" (Brandeis & Warren, 1890, p. 193).

Though the right to privacy is not expressly delineated in the U.S. Bill of
Rights, the U.S. Supreme Court has inferred such a right into the U.S. Constitution — as a "penumbra" right — and has held that it includes, to mention a
few examples, freedom from having details of one's intimate life published in
newspapers (*Olmstead v. United States*, 1928; dissent); freedom to rear children
in accordance with one's beliefs and values (*Wisconsin v. Yoder*, 1972); to decide
whether to procreate (*Skinner v. Oklahoma*, 1942) or not to procreate (*Griswold
v. Connecticut*, 1965, using the term "penumbra"; *Eisenstadt v. Baird*, 1972); to
have an abortion (*Roe v. Wade*, 1973); to marry a person of one's choice (*Loving
v. Virginia*, 1967); to engage in consensual homosexual relations (*Lawrence v.
Texas*, 2003); and to refuse medical treatment (*Cruzan v. Missouri Department
of Health*, 1990). Israel has embraced the right to privacy in its Basic Laws and
in a series of laws that protect individuals from invasion not only of the state
but also of other individuals. Israeli law greatly limits the circumstances under
which it is possible to eavesdrop (Eavesdropping Law, 1979); to do an invasive
body search on a person suspected of a crime (Criminal Procedure Law, 1996);
to release medical information about a patient (Rights of the Sick Law, 1996);
to publish information about a trial conducted behind closed doors (Courts

Laws, 1984, §70); and to reveal information about Israeli citizens on record with state administrative bodies (Freedom of Information Law, 1988).

But despite Israel's vigilant protection, for example, of its citizens' bodies from invasive searches by police, from drawing blood for evidentiary purposes (cf. Frimer, 1982), or even from undergoing medical procedures that are in their best interest but against their will (*Da'aka v. Carmel Hospital*, 1999), the state itself, by means of the chief rabbinate, which it sponsors and accords official status, conducts "surveillance" of women's bodies on the eve of their weddings. When a woman wants permission from the state to get married, she must coordinate the date with a female official at the local (state-sponsored) rabbinic council office to make sure the wedding is not scheduled for a day on which the bride is considered impure — during her menstrual cycle and for seven days afterward. The official then sets a date for the bride to take at least one mandatory class on the religious laws of family purity, which pertain to when she is allowed and not allowed to have intercourse. The bride-to-be is also told that she must attend the mikveh on the evening before her wedding and obtain a note from the mikveh attendant that she indeed did so, which she must, in turn, deliver to the officiating rabbi prior to the ceremony. Local rabbinic councils ask officiating rabbis to send them authorization of such immersion, along with a copy of the ketubah, after the wedding ceremony is over (see chapter 1).

In 2004 the Center for Jewish Pluralism (the Movement for Progressive Judaism), the Israeli branch of the Reform Movement, petitioned the Supreme Court in connection with the classes on religious purity. It did not ask the court to order the chief rabbinate to discontinue this premarital state-sanctioned administration of the bodies of women, but simply to refrain from proselytizing while conducting the classes. The center filed affidavits with the court in which women described in great detail the different ways in which they were encouraged to obey not only the laws of ritual purity but other commandments as well and how they were advised to take traditional "wifely" roles in their marriages (*Israel Movement v. Sharon* [petition], 2004). The Supreme Court, hesitant as it is to interfere with anything done by the chief rabbinate or rabbinic courts, strong-armed a compromise. It convinced the center to withdraw its demand after the rabbinate affirmed that it had issued new directives from which "it could be understood" that "family purity classes were [to be] obligatory only insofar as they prepared the bride for marriage" and only "with respect to those matters that dealt with a woman in her state of impurity, how she purifies herself, inspects her body at the end of her menses and on the ensuing seven clean days, prepares her body for immersion, and [the rules of] immersion" (*Israel Movement v. Sharon* [agreement], 2004). Thus, with the warrant of the state and the blessings of the Supreme Court sitting as the High Court of Justice, all Jewish women who want to marry in Israel and receive a marriage certificate are informed that they must undress, inspect their private parts for blood for a week after their period ends, and immerse naked in ritual waters before a strange woman who plucks stray hairs off their bodies (as described in chapter 1). We are not disparaging these practices in themselves. We are merely describing them in detail to highlight our argument that decisions such as whether to undergo ritual ablutions and when to sleep with one's husband should be left to the free will and discretion of individuals without the interference of the state.

The Israeli state also effectively warrants surveillance of some women's bodies at the time of divorce. Wives who have extramarital sex forfeit all financial rights theoretically owed them under the ketubah and in some cases also rights that would accrue to them under modern marital property laws (*Ploni v. Plonit* [infidelity], 2006). Children born of their adulterous relationships may be branded as mamzerim and placed on a (clandestine but state-authorized) "genealogical blacklist" of those who cannot marry fellow Jews. According to attorney Akivah Miller, who wrote a seminar paper on the matter, the "blacklist" is a computerized database located and operated by the Rabbinic Courts Administration. It's not entirely clear how the blacklist is used or updated or who is included in it and on what basis. The list is not available to the public and is kept strictly for the use of the Israeli marriage registrars. It is not connected to any network, and access is limited to a small number of Rabbinic Court Administration staff. Information is not given to anyone abroad. In a conversation Miller had with an American rabbi who is familiar with these matters, he was told that American rabbis do not rely on this database when conducting marriages (2009). The state has set up a special rabbinic court meant to prevent, or greatly limit, the blacklisting of children born to women who the courts suspected engaged in extramarital relations (Amar & Rubenstein, 2003). Or, perhaps even worse, to prevent their being blacklisted, the state requires those children to be registered at birth as the children of their mother's husbands, or ex-husbands — who more often than not had refused their wives a get for years on end — denying biological fathers their paternity rights over their children and forcing families to live with lies and deceptions (Population Registration Law of 1965, §22). It even prevents any paternity testing of those children, claiming that it is in the best interest of those children not to be branded, irrespective of the stated will of those children or their parent's (Genetic Information Law, 2000, §28d).

And on top of those harsh penalties, Jewish law marks adulterous women with "Scarlet A's," explicitly in the halakhic "pronouncement of a legal act" (*maaseh beit din*) that becomes part of a couple's divorce file and, at times, obliquely by reference to such pronouncement on their divorce certificate. If a woman commits adultery, she is barred from marrying her lover and from remarrying her divorced husband (T. Bavli. Sotah 5a). So even if a couple has agreed to divorce, and the question of fault is not ever raised or adjudicated or relevant, the questions of "if she did it" and "who she did it with" are relevant to a rabbinic court and will be noted and tried, if necessary. There have been situations in which the name of the woman's partner in adultery is appended to the maaseh beit din on the basis of the skimpiest of evidence, without any adjudication of the matter whatsoever (*Izkovitch v. Jerusalem Rabbinic Court*, 1990). In chapter 2 we saw how a rabbinic court conducted a trial to allow a husband who had sued for divorce to have counsel cross-examine his wife on whether, and how, she had sexual relations with a man that her husband thought was her lover. The fact that the court ultimately ruled that the husband had not proved his claim does not diminish the humiliation and degradation that the wife endured.

A man's adultery does not carry the same harsh consequences, and his dalliances are not so closely watched, surveyed, condemned, or noted as a woman's. He loses no benefits under the marriage contract. He can marry the woman with whom he was unfaithful so long as she was unmarried at the time. Thus his privacy is not invaded in the ways that a woman's is. And while we can understand that adultery may be a relevant question in divorce proceedings (in a fault-based divorce regime, for example), our contention is that any inquiry into whom one sleeps with, or how one sleeps with that person, is certainly an invasion of privacy if it is not necessary to prove one's case. It is not necessary if the divorce is consensual.

In the case in chapter 2 the wife's privacy was trampled on when she was cross-examined in the attempt to prove her disloyalty, even though she had already agreed to divorce. What is more, the court allowed the husband to show video clips of her walking around the house in her underwear. He argued that such clips were necessary to prove that his wife had breached "the laws of Judah" (customs of modesty), establishing grounds for his claim that he no longer had to live with her but also need not divorce her. The rabbis watched the entire clip. In Israel, all Jewish women who want to marry (like the wife in chapter 1), and all those who want to divorce (like the wife in chapter 2), must expose their bodies and their sexual activities to the discipline and punishment of the Israeli state.

The Right to Due Process

Everyone is entitled in full equality to a fair and public hearing by an independent and impartial tribunal, in the determination of his rights and obligations.

Article 10 of the Universal Declaration of Human Rights

Perhaps the most egregious violation of human rights in Israeli rabbinic courts is the sheer chaos that reigns there. It is this Kafkaesque turmoil that we have tried to convey in our stories. This disorder goes beyond the problem of rabbis not coming on time to hearings, or the lack of clear and accurate protocols, and even beyond the right to a "fair and public trial." What lies at the heart of this chaos is total disregard for the rule of law, a concept implicit in the notion of due process, and the right to a fair hearing and an impartial tribunal. And although the idea of the rule of law has come into disrepute as being vague and overused (Shklar, 1999), we use it here to convey two very primal and basic notions: one with practical implications and the other with broader political and philosophical implications.

In practical terms the rule of law means that law, as a tool for ordering society, cannot be vague, confusing, or arbitrary. Defining the rule of law in this manner, the Israeli-born political philosopher Joseph Raz of Oxford University writes that it "is not to be confused with democracy, justice, equality (before the law or otherwise), human rights of any kind or respect for persons or for the dignity of man. A non-democratic legal system, based on the denial of human rights, on extensive poverty, on racial segregation, secular inequalities, and religious persecution may, in principle, conform to the requirements of the rule of law better than any of the legal system of more enlightened Western democracies" (Raz, 1979, p. 211).

Not only do Israel's rabbinic courts deny principles of democracy, justice, equality, dignity, and human rights, they also deny those rights erratically, arbitrarily, and capriciously. So while the argument can be made, at least theoretically, that states should accommodate and allow for the self-governance of (or even joint governance with) "identity groups" like rabbinic courts run by Orthodox Jews (Shahar, 1998) and turn a somewhat blind eye to group infringements on equality and privacy, for example, it cannot, we argue, turn a blind eye to unclear rules, arbitrarily imposed.

The confusion that reigns in Israeli rabbinic courts is such that even a veteran divorce advocate, if asked on what grounds a rabbinic tribunal will order a husband to give a get, will hesitate and search for an answer. No short one can be provided. Is adultery grounds? Domestic violence? How much violence? If they are grounds, what is the necessary burden of proof? If pushed, such hypothetical advocate may, in want of a definitive answer, point to the Mishnah, which declares that husbands "forced" to divorce their wives are "those afflicted with boils, a man with polyps, a *meqammez*, a coppersmith, and a tanner" (Ket. 7:10). But since those grounds are hardly relevant today and were not so clear when written — the Tosefta, contemporaneous with the Mishnah, asks, what is a *meqammez?* (Tos. Ket. 7:11) — they provide unsure footing at best. Rambam's assertion (ca. 1000 CE) that a man must divorce his wife if she is "fed up" with or "revolted" by him (Mishna Torah, Personal Status Laws 14:8) would seem to echo more modern justifications for divorce, such as the "irretrievable breakdown of the marriage." But again, there is no consensus about what the Rambam meant. Did he intend to say that a wife's subjective claim that she is "fed up" is enough, thus establishing no-fault grounds for divorce on the basis of a wife's unilateral demand? Or must a wife have good and substantial reasons for being "fed up," because of some objective "fault" of the husband? Some argue that only a wife who is sexually revolted by her husband can claim that she is fed up. Is severe emotional violence also a basis for such claim? How about physical violence?

Confusion infuses each case described in this book. It stands out when all the cases are taken as a collective. Why was the wife in chapter 2 awarded an obligatory hiyuv get, even though she claimed no strong fault grounds beyond the breakdown of her marriage? Was it because her husband accused *her* of adultery? Did he? Why wasn't the wife in chapter 4 awarded a hiyuv? Shouldn't a fourteen-year separation be grounds for divorce? Is separation grounds for divorce in Jewish law at all? (No, see *Plonit v. Ploni* [separation], 2007.) The wives in chapters 3, 4, 5, and 6 all alleged domestic violence. What constitutes domestic violence under Jewish law? Is it grounds for divorce? There are no clear answers to any of these questions.

Confusion is most palpable in chapter 3, where the question seems to be, is separation grounds for divorce under Jewish law? After four years of litigation, the district rabbinic court ruled that the husband "must" divorce his wife ("*al habal le-garesh et ishto*") since there was "zero chance of reconciliation." The husband appealed, claiming that "zero chance of reconciliation" was not grounds for divorce. Had the lower court based its ruling on the "fed up" rule of the Rambam? Or something else? Was it tantamount to an "order" against the husband? And, if not, what was it? The High Rabbinic Court "clarified" matters, holding that the ruling should be viewed only as a "suggestion" or a "moral commandment" (mitzvah) and not as an "order." (So what are the implications of a district rabbinic court ruling that a man "must" divorce his wife?) The district rabbinic court promptly reissued its ruling, this time using the coveted term "order." But it did not delineate on what rule, or on what facts, it based its determination. Again the husband appealed, and again the High Rabbinic Court reversed, saying that even if the lower court had based its rulings on the fed-up rule, that rule could *not* serve as grounds for a divorce (see generally Westreich, 2002). So what can? Only after a third round of volleying, and nearly eight years after the wife had filed a second time for divorce, did the High Rabbinic Court relent and agree to let the lower court's decision stand. This time the High Rabbinic Court held that the Rambam's rule does apply (!). Perhaps the reader would agree with us that the fed up rule is, "When a rabbinic court is fed up with the husband, it will order him to give a get."

Rabbi Sherman, in a minority opinion, saw no reason to change his mind. He wrote, "It appears from the reasoning of the lower court that it adheres to its original position that it is possible to obligate a get if the [wife] argues [that her husband is] repulsive to her, as it has so held in the past. This court has already decided this matter and rejected that position in its decision of . . . 1994." Significantly, it took many more years before the wife in chapter 3 was finally divorced. And after all those years and all those decisions, it is still not clear on what facts the court ordered the husband to give a get, and the case provides no guidance whatsoever for any future determination regarding the fed up rule. Is the fed up rule grounds for divorce? Maybe.

We see another significant example of confusion when we examine the three different decisions rendered by a single rabbinic tribunal in chapter 5. There the questions at large seemed to be, is domestic violence grounds for divorce, and what is the burden of proof? The wife claimed that her husband subjected her and the children to severe emotional cruelty and displayed threatening behavior that at times turned into outbursts of physical violence. In support of her claims, the wife testified and submitted findings rendered by a criminal court that had examined similar facts. In the criminal trial, the judge held that the wife had proven that the husband subjected the family to a constant rule of terror, including physical and emotional violence, but that she had *not* proven that her husband attacked their daughter on the particular occasion for which he was being tried, since she was unable to provide the cor-roborating evidence required by law for that specific act. The court sentenced the husband to a suspended jail sentence and community service.

The rabbinic judges who heard the wife's allegations could not agree as to what all this meant. One rabbinic judge held that the wife "lied" both to the criminal court and to the rabbinic court in alleging physical violence and that she had not proven her allegation of threats, since the "husband claimed that the criminal courts finding on this matter were inconclusive." This judge also stated that the wife's statements that she had been "raped" by the husband were also "not true," because she did not file complaints to the police about this. Another judge held that although he agreed that the wife was a "liar" when she complained about rape and physical violence, he felt that the husband's "anger did not add to the possibility of reconciliation" and that the couple was "emotionally divorced." He "recommended" that the couple divorce. A third rabbinic judge held that the wife had proved that her husband had threatened to burn the house down when angry and that he had created an atmosphere of terror. He held that such findings supported the wife's claim of being "fed up" but (alas) were not grounds for ordering a divorce. He ruled that the husband "should" divorce his wife.

Confused? So are we. It is totally unclear what type of violence, if any, serves as a basis for "ordering" a husband to give a get, or what type of violence, if any, is basis for "recommending" that he give a get. It is also unclear how one would go about proving that violence occurred. What is the burden of proof?

Certainly it should be less than the burden required by a criminal court? The court does not seem able to make those types of distinctions. And what is the difference between "should" and "recommending"? In 2011, seven years later, the same tribunal held that the husband was not a "get recalcitrant," even though its consensus had been in 2004 that it was recommended that he divorce his wife.

In chapter 4 the wife also tried to claim domestic violence as grounds for her divorce. There the court held that she had not proved her claims, even though she brought, in addition to her own testimony, extensive corroborative evidence that included the testimony of two neighbors who heard her scream-ing, and the rent collector who told the court that the husband had admitted to him that he hit his wife and even gesticulated to show him how he did so. Since no one except for the wife (who didn't count) had actually witnessed the violence, the court held that it could not be sure of what had happened, suggesting that proof of domestic violence in a rabbinic court must be beyond any doubt at all. (See Frishtik [1991], regarding domestic violence as grounds for divorce under halakha, and Shenrav [2011], expounding on the problem of evidence in halakha and on the difficulty of suggesting "din-Torah" as a practical alternative to secular law.)

Compounding the confusion with respect to the substantive law and evi-dentiary rules is the fact that many rabbinic court decisions are rendered in telegraphic brevity, replete with abbreviations and Aramaic words that are indecipherable to the average attorney and accessible only to a cadre made up mostly of male yeshiva students. Most Israeli attorneys, all of whom are qualified to appear in a rabbinic court, have not studied Talmud. They do not understand Aramaic or the shorthand that dots rabbinic court decisions. So even if their rules were clearer, rabbinic court decisions would still not be ac-cessible to most people. Divine rules, it appears, do not meet the transparency requirements of the rule of law. God's laws are to a large extent unknowable, even, at times, to the rabbis themselves.

So much for failures of the rabbinic courts to meet the practical demands of the rule of law that legal norms be clear, predictable, and not arbitrarily ap-plied. As for the theoretical implications, many political thinkers and lawyers have argued the need to expand the notion of the rule of law beyond Raz's formalistic "thin" definition that laws must be clear and not arbitrarily applied. For them the rule of law includes the "thick," substantive requirement that law incorporate certain fundamental, human, or basic rights, as well as do justice (Tamanaha, 2004, pp. 102–114). Certainly, so defined, the rule of law is not practiced by Israeli rabbinic courts. As we have shown, rabbinic courts do not try to ensure the fundamental, human, or basic rights of its litigants to equality, freedom of conscience, privacy, and so on. On the contrary, they violate those rights. Rabbinic courts are not set up to do justice in the sense of correcting wrongs (Weinrib, 1995) or redistributing capital, be it material, social, or cultural (Fraser, 1997). But what we are claiming here is that Israeli rabbinic courts fail the rule of law not only because they are unpredictable and unjust, and not only because they violate basic human rights, but because they are not accountable to anyone except God.

In a democratic government it is the law that rules, not God and not the king. No one can stand above the law, not the executive, not the legislature, not the judiciary, and not even God himself. Thus the rule of law is, most important, most substantively, a check on the potentially unbridled and coercive power of different governmental bodies. Rabbinic judges, like the rest of us, should not be allowed to do anything that they may want, without restraint.

Tellingly, rabbinic judges do not pledge their allegiance to *the laws of* the State of Israel. Israeli law requires rabbinic judges to pledge their loyalty only to "the State of Israel" (Rabbinic Judges Law, 1955, §10). All other judges pledge their loyalty to both "the State of Israel" and to "its laws" (Basic Law of the Judiciary, §6). This distinction is not meaningless. Rabbinic judges literally do not, and will not, pay even lip service to laws enacted by the Knesset, though theoretically some civil laws specifically demand their compliance, such as marital property laws (Marital Property Act [Balancing of Resources] Act, 1973, §10). It is only with the greatest of reluctance, or perhaps when it serves their purported halakhic ends (see, e.g., *Ploni v. Plonit* [infidelity], 2006), that rabbinic judges cite civil law. They defer, instead, to their understanding of the word of God, drawing on ancient authorities who have, in turn, also interpreted the word of God in contexts far removed from modern Israel. In so doing, Israeli rabbinic courts carve out for themselves a theocratic island within an otherwise democratic state. They, unlike the rest of the judges in Israel, are ruled by God, not by the laws of people.

The problem with God and his laws (assuming they are discernible) is that they cannot, by definition, be significantly challenged or changed, and they are considered by the rabbis to be impregnable to outside influences and history

(Sachs, 1989). The God of Israel's Orthodox rabbis stands unyielding to the interests of the individual, who is small and insignificant in face of his greater policy demands, whatever they may be, and the identity or recognition needs of his insular community, however they are currently defined. So, it should come as no surprise that when defending a rabbinic court decision before the Supreme Court, the rabbinic court system's legal advisor will often take refuge behind the claim that the matter in question is a halakhic one and therefore immune from judicial scrutiny. Invoking God, the rabbinic court advisor silences any bid by the Supreme Court and the Knesset to check or balance anything the rabbinic courts may be doing.

All the cases described here show that, to a large extent, the Knesset, the Supreme Court, and the Israeli public give the rabbinate free rein to act on what they say is God's word in a manner that is unquestionable and unbridled. All the women stood helpless against a legal system that has run amok. No one in Israel seriously questions how, in a modern, democratic state, the wife in chapter 1 could remain married to a husband who abandoned his family and went missing for nearly ten years, and would have remained married to him to this very day had her cousin not spotted him and called the police. Or why the wife in chapter 4 is still married fourteen years and counting after she left the home she shared with her husband for only three months. It is the will of God, and so be it. It is irrelevant what policy considerations are served, or not served, by adhering to his will.

The unquestionableness of God's rule as executed by the rabbis comes into particular relief in the case of the wife in chapter 5. There the wife dared to sue her husband for damages for refusing to give her a get for nine years. To a large extent, these damages claims, filed in Israeli family courts and of relatively recent vintage, are a way of taking judicial issue with the divine rule that allows a wife to remain tethered forever to her husband's will when it comes to divorce and questioning the reasoning behind the rule and justification for it. Distraught at what they feel is an infringement on their exclusive jurisdiction and an implicit criticism of what they think is the unquestionable will of God and his laws, the district rabbinic court declared that such damage claims are nothing less than a declaration of a world war — the rule of law versus the rule of God. As we noted in chapter 5, Rabbi Ariel calls on the Supreme Court to put things in order and to render unto Caesar what is Caesar's and unto God what is God's, since, from a pure halakhic perspective, we are dealing here with the most serious and substantive laws of personal status--the validity of the get and the fear of mamzerut. Rabbi Ariel never asks why the validity of the get is so important or if a woman's lawsuit defending her rights should have an effect on that validity. And the rule of the mamzer looms large, unquestioned, reified, immutable, tautological. Because "that's the way it is."

Theocracies do not meet the rule of law because the rule of law requires checks and balances on those who rule and those who make the laws. If it is accepted that a democratic government of the people and by the people is answerable to the people and the laws they make, those laws must be open to review and amendment by an independent judiciary capable of critical thinking and willing to correct itself, reinterpret its laws, and even discard some as time and experience and context require. No one is above the law, not even the law itself. If it cannot be acknowledged that God's laws and his rule can be checked and balanced, reviewed and amended, bridled and discarded, answerable to changing policy considerations and contexts, then the rule of God does not offer a viable alternative to those who believe in the need to keep the power of government in check and balanced.

There are thinkers who argue that halakha is "Not in the Heavens," but down on earth for us mortals to interpret (Berkovits, 1983); that halakha encapsulates such metaprinciples as morality, justice, dignity, liberty, and even human rights; and that halakha, like all religious laws, like all laws, and like all social constructs, has changed and will change with time and attempts at reinterpretation and thus can meet the requirements of review that we demand of the rule of law. (This is a favorite theme, for example, of many of the thinkers at the Shalom Hartman Institute in Jerusalem, which describes itself as a "center of transformative thinking and teaching that addresses the major challenges facing the Jewish people" (Shalom Hartman Institute, n.d.). We note, and are even sympathetic to, these claims that are dear to our traditional hearts. But this ideologically inspired conception of halakha is far removed from the historical and empirical reality that we have encountered in the rabbinic courts of Israel and cannot justify in any way the imposition of an alternative divine authority, however benevolent in conception and however utopian in its possibilities, to govern alongside a human, secular one that is subject to the limits of the rule of law and answerable to the people and not to God. We must indeed render unto Caesar what is Caesar's and unto God what is God's.

The place for God and the laws attributed to him, whether they be designated as halakha or Jewish law, culture, tradition, or religion, must be fitted into the realm of civil society and not made into a powerful arm of a significant state apparatus such as a court of law.

The Right to Property

(1)

Everyone has the right to own property alone
as well as in association with others.

(2)

No one shall be arbitrarily deprived of his property.

Article 17 of the Universal Declaration of Human Rights

One rule that has gained ground and clarity in Israeli rabbinic courts in recent years is the one described in the previous section on equality as the Maharashdam-Maharik rule. Citing it, rabbinic courts will not issue a decision against a recalcitrant husband if he has set terms for divorce that the court thinks are reasonable or easy for a wife to meet. If a husband sets such terms, a court cannot place any pressure on him (thus compromising his will), even if religious law may warrant it.

In 2005 a rabbinic court ordered a woman to pay her husband sixty thousand shekels (about eighteen thousand dollars) for having "given up his right to be married to her." She appealed to the Supreme Court, stating that such award was inconsistent both with halakha and with the Basic Law of Human Dignity and Liberty. The husband, in his defense, told the court that his wife, who had been trying unsuccessfully to convince him to divorce her for seven years, had agreed to let the rabbinic court set a price for her release. When asked by the judges how common it was for women to pay for their freedom, Rabbi Shimon Yaakobi, legal advisor to the rabbinic courts, who appears often before the Supreme Court when cases are filed that challenge rabbinic court rulings, observed, "While it is not possible to say that it is common [for a woman to pay for a divorce] what is common is the give-and-take. And there are concessions made. The rabbinic courts' position is that even if it were to issue a ruling ordering a husband to give a get [hiyuv], it cannot enforce such orders by issuing sanctions against the recalcitrant husband [alluding to the Maharashdam-Maharik rule]. And while it may not be politically correct, there are circumstances in which it is necessary to buy the get. As much as we don't like it" (*Plonit v. Ploni* [right to stay married], 2011).

The price of a Jewish divorce varies. We have seen women buying their divorce for as little as a pair of gifted earrings and as much as custody of a child, let alone cash money and the waiver of rights to marital property. The wife in chapter 3 agreed to give up her claim to half of the marital home (she received 24 percent), to lower child support, to waive her husband's debt for child support, and to let the rabbinic court rehear all matters already determined by a family court. It still took her nineteen years to be finally and officially divorced. The wife in chapter 1 had no property to give up, since it all had been squandered on her husband's debts. Nonetheless, in exchange for the get, he demanded that she provide bank assurances that the couple had no outstanding debts, agree to unrealistic visitation arrangements, lower child support, and even provide a guarantee that she would not sue for more. All these demands worked as a delaying tactic until the husband had disappeared for so long and had pushed the envelope so much, that the rabbinic court got fed up with him and put him in jail (when they finally caught him). It took the wife in chapter 1 eleven years to get divorced. The wife in chapter 4 is still entangled in this web of "reasonable and easy to fulfill" demands that serve as convenient excuses for husbands and rabbinic courts to keep wives chained to a marriage that has long ended.

Forcing a woman to give up property rights for a get is not only "politically incorrect," but a violation of a basic right. In contrast to the sentiment expressed by Rabbi Yaakobi and effectively supported by the Supreme Court, it is not consent, or innocent give-and-take, when a woman gives up her rights to marital property, child custody, or even her day in court, under circumstances in which her husband holds all the power, and that power is supported by the state and its institutions. It is unconscionable coercion.

In developing a theory of feminist jurisprudence, which draws on Marxist theories of ideology and false consciousness — that things are not always as they seem — Catherine MacKinnon writes, "Dominance reified becomes difference. Coercion legitimated becomes consent" (MacKinnon, 1989, p. 238). By this she means that the insidiousness of the domination of men over women, including that which is supported by the state, is such that the exercise of power over women manifests itself as a harmless difference between men and women. And when coercion of women is legitimated, by law or otherwise, it is made to seem as if women consented to it and did not object at all. MacKinnon's words echo deep in Israeli rabbinic courts. The subjection of women that results because they can never be released from a marriage without their husband's conscious and full agreement, whereas men can be so released, is excused as small, insignificant "differences" between men and women and the way that they get divorced. When women compromise their interests in face of a recalcitrant spouse and an indifferent or hostile legal system that supports such recalcitrance for years on end, such compromises are viewed as part of the give-and-take of negotiations, consensual rather than unlawful coercion. Thus, in addition to violating women's rights to privacy, equality, due process, and freedom of conscience, Israeli rabbinic courts make women consent to giving up their property rights in exchange for their liberty, with the blessing of the Israeli Supreme Court.

The Right to Liberty and the Right to Marry

Everyone has the right to life, liberty and security of person.
Men and women of full age, without any limitation due to race, nationality or religion, have the right to marry and to found a family.
Articles 3 and 16 of the Universal Declaration of Human Rights

In his important work *Two Concepts of Liberty,* Isaiah Berlin opens with the pronouncement that the meaning of "freedom," which he uses interchangeably with the concept of "liberty," is "like happiness and goodness, like nature and reality . . . so porous that there is little interpretation that it seems able to resist" (1958, p. 6). In his attempt to make sense out of liberty, he suggests two ways to explain the notion. One he calls "negative" liberty, the freedom from arbitrary interference with one's activities and the absence of constraints, and the other he calls "positive" liberty, the freedom to be who one wants to be, "a being conscious of myself as a thinking, willing, active being, bearing responsibility for his choices and ideas and purposes" (p. 16).

The rabbinic courts are certainly guilty of failing to ensure the negative liberty of litigants in divorce cases. They place obstacles on the very bodies of persons. They curtail the physical liberty of men by putting them in jail, constraining their freedom of movement instead of simply declaring their marriage over (see chapter 6). And they curtail the sexual and procreative liberty of women by stigmatizing and casting out children born to them as a result of their intimate relationships with men who are not their husbands.

Moreover, rabbinic courts who prevent women, in the name of halakha, from getting on with their lives because their husbands won't hand them a piece of paper also infringe on their "positive" liberty to decide how to shape their family unit and who it is they want to be close to. In support of damages for get refusals, J. Greenberger quotes Joseph Raz, who on the subject of autonomy, wrote, "the ruling idea behind the ideal of personal autonomy is that people should make their own lives. The autonomous person is a (part) author of his own life. The ideal of personal autonomy is the vision of people controlling, to some degree, their own destiny, fashioning it through successive decisions throughout their lives. . . . A person whose every decision is extracted from him by coercion is not an autonomous person" (S. v. S., 2001, para. 9).

Since the Greenberger decision, numerous family courts have agreed with this reasoning and have held that get refusal infringes on the liberty of women — and men — to control their own destiny. In one of the most recent decisions, handed down on August 17, 2011, Rishon Le'Zion Family Court judge Esther Stein awarded a woman 680,000 shekels (about $190,000) in damages for get refusal, expanding on the idea that the right to remove the shackles of a failed marriage is a constitutional one. She explains, "The rights protected by the Basic Law of Human Dignity and Liberty are basic and essential rights to which all persons are entitled. The right to liberty and freedom is of particular significance — having a sense of freedom and autonomy has an impact on one's entire way of life, on one's self confidence and general functioning. It is my opinion that when a person feels that her destiny lies in the hands of someone she does not respect, and from whom she does not know how and when she will cast off the shackles of her dependency, this is a violation of a constitutional right that can serve as a basis of a tort" (P. v. P., 2011, p. 15).

Rabbinic courts have not directly addressed the contention that the courts themselves infringe on the autonomy and positive liberty of persons by facilitating get refusal. But when asked to submit his opinion in a recalcitrant husband's appeal to the Supreme Court of a decision awarding damages to his wife, rabbinic court advisor Yaakobi did ponder the issue and rejected this allegation out of hand (see chapter 4). In his mind, Israelis who choose of their own free will to marry in accordance with the laws of the Torah have accepted the rights and responsibilities inherent in Jewish marriage and divorce and consequently have subjected themselves willingly to the exclusive jurisdiction of the rabbinic court to decide how, and under what terms, that dissolution will occur:

> The parties chose to design their life together in accordance with the laws of Moses and Israel. Couples who choose to marry and decide to marry in accordance with the laws of the Torah have exercised their right to autonomy and self-realization as free people who are in control of their destiny and write the story of their lives as free people. This type of marriage carries with it a full panoply of rights and responsibilities, including [the] fact that a marriage must be dissolved in accordance with the laws of Moses and Israel. . . . Such laws of dissolution, being part of the laws of marriage and divorce, are in the sole and exclusive jurisdiction of the rabbinic courts. (N. v. N. [Yaakobi], 2011)

In other words, Yaakobi feels that people are at liberty to curtail their liberty and that Israelis who choose to marry in Israel have, at the outset, knowingly authorized such infringements by the Israeli rabbinic courts. Yaakobi is wrong.

The right to marry and establish a legally sanctioned family unit is itself a basic human and constitutional right, and Israelis have no choice to marry except in accordance with the laws of Moses and Israel, as those laws are interpreted by the rabbinic courts. They are not making a free choice but rather a fully coerced and tormented one, to marry the rabbinic way with all its indignities and curtailments of their freedom and autonomy or do not marry at all. Furthermore, the majority of Israelis have no idea that by marrying in accordance with the sole government-sanctioned procedure they have facilitated the infringement on their liberty (see chapter 1). Even many Orthodox couples who marry in Israel do so without any understanding that by accepting the "obligations and rights" of Jewish marriage, their liberties could be curtailed forever by a recalcitrant spouse and an accommodating court (see chapters 3 and 4). And even those who may have such an inkling assume that their partner will not abuse them by exercising their "rights."

Moreover, and most important for our purposes, no state can allow for and support the institutionalization of marriage in a such a way that facilitates, accommodates, authorizes, legitimates, and legalizes infringement on the liberty of persons in the name of the law. Such an institution is slavery, not marriage. Indeed, it is possible to argue that by imposing religious laws on its citizens in the area of marriage and divorce, Israel is infringing not only on the rights of persons to marry who are barred from marrying under religious law (for example, a kohen and a divorcee) but also on the rights of persons to marry by requiring them to do so in ways that violate their liberty.

In a decision on the rights of family unification (*Adala Legal Centre v. Ministry of Interior*, 2006) and in a close examination of that right and its derivation, a former Supreme Court deputy chief justice, Mishael Cheshin, affirmed that to marry and have a family is a right that, though not expressly supported by the Basic Law of Human Dignity and Liberty, is supported by the highest right of all — the right to human dignity:

> We all agree — how could we do otherwise? — that a person, any person, has a right to marry and to have a family life. The covenant between a man and a woman, family life, was created before the state existed and before rights and obligations came into the world. First came the creation of man, and man means both men and women. "And God created man in His image, in the image of God. He created him, male and female. He created them" (Genesis 1, 27 [245]). Thus Adam and Eve were created. A man needs a woman and a woman needs a man: "Wherefore a man shall leave his father and his mother and cling to his wife, and they shall be one flesh" (Genesis 2, 24).
>
> The right to marry and to have a family life . . . is the basis for the existence of society. The family unit is the basic unit of human society, and society and the state are built on it. It is not surprising, therefore, that the right to a family life has been recognized in the international community as a basic right. This is also the law in Israel. . . . See also art. 16(1) of the Universal Declaration of Human Rights, 1948. . . . Even though this right, the right to marry and to have a family life, has not been expressly included among the basic rights that have been expressly recognized in the Basic Laws, we will all agree — agree and declare — that it is derived from the highest right of all, from human dignity. (paras. 46, 47)

Our Recommendations: Disengagement, Relocation, and Reinterpretation

Like Cheshin, we believe that the right to marry and have a family is derived from the highest right of all, human dignity. We add that by imposing religious rules on citizens in matters of marriage and divorce, the state compromises this right.

This book is not meant as an attack on halakha, religion, or as yet another Israel-bashing effort. We are well aware of how our traditions, customs, tribalism, religion, culture, or nationalism ground us in society and give us meaning and order and place. Whether we relate to our Jewishness as our individual habits of the heart and faith, or as our community way of life and tradition, or as our cultural and historical heritage, or all three intertwined, it is what identifies us, locates us in time and place, reminds us where we come from and who we are. Getting married the Jewish way, and in accordance with Jewish laws, is how we celebrate the tribe's rites of passage, and it marks us as a members of the tribe and not as anonymous individuals of the amorphous liberal, Western world. As Isaiah Berlin noted in 1958 in his letter to Ben Gurion (see introduction), our Jewish national, cultural, and religious strands seem inextricably linked.

Nonetheless, it is our contention that these strands are unwinding before us, and we must consciously and purposely pursue the unraveling as well as the proper placement of all the newly defined and disentangled strands. We cannot indulge our identity needs and community values in ways that compromise our human and individual rights. The modern woman in a Western-style democracy has a right to expect justice and equality from a court of law, as well as the protection of her autonomy and dignity, and not to have to contend with religiously motivated sophistry or identity politics.

We propose a three-pronged approach: disengagement, relocation, and reinterpretation.

DISENGAGEMENT

First, marriage and divorce must be unraveled from halakha, disengaging the two completely and making civil marriage and divorce available in Israel as they are in all Western-style democracies, even in countries where the Catholic Church once controlled these matters, such as Italy, Ireland, and Spain. Israeli men and women who want to formally commit themselves to each other must be free to marry in whatever civil or religious ceremonies suit them, and Israeli women must no longer be forced to unwittingly marry in a way that binds them unilaterally to their husbands, as they do today. Right now none of us Israelis, irrespective of our religious affiliations or value systems, have a choice — when it comes to marriage and divorce, religious rules are imposed on us (see chapters 1 and 6). There should be one set of civil divorce laws, universally applicable to all Israeli citizens, of all religions, cultures, and ethnic backgrounds, even if individuals might still feel committed to their traditional communities and may insist on continuing to abide by their own millet rules, including, of course, halakha.

These changes must take place as a matter of human rights and justice, even without regard to their impact on the problem of women and Jewish divorce. But there's no doubt that civil marriage and divorce will ameliorate the problem of women tied to failed marriage, as it does for Jews who do not marry in Orthodox or Conservative ceremonies in the Diaspora, where their civil marriages have been considered by the consensus of rabbinic authorities as halakhic "nullities."

Furthermore, to minimize the harm done to those traditionalists who would insist on Orthodox marriages despite the availability of civil marriage in Israel, the family courts should expand the civil responses to address get abuse, to include the imposition of damages on recalcitrant spouses (see chapter 5), the cancellation of contracts entered into under pressure for the get (with the presumption that contracts in which property was not evenly divided are "unconscionable"), and the denial of relief of any sort in family court to a person imposing a barrier to another for remarriage (see chapter 7).

RELOCATION

The existing rabbinic courts must be privatized as arbitration panels, that is, denuded of the force of law and separated from any connection with state apparatuses, including its courts and legislature, and relocated from the sphere of the state to the realm of discretional, nongovernmental civil society and activity, along with any new rabbinic tribunals that may be established — by, for example, the more liberal-minded modern Orthodox Zohar movement or the Conservative and Reform movements. They will flourish or not depending on the public's demand for their services. By expressly taking halakha out of the realm of obligatory law and placing it within the realm of discretionary cultures and traditions, such relocation will make it clearer that law is law and halakha is something completely different, thus enabling the state courts to better keep civil law's priorities and values straight and its spheres of influence separate and apart from religious values and rules. Human rights will take a predominant role, even in the absence of a formal constitution in Israel (see chapter 7). No tradition, no halakha, no identity politics can be allowed to trump such principles as equality before the law, freedom of conscience, and liberty. These principles must be protected by the state. With religion in its proper relocated place outside of government and politics, it should be easier for Israeli family courts, including the Supreme Court acting as the instance of appeal, to decide issues brought before them, including such issues as damage claims for infringements on liberty and dignity made in the name of God (see chapter 5).

In addition, this relocation will enable ultra-Orthodox, Orthodox, Conservative, and Reform Jews, as well as Jews of other denominations or Israelis of other faiths, to continue adhering to what they feel are their religious obligations and rules. As Professor Martha Nussbaum of the University of Chicago writes, "Loyal members of a religious group should remain at liberty to follow its teachings . . . but this does not justify imposing such teachings on people who do not so choose, especially when imposition is unequal and when it violates a fundamental right of choice" (1999, p. 100). Moreover, the relocation of religion into civil society will allow for the reinvention of Jewish tradition or, more accurately, the proliferation of different Jewish traditions and expressions that will more readily align with the values and policies of a modern western state dedicated to the protection of human rights. Professors Charles Liebman and Eliezer Don-Yehiya have argued that the Israeli state, in particular, is in need of a "civil religion" that resonates with tradition to sustain its viability as a Jewish state (1983), and Professor Benedict Anderson claimed that states in general must imagine themselves as "nations" to unite diversified groups of people into a single community with common goals and values within the limited borders of a sovereign state (1983). If these scholars are right, such proliferation, and subsequent realignment, will buttress the Jewishness of the State of Israel and not undermine it. Current attempts to align the Israeli state with ultra-Orthodox, fundamentalist Judaism is undermining the Jewishness of the state, not helping it.

With their disengagement from the state and respectable reassignment to the vital sphere of civil society, rabbinic courts of all stripes and denominations will reinterpret Jewish traditions, rules, and halakhot and find creative solutions to prevent the dilemmas that challenge the relevance of religious laws to modern society in general and the problem of women entering into marriages that they cannot exit without their husband's consent, in particular. Privatization and the resulting competition will inspire creativity that is good for the Jews.

Civil Marriage and Divorce in Israel

We have proposed a three-pronged approach to civil marriage in Israel to ensure that the rules of marriage and divorce are just and protect human rights: disengagement of the state from the rabbinic courts, relocation of religion within the public and nongovernmental sphere of civil society, and the reinterpretation of halakha.

The suggestion that Israel institute civil marriage is not a new one. It has been promoted vigorously by NGOs, including a coalition of at least twenty-four organizations calling for "Free Choice in Marriage" and referred to by that name. Academics, interestingly led by prominent modern Orthodox scholars, have been backing civil marriage for a long time, including Hebrew University scientist and philosopher Yeshayahu Leibowitz (1992), a former dean of Tel Aviv University Law School Ariel Rosen-Zvi (1995), and former Hebrew University Law professor Pinhas Shifman (1994). Periodically, Knesset members have proposed legislation to institute civil marriage and divorce in one variation or another, with no success.

Two of the most prominent proposals are those made by Hebrew University law professor Ruth Gavison and rabbi and educator Yaakov Medan in their *Covenant* (Artsieli, 2004) and by Bar Ilan University professor Shachar Lifshitz in his *Spousal Registry*, drafted for the Israel Democracy Institute (Lifshitz, 2006). Neither proposal has been adopted into legislation. Both continue to intertwine state, nation, and religion in confusing and unsatisfying ways that neither resolve the human rights' issues raised, nor answer the halakhic concerns of the ultra-Orthodox. Far superior in all respects is what could be termed the "American" model, as set forth by Pinhas Shifman in his book *Who's Afraid of Civil Marriage* (1994).

In the Gavison-Medan *Covenant* the authors state unequivocally that they want to rework the status quo arrangement. Of particular interest to them is freedom of conscience — the "principle of non-coercion" or "the right of every group to preserve its own lifestyle according to its own conception and interpretation," including how they are buried, observe the Sabbath and dietary laws, pray at the Western Wall, and get married and divorced. Their proposal envisions a system in which persons can choose to marry and divorce in civil or religious ceremonies, but when it comes to remarrying, they may do so only if they are considered "unmarried both according to civil law and according to the law of his religion" in "the most strict interpretation" (Artsieli, 2004).

Aware that the proposal restores religious coercion at the time of remarriage and subjects women to the same problems of "equality" and "humiliation and the difficulties in obtaining a get" that exist today, Gavison explains her compromise as essential. She wants to solve the mamzer problem, which she thinks is necessary to protect the best interest of the child and, most important in her mind, to address "the fear of dividing the nation." "From my perspective," she writes, " the reason for requiring a religious divorce is not a religious reason per se, but a cultural-national one" (49). Rabbi Medan echoes the same concerns as Gavison but adds that from his perspective requiring a get at the time of remarriage is essential to prevent the proliferation of mamzerim, which is also a religious problem since, according to him, "it is a sin of incalculable proportions" (54). But by compromising on the freedom of conscience of persons who want to remarry, Gavison and Medan do not solve the mamzer problem or ensure the unity of the Jewish people — that all persons who claim to be Jews can marry each other without having to enquire into their genealogy. In fact, if adopted, the Gavison-Medan proposal may create more mamzerim and divisiveness, both in Israel and the Diaspora, than prevent those phenomena. In their model, an Israeli Jewish divorcee must obtain an Orthodox get if she wants to remarry so that any children born in her new marriage will not be tainted. But this also means that should such a woman procreate without remarrying, her children would be considered mamzerim. And it also implies the need for a very Orthodox get in the event of a dissolution of a civil marriage, a position taken by the rabbis in chapter 6, but by no means the prevailing one among rabbinic authorities (see introduction). Requiring a get in the event of civil marriage places children born to Jews in the Diaspora who have married, divorced, and procreated for generations in ways that were not Orthodox at the risk of being considered mamzerim, dividing the Jewish people in ways not anticipated by Gavison and Medan.

In 1959 Yeshayahu Leibowitz, an Orthodox but iconoclastic thinker, published an article titled "A Call for the Separation of Religion and State," in which he had already anticipated this dilemma, stating, "Did religious Jewry, in its fear of Mamzeruth on the one hand and concern for the unity of the nation on the other, think of the problems that will arise the moment — perhaps not so far away — when masses of Jews from the U.S.S.R. or the United States will stream to Israel? These Jews have conducted their lives for two generations, or even more, in accordance with the legal provisions and social patterns of their countries of residence. It will not prove possible to trace their precise family status. How does religious Jewry think it could assure the unity of the nation in those conditions?" (1992).

The idea for a spousal registry was first conceived by Dr. Shachar Lifshitz in 2000 in response to a challenge raised by then justice minister Dr. Yossi Beilin to find creative ways to introduce civil marriage in Israel. Lifshitz, at the time a PhD student at Bar Ilan University, argued that by expanding the rights and privileges of cohabitating partners and by acknowledging overseas civil marriages in the attempt to address the problems raised by religious law, Israeli civil law was not sufficiently addressing the problems inherent in the current divorce regime and may instead be intensifying them. He felt, for example, that it is unfair for the law to impose economic consequences on cohabiting couples who have specifically chosen not to formalize their relationship. Moreover, he believed that existing civil law does not adequately ensure the rights and responsibilities of couples who marry overseas, by including, for example, the obligation to support each other or instructions on how to dissolve their relationship. Lifshitz proposed that an entirely new system be conceived that, in addition to addressing the human rights violations outlined earlier, develops a clear civil policy of divorce law.

With the support of the Israel Democracy Institute, Lifshitz composed the proposal known as the *Spousal Registry*. In its initial conception, the proposal recommended establishing a new civil legal body known as the Spousal Registrar, which would operate alongside the current Orthodox one. Orthodox marriages would remain as the only marriages recognized officially by the state, but couples who wanted to live together with legal implications and did not want to marry in an Orthodox ceremony could choose to register as a couple in the Spousal Registrar. This new category would be added to all Israeli I.D. cards and the population registry.

Registering couples would sign affidavits in which they would specifically declare that they do not intend to marry in accordance with religious law, thus minimizing the chance that a rabbinic court will view the registering couple as married and in need of a get. Thus, according to Lifshitz (2006), the *Spousal Registry* would solve both the dilemma of those who cannot marry, as well the problem as those who cannot divorce.

The Lifshitz proposal has its clear benefits. It is politically expedient and would serve as a wonderful interim position to civil marriage and divorce. Unlike the Gavison and Medan proposal, it at least attempts to save those couples who are perspicacious and audacious enough to register with the *Spousal Registry* from having to divorce in state rabbinic courts. And it would also seem to have the pragmatic advantage of not presenting a threat to religious parties in the Knesset. But it is not enough, and in fact it also causes Lifshitz some discomfort: "It is important to note that the draft legislation is, in fact, a compromise. It does not purport to be a perfect proposal that answers every need of every party involved. On the contrary, it contains painful compromises from both the religious and the civil-liberal points of view. As someone religious who holds a liberal world view, I must say that the concessions made from both perspectives often left me frustrated and in distress."

Indeed, the proposal perpetuates, in the name of the state, a legal regime that infringes on the human rights of some of its citizens. It infringes on the freedom of conscience of those who want to marry in religious ceremonies that are not Orthodox. And by allowing the current rabbinic courts to stand and religious laws to govern some of the people, the Spousal Registrar supports a legal regime that infringes on the equality, liberty, due process, and property of those persons who chose to marry in an Orthodox manner, albeit out of their informed and conscious choice. The spirit of liberalism may allow for people to be free to choose to marry and divorce and generally live their lives in an illiberal way and in ways that may infringe on their own human rights. But the state has no right to support such illiberal institutions and laws and to perpetuate them in ways that fly in the face of human rights, irrespective of those laws' genealogies or ascription to Jewish traditions, customs, or halakhot. Neither should the state prevent persons from "opting out" of those alternative illiberal legal regimes and courts should they choose to in the future.

The *Spousal Registry* also does nothing for the "symbolic" Jewish character of the state, which is one of the reasons Lifshitz claims for suggesting a dual regime, except, perhaps, as that character may be imagined by some Nationalist Zionist Orthodox citizens. If there is significance and importance to religious marriage in the construction of the symbols and values of the Jewish state — what Charles Liebman and Eliezer Don-Yehiya refer to as Israel's civil religion (1983) — such symbols should be wide enough and embracive enough to include all forms of Jewish marriage. By ceding symbolic status to ultra-Orthodox marriages and divorces, Lifshitz boxes the state's Jewishness into a very small framework indeed. (Interestingly, Liebman and Don-Yehiya do not include religious marriage at all among the symbols they say the state has taken from Jewish tradition and reformulated to reflect the values of Israeli society and its public image.)

And finally, it is questionable whether Lifshitz's proposal will solve the dilemma of the halakhic civil marriage. When rabbinic courts and authorities attribute halakhic status to civil marriages, drawing on opinions based on texts written long before civil marriages ever existed, even though more modern authorities have held otherwise, they do so because they can and because it serves their particular needs (see chapter 6). In the case of the Israeli rabbinic courts, those needs seem to be the very fundamental ones, in which a small group of Orthodox Jews call on their sacred texts to ground their political power and identity on the backs of women. This thesis, however disturbing, is eerily echoed in the words of the Muslim anthropologist and feminist Ziba Mir-Housseini, writing about Islamic family law and the place of the Shari'a in that system: "Where modern and patriarchal orders coexist, often in a contradictory union, the Shari'a has come to acquire a special place. It symbolizes a golden past. . . . It acts as a buffer against rapid erosion of the traditional way of life and the aggressive invasion of Western values; it provides a refuge in a world permeated by uncertainty and chronic economic crisis; it is an innate answer to the crisis of identity; and, above all, it is an ideology which is used to justify unequal relations, of which gender relations are only one facet. An ideology which can claim divine roots is thereby more persuasive" (1993, p. 199).

In 2004 a legislative committee set up by the Ministry of Justice and headed by Dr. Peretz Segal, the ministry's legal advisor, modified and drafted Lifshitz's *Spousal Registry* proposal in the form of a bill. To date, it has not been approved by the Knesset. On March 15, 2010, the Knesset passed a very truncated form of the bill to cover the very limited circumstances in which both parties requesting to register as married are deemed by a rabbinic court to be "without religion." In response, Lifshitz (2010) has lamented, "This is not the baby we prayed for."

WHAT WE WANT: THE U.S./SHIFMAN MODEL

To best protect the human rights of its citizens, as well as to best safeguard the unity of the Jewish people, Israel would do well to adopt the approach to civil marriage and divorce based on the model used in the United States. Persons would have the right to marry and divorce in the religious or civil ceremony of their choice, which, assuming that it is performed by a licensed civil servant, would be recognized by the state and afford whatever rights and obligations the state has to confer on married couples. A divorce would occur only on a state proclamation that such divorce has occurred, and on the conditions to be set forth by the state, which should include consensual divorce, divorce after the irretrievable breakdown of the marriage, and separation for a period to be determined by the legislature.

The State of Israel must disband its religious courts and, most important, be rid of the blacklist set up as a response to the functioning of those courts. In turn, the state should support (perhaps even subsidize) the setting up of private rabbinic arbitration panels of all denominations to which persons can, at their choice, discretion, and cost, opt to go to. While this may not completely solve the problem of Jewish women in divorce cases, since some couples will still choose to marry in Orthodox ceremonies and to arbitrate the delivery of a get in rabbinic courts, it will significantly ameliorate it. But those who don't opt for the Orthodox option won't be held hostage by it. And without an official state-sanctioned religious court system and blacklist operated by civil bureaucrats intent on protecting the fundamentals and identity of a new ultra-Orthodoxy, mamzerim will not be targeted or followed by a powerful state apparatus but hopefully will be allowed to blend indiscernibly among the Jewish population, as they did for centuries — before their capture within the iron cage of modern tribunals, computers, and electronic communication.

With regard to those who still choose, whether out of their free will or because of societal pressure, to marry in Orthodox ceremonies and may still want a get, the state must take an active role in curtailing the abuses of power they may suffer. The family courts and the Knesset must adopt and expand on all available civil remedies to help those who are the victims of get refusal and abuse. Israeli courts, like those in New York, Canada, England and Wales, Scotland, and South Africa (Weiss & Dainow, n.d.), should have the discretion to withhold any judicial remedy requested by a person who refuses to remove religious barriers to the remarriage of his or her spouse, as well as to void contracts, or parts of contracts, signed under pressure for the get and which give a party financial benefits otherwise not due them under law (see introduction). Under very limited and circumscribed circumstances, it might also be possible for the civil courts to put recalcitrant spouses in jail at the recommendation of a religious arbitration panel.

But for the continued existence of the Jewish state as a state of all the Jewish people, as well as for the continued vibrancy of the State of Israel as a democratic state loyal to human rights, it is necessary, essential, and even crucial to sever all connections of the state to halakha — of any denominational interpretation, from the most lenient to the most strict. And the sooner the better. The place in the State of Israel for halakhic dialogue, as well as for *mishpat ivri* (Hebrew law) or *din torah* (Torah law), as those terms may differ or overlap, should be in what is often referred to as "civil society" (Avraham, 2005). The State of Israel cannot share authority over its citizens in any way with a legal system that admittedly and unabashedly ignores the rule of law and human rights.

According to the former Czech president, playwright, and thinker Václav Havel, civil society is a place that gives "power to the powerless," where the social contract can be renegotiated, and where value-based activity can occur (Reverter-Banon, 2006). It is a place of collective action and organization that stands distinct from state institutions and includes nongovernmental organizations, registered charities, women's organizations, self-help groups, and social movements, for example. It is into the arena of civil society that we would put rabbinic courts that currently operate under the auspices of the state and at the expense of the Israeli taxpayer. There, in civil society, courts will have to be user-friendly to survive and attract litigants, and it is there that courts may find a way to reinterpret halakha to meet the needs of a modern world.

In Summation

These are not just stories about agunot, individual women caught up by happenstance and bad luck in extreme situations; though they are, of course, all that as well. These are not just texts of terror or narratives of pain; though they are, of course, all that. Nor are these cases about singular failings of a good-as-it-gets legal apparatus meant to do justice. The system is not as good as it gets. And it does not do justice.

It is our primary intention that this book be about how the Israeli state has, on the backs of women, attempted to identify itself as a Jewish, democratic state--different from all other states--by using as its focal point for such identification a movement that is religious, fundamentalist, transnational, cultural, and "churchlike." By doing so, not only has Israel sacrificed its women, it has sacrificed its identification as a democratic state with its commitment to human rights and the rule of law. And by taking this fundamentalist movement as its focal point, Israel has compromised its identity as a Jewish state.

It is essential, almost axiomatic, that the Israeli state readjust its moorings to allow for the incorporation of human rights and the rule of law into the parameters of its points of identification. Religious movements must defer to the state and its laws and acknowledge that it is not their place, even to the extent that it is in the public sphere, to challenge the primacy of human rights or try to replace state laws with God's. Without such reidentification, the current (de facto, if partial) theocracy is not working. We are not suggesting replacing the current fundamentalist and dictatorial theocracy with a benevolent one. We are advocating for no theocracy, something promised by Ben-Gurion to the United Nations in 1947 and reiterated in the status quo agreement, in those words.

It is also necessary for the state to readjust its moorings to allow for the incorporation of a multitude of Jewish expressions into the parameters of its points of identification, this for it to fulfill its own stated purpose of being a homeland for all Jews. Judaism is much more than just Ashkenazi Orthodoxy, or what is seen by some, paradoxically, as a very modern interpretation of what it means to be a Jew (Soleveitchik, 1994). And, despite Ben Gurion's desire to keep the people together, life and reality have already fragmented us into many different variations on a theme that should be looked at as a beautiful mosaic, instead of a monolithic and coherent whole.

And with regard to the Jewish nature of the state and the possible fragmentation of the Jewish people, such fears are unfounded. Israeli state institutions will always serve kosher food; the Jewish Sabbath will always be the official day of rest; Jewish holidays and historical events will be commemorated; and the Israeli flag will host the Jewish Star of David. And if given support and respect in civil society (and especially if financed to some extent by the state), Jewish culture, tradition, and even halakha will flourish in all its various and sometimes contradictory and ever-changing permutations, uncoerced and contributing to the Jewish nature of the state and to the resolution of such dilemmas as the sabbath year, the convert, mamzer, and, of course, the agunah, just as many such actors are doing right now and even as we do so with the publication of this book. And as for the fragmentation of the Jewish people, we are already a diverse and varied group, and more power to us.

BIBLIOGRAPHY

Legal Cases

INTERNATIONAL CASES

Brett v. Brett. England and Wales Court of Appeal, Civil Division (1968) 1 All ER
1007. 1 WLR 487 2 (1969)

Bruker v. Marcovitz. File No. 31212. MontSC (2007). 3 SCR 607 SCC 54.

ISRAELI CASES

*Academic Institute for Law and Business, Human Rights Clinic v. Minister of
Finance.* HCJ 2605/05 (2009). Nevo Database. Retrieved April 18, 2011 from
http://elyon1.court.gov.il/files_eng/05/050/026/n39/05026050.n39.htm [English].

Adalah Legal Centre v. Minister of Defense. HCJ 8276/05 (2006). Nevo Database.
IsrLR, 352 (2), 2006 [English].

Adalah Legal Centre v. Minister of Interior et al. HCJ 7052/03. Opinion of Michael
Cheshin. *IsrSC*, 61(3), 537 (2006). *IsrLR*, 1, 443 (1), 2006 [English].

Bank Mizrahi v. Migdal Cooperative Village. CA 6821/93. *IsrSC*, 49(4), 221 (1995).
IsrLR, 1 (1995) [English].

Ben Ari v. Director of Population Registrar of the Ministry of Interior. HCJ 3045/05.
IsrSC, 61(3), 537 (2006).

B. v. K. (1). 038372306-21-1 HRabC (Shahar, Edri, Oshinshky) (2010). *Law and Its
Decisor* 26(case 4) 2011.

B. v. K. (2). 587922/5 HRabC (Shahar, Edri, Oshinshky) (2010). Unpublished.

Center for Women's Justice v. Rabbinic Court Administrative Offices. LC3252/08
JmLC (2008). Nevo Database.

C. S. v. C. P. 19270/03 JmFamC (HaCohen) (2004). Nevo Database.

C. v. C. 041987009-24-1 HRabC (Shlosh, Herzberg, Gimzo) (2003). *Law and Its
Decisor* 9(case 6) 2005.

C. v. C. RabA 009/54 HRabC (Eliyahu, Tufik, Nadav) (1994). Unpublished.

C. v. C. RabA 009/56 HRabC (Eliyahu, Tufik, Nadav) (1997). Unpublished.

C. v. C. RabA 041987009-24-1 HRabC (Amar, Sherman, Izerer) (2006). *Law and Its Decisor* 12(5) 2006.

C. v. High Rabbinic Court et al. (2001). Available from authors.

Da'aka v. Carmel Hospital. CA 2781/93. *IsrSC,* 53(4), 526 (1999). *IsrLR, 409* (1998-1999) [English].

Gaza Coast Regional Council v. Knesset of Israel et al. HCJ 1661/05. *IsrSC,* 59(2), 481 (2005).

Israel Movement for Progressive Judaism v. Sharon (agreement). HCJ 4934/04. *IsrSC* (2004). Unpublished.

Israel Movement for Progressive Judaism v. Sharon (petition). HCJ 4934/04. *IsrSC* (2004). Retrieved May 10, 2012, from http://www.humanrights.org.il/main.asp ?MainCategoryID=15&CategoryLeve102ID=194.

Israel Women's Network v. Government of Israel. HCJ 453/94. *IsrSC,* 48(5), 501 (1994). *IsrLR, 425* (1992-1994) [English].

Izkovitch v. Jerusalem Rabbinic Court. HCJ 2260/90. *IsrSC,* 44(4), 699 (1990).

K. S. v. K. S. 44248-05-10 JmFamC (Felix). (2011). Nevo Database.

K. v. K. 6743/02 JmFamC (Greenberger). (2008). Nevo Database.

L. v. L. 054568514-21-2. NetRabC (2004),(2006), (2007[1]), (2007[2]). Unpublished.

L. v. L. 272088/6 NetRabC (Amos, Pardes, Yanai). (2011). *Law and Its Decisor 27* (case 7) 2011.

Miller v. Minister of Defense. HCJ 4541/94. *IsrSC,* 49(4), 94 (1995). *IsrLR, 178* (1995-1996) [English].

N. v. N. (Yaakobi). FHRA 2374/11. *IsrSC* (2011). Unpublished.

N. v. N. 24782/98 TAFamC (Sivan) (2008). Nevo Database.

N. v. N. 311698393-21-1 TARabC (2000). *Law and Its Decisor 18*(case 9) 2008.

N. v. N. 311698393-21-1 TARabC (2005). Unpublished.

N. v. N. FamA 1020/09 TADC (Kovo, Rubenstein, Cherniak) (2011). Unpublished.

N. v. N. FHR 2374/11. *IsrSC* (Hendel) (2012). Nevo Database.

Office of Israeli Financial Planners v. Minister of Finance. HCJ 1715/97. *IsrSC,* 51(4), 367 (1998).

Oron v. Knesset Speaker. HCJ 1030/99. *IsrSC,* 56(3), 640 (2002).

Plonit v. Ploni (Benai Noah). RabA 4276/63. HRabC (Dichovski, Sherman, Izerer) (2003). *Law and Its Decisor 5*(case 3) 2004.

Plonit v. Ploni (HaCohen). 021162/07 JmFamC (HaCohen) (2010). Nevo Database.

Plonit v. Ploni (right to stay married). HCJ 2609/05. *IsrSC* (2011). Nevo Database.

Plonit v. Ploni (separation). RabA 034524637-21-1. HRabC (Sherman, Elgrabli,
    Elhadad) (2007). *Law and Its Decisor 18*(case 8) 2008.

Plonit v. Tel Aviv Rabbinic Court et al. (civil marriage). HCJ 2232/03. *IsrSC, 61*(3),
    496 (2005).

Ploni v. Plonit (infidelity). RabA 1219-21-1 HRabC (Dichovsky, Sherman, Izerer)
    (2006). Retreived May 12, 2012, from www.rbc.gov.il/judgements/docs/270.doc.

Ploni v. State of Israel. MCrim 8823/07. *IsrSC* (2009). Nevo Database.

Plotkin v. Eisenberg Brothers. LC 3-129. *IsrNLC* (1997). *33IsrLL, 481* (1999).

Poraz v. Lahat. HCJ 953/87. *IsrSC, 42*(2), 309 (1988).

Punk Schlesinger v. Ministry of Interior. HCJ 143/62. *IsrSC, 17,* 249 (1962).

P. v. P. FamC 9877/02 Rishon LeZion (Shtein) (2010). Nevo Database.

Regan v. Transportation Ministry. HCJ 746/07. *IsrSC* (2011). Nevo Database.

Sabag v. High Rabbinic Court. HCJ 6751/04. *IsrSC, 59*(4), 817 (2004).

Shakdiel v. Minister of Religious Afairs. HCJ 153/87. *IsrSC, 42*(2), 221 (1988). *IsrSJ 8,*
    186 [English].

Shalit v. Minister of Interior and Regisration Clerk of Haifa. HCJ 587/68. *IsrSC, 23*(2)
    477 (1970). *IsrSJ, 35* (1971) [English].

State of Israel v. Ofir Beeri. CA 5612/92. *IsrSC, 48*(1), 302 (1993).

S. v. S. 3950/00 JmFamC (J. Greenberger) (2001). *IsrDC, 29* (2001).

Taib v. State of Israel. CA 115/00. *IsrSC, 54*(3), 289 (2000).

Training Institute for Rabbinic Court Pleaders v. Minister of Religious Affairs. HC
    6300/93. *IsrSC, 48*(4), 441 (1994).

T. v. T. 022158/97 Motion 056986/07 JmFamC (HaCohen) (2007). Unpublished.

Tzemach v. Minister of Defense. HCJ 6055/95. *IsrSC, 53*(5), 241 (1999). *IsrLR, 635*
    (1998-1999) [English].

United Mizrahi Bank Ltd. v. Migdal Cooperative Village. CA 6821/93. *IsrSC, 49*(4),
    221 (1995). *IsrLR, 1* (1995) [English].

Yaakobi v. Yaakobi. CA 1951/91. *IsrSC, 49*(3), 529 (1995).

Ziv v. DeFacto Head of the Tel Aviv Municipality. HCJ 10/48. *IsrSC, 1,* 85 (1948).

U.S. CASES

Cruzan v. Missouri Department of Health. 497 U.S. 261 (1990).

Eisenstadt v. Baird. 405 U.S. 438 (1972).

Griswold v. Connecticut. 381 U.S. 479 (1965).

Lawrence v. Texas. 539 U.S. 558 (2003).

Loving v. Virginia. 388 U.S. 1 (1967).

Olmstead v. United States. 277 U.S. 438 (1928).
Perl v. Perl. NY S. Ct. 126 A.D. 2d 91 (1987).
Roe v. Wade. 410 U.S. 113 (1973).
Skinner v. Oklahoma. 316 U.S. 535 (1942).
Wisconsin v. Yoder. 406 U.S. 205 (1972).

Published Works

Adler, R. (1973, Summer). "The Jew Who Wasn't There: Halacha and the Jewish Woman." *Response: A Contemporary Jewish Review.*

Almond, G., Appleby, R., & Sivan, E. (2003). *Strong Religion: The Rise of Fundamentalisms around the World.* Chicago, IL: University of Chicago Press.

Amar, R. M., & Rubenstein, E. (2003, December 23). *Procedural Guidelines for Those Ineligible for Marriage* [in Hebrew]. Justice Department. Retrieved May 22, 2011, from http://www.justice.gov.il/NR/rdonlyres/EC880D06-9620 -44AC-9CC2-3A1ED52643F8/0/lineage.pdf.

Americans for Divorce Reform. (2002). "World Divorce Statistics: Percentage of New Marriages Which End in Divorce, in Selected Countries." *DivorceMagazine .com.* Retrieved August 8, 2011, from http://www.divorcemag.com/statistics /statsWorld.shtml.

Anderson, B. (1983). *Imagined Communities: Reflections on the Origin and Spread of Nationalism.* London, England: Verso.

Artsieli, Y. (2004). *Foundation for a New Covenant among Jews in Matters of Religion and State in Israel: The Gavison-Medan Covenant; Main Points and Principles.* Israel Democracy Institute/Avi Chan Israel. Retrieved August 15, 2011, from http://www.gavison-medan.org.il/Admin/fileserver/ikarim%20English.pdf?file=6.

Avraham, H. M. (2005). "Is Halacha the Same as Mishpat Ivri? On Religion, Morality, and the Law" [in Hebrew]. *Akdamot, 15,* 141-163.

Barak-Erez, D. (1995). "From an Unwritten to a Written Constitution: The Israeli Challenge in American Perspective." *Columbia Human Rights Law Review, 26,* 309-355.

Barak-Erez, D. (2009). Law and Religion under the Status Quo Model: Between Past Compromises and Constant Change. *Cardozo Law Review, 20*(6), 2495-2507.

Ben-Gurion, D. (1958, October 27). "Letter to Isaiah Berlin, and Other" [in Hebrew]. Unpublished manuscript. Jerusalem, Israel: Ben Gurion University.

Ben-Hayyim, A. (2007, June 26). *Rabbinic Court: More Men Denied Divorce*

Than Women [in Hebrew]. NRG, Ma'ariv. Retrieved August 29, 2011, from
http://www.nrg.co.il/online/1/ART1/600/643.html.

Berger, P. (1997, Winter). "Secularism in Retreat." *National Interest, 46*, 3–13.

Berkovits, E. (1983). *Not in Heaven: The Nature and Function of Halakha*. Jerusalem:
Ktav.

Berlin, I. (1958). *Two Concepts of Liberty*. Oxford, England: Clarendon.

Berlin, I. (2009). *Enlightening Letters, 1946–1960* (H. Hardy & J. Holmes, Eds.).
London, England: Chatto and Windus.

Bourdieu, P. (2001). *Masculine Domination* (R. Nice, Trans.). Cambridge, MA:
Polity.

Brandeis, L. D., & Warren, S. (1890). *Harvard Law Review, 4*(5), 193–220.

Breitowitz, I. A. (1993). *Between Civil and Religous Law: The Plight of the Agunah in
American Society*. Westport, CT: Greenwood.

Casanova, J. (1994). *Public Religions and the Modern World*. Chicago, IL: University
of Chicago Press.

Center for Pluralistic Judaism. (n.d.). "There is an Equal/Worthwhile Way to
Marry as a Jew" [Hebrew]. *Beit-Daniel*. Retrieved August 24, 2011, from http://
www.beit-daniel.org.il/imgs/site/ntext/weddings.pdf.

Convention on the Elimination of All Forms of Discrimination against Women.
(1979, December 18). Office of the High Commissioner for Human Rights.
United Nations. Retrieved May 13, 2012, from http://www2.ohchr.org/english/law
/cedaw.htm.

Cooke, R., & Cusack, S. (2010). *Gender Stereotyping*. Philadelphia: University of
Pennsylvania Press.

Department of Marriage [in Hebrew]. (n.d.). Chief Rabbinate of Tel Aviv-Yaffo,
Religious Councils. Retrieved May 15, 2011, from http://www.rabanut.co.il/show
_item.asp?levelId=60062.

Fact Sheet No. 2 (Rev. 1) International Bill of Human Rights. (n.d.). United Nations
Human Rights. Retrieved May 18, 2011, from http://www.ohchr.org/Documents
/Publications/FactSheet2Rev.1en.pdf.

Falk, Z. (1964). *Hebrew Law in Biblical Times*. Jerusalem, Israel: Wahrmann Books.

Fineman, M. A. (1991). *The Illusion of Equality: The Rhetoric and Reality of Divorce
Reform*. Chicago, IL: University of Chicago Press.

Fraser, N. (1997). "From Redistribution to Recognition? Dilemmas of Justice
in a 'Postsocialist' Age." In *Justice Interruptus: Critical Reflections on the
"Postcolonialist" Condition* (pp. 11–40). New York, NY: Routledge.

Friedman, M. (1990). "The Chronicle of the Status-Quo: Religion and State in Israel" [in Hebrew]. In V. Pilowsky (Ed.), *Transition from Yishuv to State 1947-1949: Continuity and Change* (pp. 47-80). Haifa, Israel: University of Haifa, Herzl Institute for Research in Zionism.

Frimer, D. (1982). "Medical Examination by Order of the Court and the Right to Privacy: The Common Law and Jewish Law Experiences." *Israel Law Review, 17,* 96-103.

Frishtik, M. (1991). "Physical and Sexual Violence by Husbands as a Reason for Imposing a Divorce in Jewish Law." *Jewish Law Annual, 9,* 145-169.

Genovese, E. D. (1976). *Roll, Jordon, Roll: The World the Slaves Made.* New York, NY: Vintage Books.

Glendon, M. A. (1989). *The Transformation of Family Law, State, Law and Family in the United States and Western Europe.* Chicago, IL: University of Chicago Press.

Halbertal, D. (2010, December 22). "Israel Must Separate Religion from Politics." *Haaretz.* Retrieved May, 5, 2012, http://www.haaretz.com/print-edition/opinion /israel-must-separate-religion-from-politics-1.331937.

Halperin, R. (1989). "Adultery on the Part of the Husband as Grounds for Compelling Him to Divorce His Wife" [in Hebrew]. *Mehkarei Mishpat, 7,* 297-329.

Halperin-Kaddari, R., & Adelstein-Zeckback, T. (2011). *Pi Project: Supervision Enforcement and Implementation of Family Law in Israel. Report No. 1: The Rabbinical Courts Law (Implementation of Divorce Judgements, 1995).* Ramat Gan, Israel: Bar Ilan University, Rackman Center.

Halperin-Kaddari, D. R., & Karo, I. (2009). *Women and Family in Israel: Statistical Bi-Annual Report* [in Hebrew]. Ramat Gan, Israel: Bar Ilan University, Rackman Center.

Halperin-Kaddari, R., & Yadgar, Y. (2010). "Between Universal Feminism and Particular Nationalism: Politics, Religion and Gender (In)Equality in Israel. *Third World Quarterly, 31*(6), 905-920.

Harris, R. (2002). "Absent Minded Misses and Historical Opportunities: Jewish Law, Israeli Law and the Establishment of the State of Israel" [in Hebrew]. In M. Bar-On & Z. Zameret (Eds.), *On Both Sides of the Bridge: Religion and State in the Early Years of Israel* (pp. 21-54). Jerusalem: Yad Yizhak Ben-Zvi.

Hauptman, J. (1998). *Rereading the Rabbis: A Woman's Voice (Radical Traditions).* New York, NY: Westview.

Hawthorne, N. (1994). *The Scarlet Letter.* London, England: Penguin Books. (Original work published 1883.)

Herzog, H. (1992). "The Fringes of the Margin: Women's Organizations in the Civic Sector at the Time of the Yishuv." In D. S. Bernstein (Ed.), *Pioneers and Homemakers: Jewish Women in Pre-State Israel* (pp. 283–304). Albany, NY: State University of New York Press.

Herzog, H. (2004). "Women in Israeli Society." In U. Rebhun & C. I. Waxman (Eds.), *Jews in Israel: Contemporary Social and Cultural Patterns* (pp. 195–220). Lebanon, NH: Brandies University Press/University Press of New England.

ICAR. (n.d.). "About ICAR." Retrieved May 16, 2012>> from http://www.icar.org.il /about-icar.html.

Jerusalem Post. (2011, June 18). "154 Couples Tie Knot in Cyprus in Attempt to Break Record." *JPost.com.* Retrieved August 4, 2011, from http://www.jpost.com /LifeStyle/Article.aspx?id=225543.

Krauss, N. (Ed.). (1962). *The Encyclopedical Religious Yearbook.* Tel-Aviv: Sifriati.

Lavie, A. (2006). "Arranging a Get after a Husband Is Ordered to Pay Damages to His Wife" [in Hebrew]. *Tehumin, 27,* 160–172.

Leibowitz, Y. (1992). "A Call for the Separation of Religion and State." 1959. In Y. Leibovitz & E. Goldman (Eds.), *Judaism, Human Values, and the Jewish State.* Cambridge, MA: Harvard University Press.

Liebman, C. S., & Don-Yehiya, E. (1983). *Civil Religion in Israel: Traditional Judaism and Political Culture in the Jewish State.* Berkeley, CA: University of California Press.

Lifshitz, S. (2001). "Law of Secular Cohabitants in the Next 50 Years" [in Hebrew]. *Mechkarei Mishpat, 17,* 157–187.

Lifshitz, S. (2006). *The Spousal Registry.* Israel Democracy Institute. Retrieved August 15, 2011, from http://www.idi.org.il/sites/english/ResearchAndPrograms /Religion%20and%20State/Pages/ReligionandStateArticle1TheSopusalRegistry .aspx.

Lifshitz, S. (2009). "Family Law in the Civil Era: From the Laws of Marriage of Persons Who Married outside Israel to the Day after Civil Marriage Is Instituted within the Country" [In Hebrew]. *Mishpat ve'Asakim, 10,* 447–498.

Lifshitz, S. (2010, September 13). *This Is Not the Baby We Prayed For* [in Hebrew]. Israel Democracy Institute. Retrieved August 15, 2011, from http://www.idi.org.il /BreakingNews/Pages/177.aspx.

Lorde, A. (1984). *Sister Outsider: Essays and Speeches.* Berkeley, CA: Crossing.

MacKinnon, C. (1987). "On Sex Discrimination." In *Feminism Unmodified: Discourses on Life and Law, Difference and Domination* (pp. 32–45). Cambridge, MA: Harvard University Press.

MacKinnon, C. (1989). *Toward a Feminist Theory of the State.* Cambridge, MA: Harvard University Press.

Marty, M. E., & Appelby, R. S. (1994). *Accounting for Fundamentalisms.* Chicago: University of Chicago Press.

Mazie, S. V. (2006). *Israel's Higher Law: Religion and Liberal Democracy in the Jewish State.* Landham, MD: Lexington Books.

Miller, A. (2009). "The Blacklist." Unpublished manuscript.

Mir-Housseini, Z. (1993). *Marriage on Trial: A Study of Islamic Family Law.* London, England: Tauris.

Mualem, M. (2011, May 15). *Israeli Author Yoram Kaniuk Asks Court to Cancel His "Jewish" Status.* Haaretz.com. Retrieved August 1, 2011, from http://www.haaretz.com/print-edition/news/israeli-author-yoram-kaniuk-asks-court-to-cancel-his-jewish-status-1.361720.

Newhouse, A. (2010, July 15). "The Disapora Need Not Apply." *New York Times.* Retrieved August 24, 2011, from http://www.nytimes.com/2010/07/16/opinion/16newhouse.html.

Nussbaum, M. C. (1999). *Sex and Social Justice.* Oxford, England: Oxford University Press.

Okin, S. M. (1999). "Is Multi-Culturalism Bad for Women?" In J. Cohen, M. Howard, & M. C. Nussbaum (Eds.), *Is Multi-Culturalism Bad for Women?* Princeton, NJ: Princeton University Press.

Provisional Government of Israel. (1948, May 14). "Proclamation of Independence." Knesset English home page. Retrieved May 17, 2012, from http://www.knesset.gov.il/docs/eng/megilat_eng.htm.

Rabinovich, I., & Reinharz, J. (Eds.). (2008). *Israel in the Middle East: Documents and Readings on Society, Politics, and Foreign Relations, Pre-1948 to the Present.* Lebanon, NH: Brandeis University Press.

Raday, F. (2005). *A Free People in Our Land: Gender Equality in a Jewish State.* Israeli Ministry of Foreign Affairs. Retrieved July 10, 2011, from http://www.mfa.gov.il/MFA/Government/Facts+about+Israel-+The+State/A+Free+People+in+Our+Land-+Gender+Equality.htm.

Radzyner, A. (n.d.). *The Problem of the Appeal in Jewish Law.* Jewish Virtual Library.

Retrieved August 8, 2011, from http://www.jewishvirtuallibrary.org/jsource/judaica
/ejud_0002_0002_0_01192.html.

Radzyner, A. (2004). "Rabbi Uziel, the Tel Aviv Rabbic Court and the High
Rabbinic Court: A Tale of Four Battlefronts" [in Hebrew]. *Legal Research, 21,*
129–242.

Raz, J. (1979). "The Rule of Law and Its Virtue." In *The Authority of Law: Essays on
Law and Morality* (pp. 210–229). Oxford, England: Clarendon Press, 1979.

Reservations to CEDAW. (n.d.). UN Women. Retrieved May 15, 2011, from
http://www.un.org/womenwatch/daw/cedaw/reservations.htm.

Reverter-Banon, S. (2006). *Civil Society and Gender Equality: A Theoretical
Approach, Civil Society Working Paper No. 24.* London School of Economics and
Political Science. Centre for Civil Society. Retrieved September 12, 2011, from
http://eprints.lse.ac.uk/29077/1/CSWP24.pdf.

Ripple, Y. (1998). "Where's the Status Quo?" In S. Aharoni & M. Aharoni (Eds.),
Personalities and Events in the State of Israel (50 Year Jubilee) (pp. 127–128)
[in Hebrew]. Kfar Sava, Israel: Maksim.

Rosen-Zvi, A. (1995). "The Rabbinic Courts, Halakha, and the Public: A Very
Narrow Bridge" [in Hebrew]. *Misphat ve'Mimshal, 3*(1), 173–220.

Sachs, J. (1989). "Creativity and Innovation in Halakha." In J. Sachs (Ed.), *Rabbinic
Authority and Personal Autonomy* (pp. 123–168). Northvale, NJ: Aronson.

Scheinbaum, J. E. (1986). "Ministry of Justice Report of the Committee to
Evaluate the Application of Family Law, Jerusalem" [in Hebrew]. In *Mishpacha
be'Mishpat, 2* (2009), 278–374. Shaarei Mishpat Law School. Retrieved July 10,
2011, from http://www.mishpat.ac.il/family2/02.pdf.

Shahar, A. (1998). "Group Identity and Women's Rights in Family Law: The Perils
of Multicultural Accommodation." *Journal of Political Philosophy, 6*(3), 285–305.

Shalev, C. (1995). "Freedom of Contract for Marriage and a Shared Life." In F.
Raday, C. Shalev, & M. Liban-Kooby (Eds.), *Women's Status in Israeli Law and
Society* [in Hebrew] (pp. 459–502). Tel Aviv, Israel: Schocken.

Shalom Hartman Institute. (n.d.). "About Us." Shalom Hartman Institute.
Retrieved May 10, 2012, from http://www.hartman.org.il/About_Us_View
.asp?Cat_Id=187&Cat_Type=About.

Shamir, R. (1996). "Religion, Feminism, and Professionalism: The Case of Rabbinic
Advocates." *Jewish Journal of Sociology, 38*(2), 73–88.

Shamir, R. (2000). *The Colonies of Law: Colonialism, Zionism and Law in Early
Mandate Palestine.* New York: Cambridge University Press.

Shavit, V. "I'll Dance on the Steps of the Rabbinate-Divorce Clip (LipDub)." Adapted from the song by Amnon Dankner. YouTube video. January 7, 2011. Retrieved April 18, 2012, from http://www.youtube.com/watch?v=R1rsuDYFOaA.

Shenrav, N. (2011). "'Because There Is No Law': On the Difficulty of Suggesting 'Din-Torah' as a Practical Alternative" [in Hebrew]. *Akdamot, 26*, 75-88.

Shifman, P. (1990). "Family Law in Israel: The Struggle between Religous and Secular Law." *Israel Law Review, 24*, 537-552.

Shifman, P. (1994). *Who's Afraid of Civil Marriage* [in Hebrew]. Jerusalem, Israel: Jerusalem Institute for Israel Research.

Shklar, J. (1999). "Political Theory and the Rule of Law." In S. Hoffman (Ed.), *Political Thought and Political Thinkers* (pp. 21-37). Chicago, IL: University of Chicago Press.

Shmueli, B. (2007). "Tort Compensation for Abandoned Wives (*Agunot*)." *HaMishpat, Volume in Memory of Judge Adi Azar* [in Hebrew], *12*, 285-342.

Soleveitchik, H. (1994). "Rupture and Reconstruction: The Transformation of Contemporary Orthodoxy." *Tradition, 28*(4), 64-128.

Tamanaha, B. Z. (2004). *On The Rule of Law: History, Politics, Theory.* Cambridge, England: Cambridge University Press.

Universal Declaration of Human Rights. (n.d.). United Nations. Retrieved May 13, 2012, from http://www.un.org/en/documents/udhr/.

Weinrib, E. J. (1995). *The Idea of Private Law.* Cambridge, MA: Harvard University Press.

Weiss, S. (2002). "The Three Methods of Jewish Divorce Resolution: Fundamentalism, Extortion and Violence" [in Hebrew]. *Eretz Aheret, 13*, 42-47.

Weiss, S., & Dainow, S. (n.d.). "Four Methods of Civil Response to Get Recalcitrance." Work in progress.

Westreich, E. (2002). "The Rise and Decline of the Law of the Rebellious Wife in Medieval Jewish Law." *Jewish Law Association Studies, 12*, 207-218.

Wolf, L. (1904). "The Zionist Peril." *Jewish Quarterly Review, 17*(1), 1-25. Rebound, New York: Ktav, 1966.

Zangwill, I. (1905). "Mr. Lucian Wolf on 'The Zionist Peril.'" *Jewish Quarterly Review, 17*(3), 397-425. Rebound, New York: Ktav, 1966.

INDEX

jurisdiction over, 14; in Shira's case, 49, 50, 52–53, 55; in Tikvah's case, 105–9, 111–12, 113

chuppah, 43, 46

civil courts: polarization of Israeli courts, 12; get extortion condoned by, 93; women turn to, 12, 63. *See also* family courts

civil divorce: and *Benai Noah* decision, 162; making it available in Israel, 189–90; nonexistent in Israel, 2, 4, 51; one set of laws for, 190; proposals for, 192–97; Reform women as unaware of its nonexistence in Israel, 61; and "status quo" arrangement, 10; U.S. model for, 197–98

civil marriage: in Cyprus, 28, 39, 53, 149, 150–52; in Efrat's case, 148–63; get compelled for, 156–57, 159; making it available in Israel, 189–90; nonexistent in Israel, 2, 4; in Prague, 43; proposals for, 192–97; rabbinic authorities who believe a get is not required for, 28, 32; rabbinic courts' jurisdiction over dissolution of those performed abroad, 22, 148, 149, 154, 161, 162–63; and Shira's case, 44, 53; and "status quo" arrangement, 10; U.S. model for, 197–98

civil society: Jewishness of Israel supported and respected in, 200; rabbinic courts and operation within, 190–91, 198–99; relocating religion within, 25, 33, 183, 191, 192

cohabitation arrangements, 21, 22, 28, 29, 33, 194

Colon, Yoseph (Maharik), 8, 54, 76, 92, 168, 183, 184

"common law" marriages, 21, 151

Convention on the Elimination of All Forms of Discrimination against Women (CEDAW), 18, 19–20, 166

Cyprus, Jewish marriages in, 28, 39, 53, 149, 150–52

CWJ. *See* Center for Women's Justice (CWJ)

damages: in Dalia's case, 96–97; family courts award to women, 16, 35, 80, 114, 186; foreign courts' award of, to women, 27; get received

in exchange for dropping tort claims, 138–40, 146–47; in Nava's case, 122, 123, 135–47, 181; rabbinic courts' opposition to, 16, 39, 100, 122, 123, 137–38 142–145, 181; in Tikvah's case, 100, 114, 117

Davidson, Benny, 64

Declaration of the Establishment of the State of Israel, 3, 17, 18–19, 20, 24

Deuteronomy, 4–5, 6, 16

Diaspora: assimilation confronts, 23; civil marriages in, 190; divorce in, 26–28; effect of Efrat's case on, 162–63; Gavison-Medan *Covenant* and, 194; Israeli rabbinic courts' influence in, 161

Dichovsky, Shlomo, 28, 158, 159, 161, 162, 163

divorce: attorneys, 63–64, 85, 179; ceremony, 58–59; civil penalties for refusing get, 116–19; consensual, 170, 174, 197; contests as complicated and cerebral, 65; disengaging from halakha, 119, 189–90; get received in exchange for dropping tort claims, 138–40, 146–47; grounds for, 176–77; halakha in Israeli, 2, 12, 51, 149; if marriage is over in fact, 38; increase in, 13; Israel not hospitable environment for, 122; in Jewish law, 4–28; men's upper hand in Israeli, 61, 167–68; money as obstacle to reaching agreement about, 105–6; move from fault to no-fault grounds, 22, 176; in Rabbinic Courts Jurisdiction (Marriage and Divorce) Law of 1953, 2, 12; "race to the courthouse" for, 12; recommendations of the authors for, 189–92; revoking a get for bad behavior, 93–94; statistics on, 29–30; against wife's will, 31, 59; Wolf-Zangwill debate on, 16–17; women paying for, 183–84. *See also* civil divorce; "forced" divorce

domestic violence: in Allison's case, 62; in Dalia's case, 79, 82–83, 87, 92; in Efrat's case, 153; as grounds for divorce, 176, 177, 178–79; Law against Family Violence of 1991, 126, 135, 141, 147; in Nava's case,

port, 108; *mishpat ivri* compared with, 11; no judicial review regarding, 92, 181; Orthodox Jews' distancing themselves from state involvement in, 34; patriarchal underpinnings of, 37, 93; pressuring men as against, 54; in Rabbinic Courts Jurisdiction (Marriage and Divorce) Law of 1953, 2, 12; rabbinic courts' minority views of, 122; rabbinic will and, 58; registration law changed to reflect, 24; relocating to discretionary realm, 191; and rule of law, 182–83; severing Israeli state from, 198; in Wolf-Zangwill debate, 16–17; women versed in, 15

Halbertal, Dov, 34

Handel, Justice, 120

Harris, Ron, 11–12, 22

Havaya, 43

Havel, Václav, 198

Hawthorne, Nathaniel, 60

Herzog, Yitzhak HaLevi, 28

High Rabbinic Court: Allison's case, 75–77; Dalia's case, 84, 86, 89–92, 94–96, 177; and Efrat's case, 158–59; lower courts may ignore, 7; Tikvah's case, 111, 114; on tort claims and get refusal, 143–44, 145

hiyuv get, 8, 75

human rights, 17–20; civil marriage and divorce as matters of, 190; halakha seen as encapsulating, 182; Israeli state and incorporation of, 199; Lifshitz's *Spousal Registry* proposal and, 195; misusing religious freedom to violate, 119; rabbinic courts' violations of, 40, 164–89; replacing halakha with, 191; in "thick" definition of rule of law, 180

infidelity: in Allison's case, 67, 68–78; as grounds for divorce, 176; in rabbinic divorce law, 5, 7; unequal treatment of men and women regarding, 31, 77, 167–68, 174; and women's right to privacy, 173–75

International Bill of Human Rights, 18, 19–20

International Coalition for Agunah Rights (ICAR), 15, 35

International Covenant on Civil and Political Rights (ICCPR), 17–18

International Covenant on Economic, Social and Cultural Rights (ICESCR), 18

Israel: alignment with ultra-Orthodox Judaism, 191–92; civil religion for, 191, 196; Declaration of the Establishment of, 3, 17, 18–19, 20, 24; diversity of expressions of Jewishness in, 199–200; divorce in, 8–17; halakha governing marriage in, 2; human rights incorporated into, 199; secularism in, 33–34, 43–44; severing state from halakha, 198; status quo arrangement, 10–11, 12, 193; symbolic Jewishness of, 196; women in contemporary, 3–4. *See also* Basic Laws

Israel Movement v. Sharon (2004), 172–73

Israel Women's Network, 15

Isserles, Moses (Rema), 6, 7, 131, 156

Itzik, Dalia, 3

Jacob ben Meir (Rabbeinu Tam), 6, 160

Jewish identity, 23–25

Jewish Life Information Center (ITIM), 43

Kahat, Hannah, 34

Kaniuk, Yoram, 24

Katsav, Moshe, 4

Knesset Israel, 10

Kolech, 34, 35

Kook, Isaac HaCohen, 28

Lalouz, Amnon, 140

Landau, Yechezkel ben Yehuda (Noda BeYehudah), 76

Law against Family Violence (1991), 126, 135, 141, 147

Law and Administration Ordinance (1948), 11

Leibowitz, Yeshayahu, 192, 194

Leviticus, 4

liberty: rabbinic courts' violation of right to,

185-87; tradition not permitted to trump, 191. *See also* freedom of conscience

Liebman, Charles, 191, 196

Lifshitz, Shachar, 192-93, 194-97

Livni, Tzippi, 3

Lubitch, Rivkah, 36; in Allison's case, 68; in Dalia's case, 94, 96; in Efrat's case, 157, 158; in Nava's case, 146, 147; in Shira's case, 41, 56, 58, 59

Luria, Marc, 15

MacKinnon, Catherine, 169, 184-85

Maharashdam (Samuel ben Moses de Medina), 1-2, 8, 54, 88, 89, 92, 168, 183, 184

Maharik (Yoseph Colon), 8, 54, 76, 92, 168, 183, 184

mamzerim: blacklisting of, 120, 173-74, 197-98; civil marriage seen as leading to, 10; in Efrat's case, 155; in Gavison-Medan *Covenant*, 193-94; prohibited from marrying Jews, 6, 31; rabbinic courts' concern with, 39, 121, 123, 142, 144, 145, 182; rabbinic courts' increase in number of, 165; in Shira's case, 54; in Tikvah's case, 119-20

marital property: in Allison's case, 64-65, 66, 68, 77; in Dalia's case, 83, 88, 90, 91, 92, 93, 95, 184; double bind in law of, 13, 35; foreign courts on, 27-28; Marital Property Law, 13, 15, 180; in Nava's case, 125, 127, 132, 133, 134, 136, 145; as price for divorce, 184; rabbinic courts' jurisdiction over, 12, 14; in Shira's case, 49, 50

Marital Property (Balancing of Resources) Law (1973), 13, 15, 180

marriage: in accordance with laws of Moses and Israel, 43, 46, 156, 187; Ben-Gurion on, 9-10; bigamy, 31, 53, 154; "common law," 21, 151; Convention on the Elimination of All Forms of Discrimination against Women on, 18; disengaging from halakha, 189-90; empty shells of legal, 22; halakha in Israeli, 2, 12, 51; Israeli state's infringement on right

to marry, 189; medieval nature of Israeli, 43; polygamy, 16, 168; in Rabbinic Courts Jurisdiction (Marriage and Divorce) Law of 1953, 2, 12; rabbinic courts' violation of right to marry, 187-88; recommendations of the authors for, 189-92; statistics on, 28-29; types of unions, 21-22; Wolf-Zangwill debate on, 16-17. *See also* civil marriage; divorce

Marty, Martin E., 32

Mavoi Satum, 34, 35

Mazie, Steven V., 164

Medan, Yaakov, 192-94, 195

Meir, Golda, 3

men: anchored in failed marriages, 30-32, 169, 170; dominance over Jewish women, 169-70; halakha as biased in favor of, 168; marriage statistics, 28; patriarchal family, 22, 37, 57, 93; rabbinic courts as male dominated, 71; rabbinic courts' bestowal of power on husbands, 38; their upper hand in Israeli divorces, 61, 167-68; turning to rabbinic courts, 12, 13, 63; unequal treatment regarding infidelity, 31, 77, 167-68, 174

Metzger, Yonah, 77

mikveh: in Allison's case, 61, 62, 66; required for Orthodox weddings, 43, 77, 172, 173; in Shira's case, 44-46

Miller, Akivah, 173

millet system, 8-9, 10, 11, 12, 170

Mir-Housseini, Ziba, 196-97

mishpat ivri, 11-12, 198

missing husbands unit, 55, 56

Mitchatnim (magazine), 42-43

Mordecai, Yitzhak, 4

moredet, 83

Moses ben Maimon (Rambam), 6-7, 75-76, 176, 177

Movement for Progressive Judaism, 150

multiculturalism, 33

Naamat, 153

negative liberty, 185-86

negligence, 117, 135, 141, 147

Noahide marriages, 158

Noda BeYehudah (Yechezkel ben Yehuda Landau), 76

Numbers, 4

Nussbaum, Martha, 191

Ohrbach, Frieda, 126

Okin, Susan Moller, 33

Ombudsman's Office of the Israeli Judiciary, 56, 141

"one family, one judge" arrangement, 13

Padan, Shimmy, 64, 76

Pardes, Shnuer, 145

patriarchal family, 22, 37, 57, 93

Plonit v. Ploni (Benai Noah) (2003), 28, 156, 159, 162

Plonit v. Ploni (right to stay married) (2011), 184

Plonit v. Ploni (separation) (2007), 177

Plonit v. Tel Aviv Rabbinic Court (civil marriage) (2006), 158, 162

Ploni v. Plonit (infidelity) (2006), 166, 173, 180

polygamy, 16, 168

positive liberty, 185, 186

prenuptial agreements, 35, 44

privacy: rabbinic courts' violation of right to, 171–75, 176

Procaccia, Ayala, 27

property: rabbinic courts' violation of right to, 183–85. *See also* marital property

rabbinic court pleaders: in Allison's case, 68, 70; in Dalia's case, 38, 83, 84–85, 94; Rivkah Lubitch as, 41, 56, 68, 94, 157; in Nava's case, 142; in Shira's case, 41, 56; in Tanya's case, 157; in Tikvah's case, 104, 107, 108, 115; women becoming, 14–15

rabbinic courts: Allison's case, 64–78; in ancillary matters, 12, 14; brevity of decisions of, 179; in broken *vort* cases, 102; change in focus of, 12–13; as chaotic, 175–76; as

"church," 25, 162; Conservative and Reform opposition to, 34; Dalia's case, 79, 82, 83–96, 184; on damages suits, 16, 39, 100, 122, 123, 137–38 142–145, 181; Diaspora, 161; divorce statistics, 29–30; Efrat's case, 149, 154–61; finessing the schedule in, 84; get refusal as question of fact independent of, 116; hearings as negotiations, 7, 38; human rights violated by, 40, 164–89; as ineffective in resolving divorce cases, 30; Israeli state as deferring to, 77; jurisdiction of, 26–27; Knesset Israel and opting out of, 10; Lifshitz's *Spousal Registry* proposal and, 195; loyalty only to State of Israel, 180; as male dominated, 71; men turning to, 12, 13, 63; under *millet* system, 8–9; minority views of halakha in, 122; Nava's case, 122, 125, 128–35, 136–37, 139–47, 178; polarization of Israeli courts, 12; get extortion condoned by, 93; power bestowed on husbands by, 38; power to punish recalcitrant husbands, 26; in Rabbinic Courts Jurisdiction (Marriage and Divorce) Law of 1953, 2, 12; rabbinic literature's influence on, 7–8; recommendations for reforming, 164–65; reinterpretation of tradition necessary for, 192; relocating to nongovernmental civil society, 190–92; responsibility for abuse transferred to victim by, 54–55; Rosen-Zvi's recommendation for, 13–14; rule of law absent in, 180; rules of evidence and procedure in, 14, 70; salaries for judges, 50; Shira's case, 49, 50–59, 184; Supreme Court dislike of confrontations with, 90, 172, 181; tension between family courts and, 15–16, 23, 39–40, 122–23, 147; as theocratic islands in democratic state, 180; Tikvah's case, 99–100, 104–15, 118–19, 179, 184; ultra-Orthodox protected by, 32–33, 90, 91, 197; vacuous nature of decisions of, 38–39; women becoming pleaders in, 14–15; women not represented on, 166–67; women's attitudes toward, 36; women's complaints ignored by, 34; in "world war" with family courts, 16, 23, 39, 118, 122, 142, 144, 169, 181. *See also* High Rabbinic Court

Rabbinic Courts Jurisdiction (Enforcement of Rabbinic Rulings) Law of 1995, 8

Rabbinic Courts Jurisdiction (Marriage and Divorce) Law of 1953, 2, 12, 13–14

rabbinic literature: on divorce, 5–8. *See also scholars by name*

Rackman Center at Bar Ilan University, 35

Rambam (Moses ben Maimon), 6–7, 75–76, 176, 177

Ramon, Haim, 4

rape, 4, 82, 128–29, 130, 131, 178

Raz, Joseph, 175–76, 179, 186

reconciliation. See *shalom bayit* (reconciliation)

redemption of the first born, 106–7

religious parties, 17, 32, 44

religious purity classes, 172–73

Rema (Moses Isserles), 6, 7, 131, 156

restraining orders, 125, 126, 133

revulsion: in Dalia's case, 86, 87; in Nava's case, 131; in rabbinic divorce law, 5, 6, 7, 176; in Tikvah's case, 103, 111

Rosenthal, Dayan Haim, 34

Rosen-Zvi, Ariel, 13–14, 192

Rosh (Asher ben Jehiel), 6, 75

rule of law, 79; interpreting halakha so that it meets requirements of, 182; Israeli state obligation to allow incorporation of, 199; rabbinic courts' violation of, 164, 175–76, 179–80

Sabag v. High Rabbinic Court (2004), 25, 27

same-sex marriages, 21

Samuel ben Moses de Medina (Maharashdam), 1–2, 8, 54, 88, 89, 92, 168, 183, 184

Scheinbaum, Elisha, 13–14

secular Israeli Jews, 33–34, 43–44

Segal, Peretz, 197

Sentenced to Marry (documentary), 135

separation, 177, 197

Shaanan, Haim Shlomo, 130, 132, 137

Shalit, Benjamin, 24

shalom bayit (reconciliation): in Dalia's case, 82, 86, 177; in Efrat's case, 155, 161; as impossible with woman's adultery, 168; in Nava's case, 128–29, 131, 135, 178; in Tikvah's case, 108, 110, 113

Shalom Hartman Institute, 182

Shamgar, Meir, 13

Shamir, Ronen, 15

Shari'a, 196–97

Shas, 32, 44

Shavit, Vered, 148, 149, 162

Sheinfeld, Shalom, 84–85

Sherman, Rabbi, 177

sheva brakhot, 102–3

Shifman, Pinhas, 15, 192

Shinnui party, 34

Shmueli, Benjamin, 117

Shulhan Arukh, 6, 7, 34, 65, 131, 156

Sivan, Emmanuel, 33, 147

Sivan, Tova, 115

Spousal Registry proposal, 192–97

status quo arrangement, 10–11, 12, 193

Stein, Esther, 186

Stoleman, Pinhas, 83

Supreme Court: and Basic Laws of Human Dignity and Liberty and of Freedom of Occupation, 19; and civil marriage, 157–58; Dalia's case, 89–90, 91–92, 94, 96–97; dislike of confrontations with rabbinic courts, 90, 172, 181; halakha as immune from judicial scrutiny, 92, 181; get extortion condoned by, 93; rabbinic courts contrasted with, 14; on registration of children as Jewish, 24; on religious purity classes, 172–73; *Sabag v. High Rabbinic Court*, 26–27; Shira's case, 50; Tikvah's case, 118–19, 120; and tort claims and get refusal, 144; on women forced to give up property rights, 185; Women's Equal Rights Law of 1953 used by, 3; women's rights' infringements ignored by, 20

Talmud, 5–6
Tam, Rabbeinu (Jacob ben Meir), 6, 160
theocracy, 2, 17, 40, 199
Torah law *(din torah)*, 2, 12, 113, 114, 198
tort claims. *See* damages
Training Institute v. Minister of Religious Affairs (1994), 15
Tzohar, 43

ultra-Orthodox *(haredi):* civil marriage opposed by, 10; funding of husband in Tikvah's case, 114–15, 117; Israeli state aligned with, 191–92; men's preference for younger women, 99; political parties, 17, 32, 44; rabbinic courts protection of, 32–33, 90, 197; relocation of religion and, 191; secular authorities avoided by, 104; Supreme Court as reluctant to antagonize, 91; and women's deportation, 98, 100
Universal Declaration of Human Rights, 17-18
Uziel, Ben Zion Meir, 28

violence. *See* domestic violence
visitation: in Efrat's case, 154; in Nava's case, 127; as price for divorce, 184; in Tikvah's case, 100, 107–8, 111–12, 113, 117
vort, 101–2

Waldenberg, Eliezer, 28
Warren, Samuel D., 171
Weisenfeld, Tamara, 153–54
Weiss, Susan, 135, 141, 146
Wolf, Lucien, 16–17

women: becoming pleaders in rabbinic courts, 14–15; civil courts used by, 12, 63; civil marriage and divorce as ameliorating problem of failed marriages for, 190; in contemporary Israel, 3–4; at divorce ceremony, 58–59; and feminism, 3, 34, 35, 57, 184; foreign courts' assistance to, 27–28; human rights conventions on, 17–20; in illicit unions, 31; inadequate responses to complaints of, 34–35; Israeli state's power over lives of, 77–78; Jewishness of Israel as resting on backs of, 199; marriage statistics, 28; men's dominance over, 169–70; nonprofit organizations and legal aid clinics for, 15; as not represented on rabbinic courts, 166–67; pressure of rabbinic judges on, 8, 54; staying in bad marriages rather than face rabbinic courts, 30; suing recalcitrant husbands for damages, 16, 35, 80, 96–97, 100, 114, 122, 123, 135–47, 186; system as discriminating against, 30–32; and unequal treatment regarding infidelity, 31, 77, 167–68, 174; reasons for staying in bad relationships, 121–22
Women's Equal Rights Law (1953), 3

Yaakobi, Shimon, 118–19, 183, 184, 187
Yaakobi v. Yaakobi (1995), 13
Yad L'Isha, 35
Yanai, Ariel, 144, 145, 181, 182
Yashar, David, 104
Yerucham ben Meshulam, 156
Yonath, Ada, 3

Zangwill, Israel, 16–17
Ziv, Neta, 1
Zuria, Anat, 135